TH
I HAVE SEEN

Memoirs from the Case Files of
Lt. Detective Robert (Robbo) Davidson

Lt. Detective Robert (Robbo)
Davidson and
P.J. Jones

This book is dedicated to victims of violence and their families. It would not be possible without the love and encouragement of my wife, Linda and our daughters Allison, Ann, and Ashley.

Acknowledgments

This book was two years in the making. It would not have been possible without the patient assistance of many people.

From the beginning, DeSoto Parish Clerk of Courts Jeremy Evans and his staff willingly rounded up old case files, trial transcripts and appellate documents for review. DeSoto Parish Sheriff Jayson Richardson interviewed and allowed access to closed case files and the staff of the DeSoto Parish Public Library waded through old files on microfilm to help pull all the facts together.

I thank my former co-workers and friends—who are family to me—law enforcement family members who always had my back and who interviewed for these stories. Case by case, they helped jog my memories, fill in holes to bring these stories to life. I dare not name them all for fear of absent-mindedly leaving one out. They know who they are. Thank you.

I am grateful to members and former members of the Louisiana judicial system who interviewed.

Vickie Welborn played an invaluable role providing her own memories of cases she covered, pulling up old stories she wrote for the *Mansfield Enterprise* or *Shreveport News*. And I am grateful to the *Mansfield Enterprise* for giving permission to publish photographs of news stories they carried on different cases.

I am indebted to the families and friends of these victims of crime who were willing to speak on the record as well as three men who are serving life sentences in prison for crimes they committed.

Finally, thanks to my writing partner, P.J. Jones, editor Susan Mary Malone, and the staff of White Bird Publications.

Table of Contents

THE EVIL
I HAVE SEEN

Memoirs from the Case Files of
Lt. Detective Robert (Robbo) Davidson

White Bird
Publications

Introduction

An icy wind rattled the windows, waking me from a deep sleep. Drawing back the bedroom curtains, I was jolted to see people bundled in jackets and toboggans gathered around a roaring bonfire, rubbing their hands, and holding them out to feel the warmth of the flames. Their breath crystallized in the air.

Who were they? What were they doing in my pasture?

Grabbing a coat, I headed outside. The full moon bathed the frozen landscape in silver and white, showing the way for me to approach in silence. I didn't want them to run away before I could see who they were. Nearing the fire, still not close enough to discern faces, a knotty pine exploded atop the pyre, shooting embers into the sky, carrying cinders on the wind. *My God, they could catch the woods on fire!* Panic gripped my throat; I tried to yell, but nothing came out as I raced to smother the fiery pieces before they reached the tree line. Jumping to snatch the first, I saw a face, ringed in fire, in my hand. It was a face that I knew. Swirling around it were more faces, each ringed in fire, each a face pulled from my past.

I bolted upright in bed, recognizing my surroundings.

"What's the matter?" Linda asked. "You can't sleep again?"

A glance at the clock told me it was only thirty minutes past midnight. "I'm going to get something to eat."

In the kitchen, I scrounged for my favorite cast-iron frying pan (which for some reason Linda likes to hide) and I threw on a thick slice of bologna. Bologna gets a bad rap. My kids won't eat it, but I love it. Midnight bologna and salami sandwiches have become a routine since I retired in 2014 after working almost four decades in law enforcement.

Seems the older I get the less I sleep, awakened night after night by the memory of one case or another. As long as I was working, I stayed busy with a specific case (or several) either investigating, tracking down and interviewing witnesses, building a case for a prosecutor, testifying to a grand jury, in pre-trial or trial or on appeals. Criminal cases, especially murder cases, take on a life of their own.

Now I ruminate on those old investigations, realizing some things seen stain the brain as surely as the iron-laden soil of western Louisiana forever changes the color of whatever it touches. You cannot wash red dirt out of clothing, and you cannot unsee what you have seen. You cannot look into the empty eyes of death staring back at you as many times as I did and say you were not changed by what you saw. I stopped trying to count homicide cases a long time ago. There are ghosts waiting for me in every corner of DeSoto Parish.

The other day, driving down a country lane, Linda cried out, "Oh, what a pretty yard!"

Turning to see the object of my wife's admiration, I recalled the night I kneeled over a man lying on that lush Saint Augustine lawn, a hole between his eyes with the back of his head blown off. She saw Mobile azaleas, and I saw a just-dead man lying in a puddle of brains and blood.

I cannot drive past the railroad trestle in Logansport and not see an old woman with a knife plunged into her forehead, nor can I drive to Many down Louisiana Highway 171 and not see a young man who should have been allowed to live, to love his children and grandchildren, instead, bleeding to death on the asphalt, a four-inch blade plunged directly into his heart.

And then, of course, there is the pond. Dew Pond. A fisherman's paradise as picturesque as any artist could paint, forever spoiled by carnage.

I am not a man prone to melancholy. To the contrary, I have led a blessed life in every way. I loved my work, and the decision to retire was extremely difficult. But there comes a time for each of us, and I knew it was mine.

Still, I cannot stop waking up in the middle of the night, the face of some innocent victim looming in the blackness over my bed. I have come to live with them, these ghosts of DeSoto Parish, but I cannot say I do so peacefully. I struggle to define the emotions the disturbing images evoke, though I am certain regret is one element—regret that we could not save any of them, just come along after the fact to try and find justice for each, knowing justice is a poor substitute for life.

I think about the seemingly insignificant decisions that led each one to their demise—a decision to take this turn instead of that, to trust the wrong person, to open their door to a stranger. In each case, if they just had not done *that*, they might still be alive.

Sitting at the kitchen table, slathering mayonnaise on bread, peppering my bologna sandwich, it occurred to me— maybe their images were meant to remind me my job was not yet done. Maybe I needed to tell their stories, to lend them a voice, for better or for worse.

I think if I do not, the evil I have seen may never let me sleep.

My law enforcement career did not take a traditional path. After graduating Mansfield High School in 1966, I went to college in Natchitoches—the Louisiana town made famous by the movie *Steel Magnolias*, and yes, that's a pretty fair portrayal of life in a small Louisiana town. When I was in Northwestern University, the war in Viet Nam was exploding and I figured it would not be long until Uncle Sam tapped me on the shoulder. Hoping to avoid the jungles of Southeast Asia, I enlisted in the United States Air Force. That was 1968.

I'd been studying criminal justice aiming for a career in law enforcement. Everyone I knew in the military said, "Don't tell them what you *really* want to do because you won't get your first pick. Whatever you want to do, list it as second choice, that way you'll be more likely to get it." So, I listed medic as my first choice for an assignment, and military police as second.

Guess what I got? Medic. So much for the quality of some advice. I served as a military medic for two years. Helped deliver a lot of babies.

When I got out, I still wanted to work in law enforcement. In 1970, illegal drugs, mostly marijuana and LSD, were flowing into Louisiana like the Mississippi River in spring. I had a friend who worked narcotics for Shreveport Police who told me about a new group being formed in Beauregard Parish by Sheriff Bolivar Bishop, a man who went on to become a legend in Louisiana law enforcement serving thirty-six years in office. Bolivar Bishop was a four-star general in the state's war on drugs, which he was just getting started in 1970 by taking this initiative to create a partnership with the Louisiana State Police, assembling a team of undercover agents who would infiltrate the bayou drug world.

My friend introduced me to Sheriff Bishop. We hit it off, and I was commissioned as a law enforcement officer to work undercover wherever Sheriff Bishop and or the Louisiana State Police needed me. I worked in nine parishes.

There weren't a lot of rules back then—that kind of undercover work was in its infancy, at least in Louisiana—so you could say we had a lot of "on the job training."

We called ourselves the Dirty Dozen, as there were twelve of us. Sometimes we worked in teams and sometimes alone. Any time another parish sheriff called Sheriff Bishop saying, "We've got a problem," depending on the problem and the place, one or more of us was dispatched with a cover story.

One time I was a music promoter by the name of Ricardo DeVecchio, supposedly sent to Deridder to gather signatures for a rock festival. I used that name because I had an initial ring with the letters R.D., which helped make a convincing cover. With my coloring, I could pass for Italian or Mexican, easy.

I told people I needed 1,000 signatures on a petition to bring a rock festival to town, to comply with state law, which was true. The petition part was, anyway. The Louisiana legislature had passed a law requiring such a petition before any festivals could be held. As a music promoter, of course, everyone thought I either had drugs or wanted drugs. I worked there several weeks, gathering signatures on my bogus petition, buying drugs until word of a Woodstock-like festival got to the newspaper.

The Beauregard Daily News headline July 26, 1972 read: "Rock festival site sought in Beauregard Parish." The story read, "A rock festival, which promoters say could attract five to ten times as many spectators as there are residents in Beauregard Parish, is being talked about for an area north of DeQuincy—somewhere in rural Beauregard. A festival promoter who has been securing signatures on a petition from local people backing the festival said the event could draw between 100,000 and 200,000 people. Beauregard Parish only has a population of about 22,000."

Chamber of Commerce leaders went nuts, calling the sheriff, demanding, "How are you going to stop this? We don't want a big rock festival in our town."

Sheriff Bishop assured them, "I'll take care of it."

He did. I was arrested—pre-planned, of course—picked up and held overnight on a "traffic violation." When I "bonded out" the next day, I disappeared, and not long afterward, the sheriff's department made twenty-eight arrests for sale and distribution of narcotics.

That went on for years until I realized it wasn't the best line of work for a family man. After a brief stint as a guard at Angola Prison, I became the investigator for the 11th Judicial District Attorney's Office, serving Sabine and DeSoto Parishes under newly elected DA James Lynn Davis.

Five years later, in 1980, I became a narcotics investigator for the DeSoto Parish Sheriff's Office under Sheriff Frenchie Lambert. It was my niche. I never left the department, moving from narcotics to the Criminal Investigations Division and eventually Chief Detective. I served on the Joint Terrorism Task Force from 2000 to 2013 and retired in 2014. I still serve on the Louisiana Commission on Law Enforcement and handle cold cases for DeSoto Parish.

For decades, I kept a rack of file folders containing my cases, open and closed. Every now and then, I'd pick one up, re-read it, and think, why didn't I ask *that*? Or let's check *this* out.

My office had two bulletin boards. One had the pictures of the victims of the cases I had worked. The other had notes of things I needed to remember to do. The victim's bulletin board was directly across from my desk, so that when I looked up, they were always there, looking back at me.

Son of a gun.

And I wonder why their faces are embedded in my brain?

Deadly Cocktail

In March 1981, a young couple quarreled at a bar in DeSoto
Parish. Fuming, the man stormed off, abandoning his wife
in the crowded club. Having overheard the argument, a man
sitting nearby struck up a conversation with the woman. Late
in the evening, when her husband did not return, the woman
asked the man, if he would he be kind enough to take her
home.

"Of course," he replied.

He did not take her directly home. He drove her to a
wilderness area known as the Big Woods, where he held a
knife to her throat and forced her to have sex.

His appetite satisfied, the burly man warned, "You go
to the cops with this, and I'll kill you."

She believed him.

It was too early in the day to be so damned hot. I shifted my
shoulders and rolled my neck, reactions to sweat sliding

down my spine, dripping off my brow, stinging my eyes. The late-morning sun scorched my face and arms. When I stopped walking long enough to mop my forehead with my sleeve, I gave myself a talking-to.

"Tomorrow's the Fourth of July, for crying out loud. What do you expect?"

Somewhere, people were packing picnic baskets and popping firecrackers. Celebrating. They were a long way from where I was—shin deep in a tangle of blackberry vines, saw briars, privet, and sumac filling the ditch of a lonesome logging road deep in the belly of the Big Woods.

Looking ahead, getting a lay of the land, a swarm of flies caught my eye, maybe a hundred-fifty feet ahead on the other side of the rutted red dirt road. I lifted my sunglasses and squinted. Beneath the swarm, I thought I saw something—something that did not belong. Rushing forward, forgetting the heat, humidity, and sun, as the hum grew louder and louder, I became certain I would find what I was looking for. Blow flies deposit their eggs in decaying flesh. They are as good as any cadaver dog.

Halting a few feet from the swirling, buzzing green flies, I saw her naked body half-hidden by thorny brush, flies, and ants crawling on her porcelain skin, feeding on her breasts, her shoulders, her neck, and face. Her face. He had not hurt her face. My God, she was—she had been—a pretty woman. Late twenties. Maybe early thirties. Tall. Slim. Voluptuous. She lay sprawled on her back, her eyes closed. That was a relief.

For whatever reason, it is a little easier when their eyes are closed.

In the wee hours of that sultry summer morning in 1981, Dewayne George drove to Converse through the woodlands of western Louisiana along State Highway 171, skirting the eastern edge of the Big Woods. It is a sparsely populated, remote region of towering trees—long-leaf pine, oak, pecan, hickory, cottonwood, elm, sweet gum—so thick they blocked the sky except for the sliver of stars directly over the road. The car's headlights pierced the abysmal darkness of the new moon.

Thursday night—payday—had turned into Friday morning as Dewayne and his wife Suzette partied at the Rendezvous Club outside Mansfield. About three o'clock after the club closed, they headed home on what was normally a thirty-minute drive. Not long after they crossed from DeSoto into Sabine Parish, a speeding truck appeared in the rear-view mirror, overtaking them. The driver flashed the headlights, honked the horn, and pulled alongside the Oldsmobile Cutlass, signaling for the Georges to pull over.

Dewayne recognized the blue truck.

Obligingly, he slowed to stop at the road's edge with the passenger side tires in the grass. The remainder of the vehicle partially blocked the southbound lane of traffic. The truck came around to stop directly in front of him.

What was wrong? Dwayne George got out of his car to find out.

Their night started at the Rendezvous Club, a private bar opened the year before outside Mansfield by a young entrepreneur named Alan Yarbrough, a bird dog for opportunity who could sniff a dollar before he saw it.

What he sniffed out in 1980 was the fact that—contrary to what had been believed for the preceding 137 years— DeSoto Parish was wet unless voted otherwise, which it had not been. His discovery meant that if you had a liquor license, which Yarbrough already had, you could sell liquor for on-premise or off-premise consumption anywhere in DeSoto Parish that was not incorporated. It was the opposite of what had been believed and it was like discovering gold.

Up until that time, DeSoto Parish had no bars. Of course, at the country club members of the old-money upper-crust could imbibe and socialize, but no places existed where common people could congregate and enjoy a drink. Alan Yarborough changed that.

Still in his twenties, Yarborough sold his liquor store in South Mansfield, a tiny burg incorporated for the sole purpose of selling liquor for off-premise consumption, and moved on down Louisiana Highway 171 to unincorporated DeSoto Parish where he opened Weekend Liquor Mart. On the same property, behind the liquor store, he placed the Rendezvous Club.

The glorified, rambling seventy-foot-long mobile home had a mirrored back wall that made it feel roomier than it actually was. It also had a bathroom on each end and a horseshoe bar in the middle. He had a cash cow, and Yarbrough laughed all the way to the bank every day. There wasn't anything any Baptist could do about it, either.

That the opening of the Rendezvous coincided with the start of construction on a $750-million-dollar-mill for International Paper Company in DeSoto Parish, being built by Brown & Root Construction Company, was no accident. Tradesmen from all over the country flocked to Mansfield. Every spare room in the parish was rented out. Trailer parks had doubled-up, squeezing in two trailers on each lot. There was even a tent city near the construction site.

"It was kind of like the wild west," Yarborough looked back on old times, recalling when ten-thousand workers, many with families, flocked to Mansfield.

His new bar stayed packed seven nights a week but was especially crowded on Thursdays—payday for Brown & Root. Ironworkers, pipefitters, welders, plumbers, electricians, masons, carpenters, concrete workers all knew Alan Yarbrough would cash your check at his bar.

A lot of his customers who worked at Brown & Root did not have a checking account to deposit their paycheck into, because they were wanted somewhere else, or they were afraid they were wanted. Yarbrough charged them one percent to cash their checks. Then most of them would hang around and spend some money with him.

Thus, Dewayne George, an electrician for Brown & Root, along with so many of his coworkers, could be found at the Rendezvous most Thursdays after work. It was the blue-collar place to be. Not that Dewayne George needed his check cashed—he was a hometown boy just back from a tour of duty in the Navy. He had no criminal record. He just liked the comradery.

His wife Suzette was dropped off at the Rendezvous about 9 p.m. to wait for him to join her when he got off second shift. It was a detail about the night that later stood out since no one could remember her ever being there without her husband.

Suzette George was a curvaceous, lanky brunette men noticed. With delicate features—a small nose, almond-shaped eyes, and chestnut hair that fell below her shoulders—you could say she was worth looking at.

"She could turn heads," her friend Linda Brown recalled. Linda grew up on the same block in Shreveport with Suzette and they had remained close. She and her husband had planned a Fourth of July get together with Dewayne and Suzette.

"She was pretty," Linda said, "But I don't know that she realized it. She was really quite bashful."

Waiting on Dewayne to join her, Suzette had a few drinks, two bartenders recalled, but neither bartender thought she had too much. She had just sipped on her beer and visited. They recalled she played the Juke Box and danced a few times. One bartender thought she'd gone outside with someone for a while. When Dewayne arrived, the bartenders recalled, he was miffed about all the attention his wife was receiving from other men.

"Wonder if I can get to see my wife," he'd cracked, bartender Bruce Rogers recalled.

When Suzette approached Dewayne at the bar, Rogers said, it appeared maybe they argued, but later the couple danced so both bartenders assumed all was well with them.

Last call was at 2 a.m. but since people lingered around

and finished their drinks, it wasn't unusual for the parking lot not to clear out until around three o'clock, as it had that morning.

The bartender Bruce Rogers recalled, among the last people to leave the Rendezvous Club the morning of July third were Dewayne and Suzette George, a regular by the name of James Caston and another man—a troublemaker—Herman Hanks.

Herman Karrel Hanks was burly and blonde, and were it not for his long, full beard you might call him baby-faced. Fair-skinned, pudgy cheeks—wide-set, light blue eyes with a long nose and flaring nostrils. What you noticed about him first, though, was his size. Herman Hanks bumped six foot-five, and he was broad as a boxcar.

Family members called him Herman Karrel or just Karrel, to distinguish him from his father, Herman Lewayne Hanks.

Herman Karrel dropped out of Shreveport's Byrd High School at the age of seventeen to join the Army. He was discharged nine months later after serving in Germany and began to drift. He worked offshore in the Gulf, tended bar in Morgan City, drove a taxi. He was working as a pipefitter for Brown & Root in Mansfield in 1981, but having injured his back, by July he was drawing disability.

His disability didn't keep him from fighting. Beneath the baby face, there was an oft-unbridled anger. Herman Hanks admitted that sometimes he just wanted to punch something.

One night, Yarbrough said, Hanks and his buddies got into three different brawls. "We were always having to call them down or throw them out," he said.

But not that night, Yarbrough said. That night there had been no fights at the Rendezvous that he or any employee could remember. And when the bar closed, Hanks was last seen driving his buddy, James Caston, home.

Army Staff Sgt. Patricia Lanagan travelled north on Louisiana Highway 171 from Fort Polk when she came upon a pickup truck approaching in her lane of traffic. She noted that it was about 4 a.m.

Forced to slow and veer, Sgt. Lanagan saw a man lying on the roadway to her left, in front of a car that was stopped on the edge of the southbound lane. His body was visible in the beam of the car's headlights. The man and car partially blocked the southbound lane, forcing traffic to veer around.

Concerned, Sgt. Lanagan flashed her headlights, trying to flag the attention of whoever was driving an Exxon tanker truck ahead of her, but the big rig just kept going. Travelling alone on such a dark night and fearing the circumstances, the sergeant did not stop to render aid but instead made a mental note of the time and mileage on her odometer. In Mansfield she pulled into an all-night gas station, ordering the attendant, "Call police!" There was a body, she said, in front of a car sixteen miles south on Highway 171.

"I didn't get the license number of the pickup truck," Lanagan reported, "and I didn't see any movement from the body."

Neither did she see anyone inside the parked vehicle.

"I was afraid to stop," she said.

When he got the call from Holicer Gas Station, DeSoto Parish sheriff's office dispatcher Wesley English radioed his only overnight patrol deputy, Ken Roberts. Roberts was a veteran with more than twenty years in law enforcement, on patrol north of Mansfield when he got the call.

"A woman just stopped at Holicer Gas and said she'd seen a body lying in front of a parked car about sixteen miles south on State Highway 171," the dispatcher relayed. "It's on the west side of the road. She advised she wouldn't stop to see what the problem was due to the darkness and her fear."

Sirens blaring, lights whirling, Roberts raced to the scene, noting he'd just left his jurisdiction when he spotted the parked car. This was Sabine Parish. The officer made a U turn to stop directly in front of the George's car—exactly where the pickup truck had been—but facing the Cutlass in order to shine more light on the scene.

More than an hour had passed since Dewayne George was flagged to stop. The Cutlass' headlights had drained the battery and were dimming.

Roberts found Dewayne George lying on his right side in his own blood.

"His head or face was pointed down toward the ditch on the shoulder," Roberts later wrote in his report. "His feet were close to the travel lane."

Kneeling over him, the deputy asked, "What happened?"

"I'll take care of it myself," Dewayne replied. His voice sounded strong enough, the deputy made a mental note. "I've been stabbed in the chest."

"Let me see."

Roberts ripped open the snaps on the plaid shirt. There was a gaping puncture wound near the center of Dewayne's chest, pulsing blood that flowed down his torso to the roadway running underneath his face, soaking his hair.

It appeared to the deputy that Dewayne George had been beaten. His face was battered.

"Who did this to you?" Roberts asked.

"Herman Hanks."

"Herman Hanks?"

"Yeah, Herman Hanks. I know him from work."

Roberts radioed Sabine Parish Sheriff's Office for an ambulance and help.

"My feet hurt," Dewayne said. His voice remarkably weaker. "Will you take my shoes and socks off?"

As Roberts removed the shoes and socks, he asked

again, "Are you sure it's Herman Hanks?"

"Yes," Dewayne mumbled, "he forced my wife out of the car and took her with him."

Noticing Dewayne's back was also soaked in blood, the deputy lifted the tail of the shirt. He was astonished to see this man had not only been stabbed in the chest but also near the center of his upper back. This wound, too, was bleeding profusely.

Roberts drew back.

How could he stop this much bleeding in time to save this young man's life?

"I'm going to die." Dewayne spoke what Roberts was thinking.

"No, you're not, son," the deputy said against reason. "I'm getting help."

Everything began to happen at once. Having overheard DeSoto Parish Patrol Deputy Ken Roberts' radio call for help, Louisiana Department of Public Safety Trooper James Napier, who was on patrol near Converse, sped to the scene. He radioed the ambulance to step on it when he saw the situation.

Like Roberts, the state trooper asked Dewayne, "Who did this to you?"

The answer was the same.

"Herman. Herman Hanks. The son of a bitch stabbed me."

Looking at one another the trooper and the deputy had the same question: Where's his wife? There was no sign of her.

Each man wondered: *Was she in on this?*

Converse Police Chief Hugh Spillard was called to the scene about 4:30 a.m. by the Sabine Parish Sheriff's Office. The Georges made up a chunk of the population of tiny Converse, and Spillard knew them all.

By the time Spillard arrived, three Sabine Parish Sheriff's deputies were already there, plus the state trooper and Deputy Roberts from DeSoto Parish. Arriving about the same time as the ambulance, the police chief saw for himself the plight of Dewayne George. His heart sank. No parent should have to bury a child, but if this boy didn't make it, Dewayne would be the third son Junies George would bury. His two oldest, D.C. and Truly, were both killed in the service, D.C. in combat in Viet Nam, Truly in a bridge collapse in Germany.

"God, have mercy," the police chief said. "Dewayne, it's Hugh. It's Chief Spillard. What happened?"

This time the reply was barely discernable.

Leaning in, Spillard heard Dewayne's answer, "The son of a bitch stabbed me."

"Who stabbed you?"

"Herman Hanks stabbed me," he said. "Would you tell my mother and father?"

"Yes," the chief assured him. "You hang in there. They'll get you to the hospital right away."

The ambulance arrived at DeSoto General Hospital in Mansfield before 5:30 a.m. where the doctor and nurses could do little. They prepped Dewayne for surgery, but he didn't live long enough to get into the operating room.

"All emergency measures were carried out," Dr. Roy Bucy would later testify. "But to no avail."

Facing his death, Dewayne George's last words were not for himself. Ambulance attendant Don Barnes recalled Dewayne George rambled incoherently as he was being bandaged, but at one point he looked squarely at the attendant and said clearly, "He's got my baby. I've got to find him."

Suzette George was half-asleep on the ride home from the Rendezvous Club when she realized Dewayne had stopped the car. She looked out her window into darkness. They were stopped on the side of the road. Where were they? Was there car trouble?

She had been at the Rendezvous since about nine

o'clock so by three the next morning, she was woozy headed and sleepy and just wanted to go home.

Dewayne was outside the car, talking to someone. Who?

He returned, opened his driver's door, and sat back down behind the steering wheel when a man jerked the door open, leaned in, and plunged a knife into Dewayne's chest. Suzette gasped as Dewayne slumped toward her.

"This turkey stabbed me," he said. "He stabbed me."

She hollered, leaning over her husband to shield him.

What was happening? Who was this?

Beside her, Dewayne fumbled for his pocketknife, but the big man jerked it from him, opened it, and plunged the pocketknife into Dewayne's back.

Suzette screamed, crawling on top of her husband, reaching across him clawing, flailing, trying to shield him as the big man pulled the knife out of Dewayne's back and withdrew from the car.

Dewayne used the steering wheel to pull himself up and out of the vehicle. Gripping the door then leaning against the car's hood, Dewayne struggled to the front of the car as the man reached in and yanked Suzette from the vehicle, dragging her by her upper left arm to his truck.

"Is he dead?" she shrieked. "Is Dewayne dead?"

The man shoved her into the open driver's side door of his idling truck.

"I don't know," he said, then peeled out, racing toward Converse. He set Dewayne's bloodied pocketknife on the dashboard in front of her.

Lying helpless on the highway, Dewayne George watched the truck speed away, his wife inside, taillights disappearing into the night.

Life drained out of Dewayne George as the sun rose over western Louisiana.

My phone rang about 5:30 a.m. That was never good.

17

"Robbo, they need you at DeSoto General." It was DeSoto Parish Sheriff's Department radio dispatcher Dick Atkins. "Can you meet Marvin Melton and Ken Roberts at the hospital?"

Marvin Melton and I were the two C.I.D. investigators for the parish. He was the senior officer—my mentor. Melton was a Marine veteran, retired from Louisiana State Police then he worked eighteen years with DeSoto SO. He was so much more experienced, but I was the one on-call.

"Sure. What's going on?" I asked the dispatcher.

"A kid from Converse has been killed. Stabbed. He just died at the hospital. His wife is missing."

"Did she do it?"

"I don't know. I don't think that's what they are thinking, but I don't know, Robbo," Dick said.

I sat up, getting my head around what Atkins was saying.

"Who's the victim?"

"Dewayne George."

"Joe's brother?"

"Yeah."

I knew the Georges. Everybody did. They were solid people. Their dad ran a gas station in Converse. Junies George had two sons, one a year older than I was. They both died in the service. Now Dewayne?

At the hospital, Melton and Ken Roberts filled me in on what had happened, about the call from the woman who saw Dewayne lying on the road. Ken explained what happened at the scene.

"I got to him in time for him to tell me who stabbed him," Ken said.

That was a surprising break.

"Who was it?"

"He said it was Herman Hanks."

"*Herman Hanks?*"

I looked at Melton and he nodded.

"Son of a bitch."

"Yeah, I know," Melton said. "He *is* a son of a bitch."

Hanks was the number-one suspect in a sexual-assault case just a few months earlier. A woman came to the sheriff's office and said Hanks offered to give her a ride home from the Rendezvous, but instead he took her out in the Big Woods and raped her, holding a knife at her throat. She said he'd threatened to kill her if she told anyone. It wasn't my case. Like I said, I worked narcotics. But the officers involved, including Melton, didn't think she would have reported it, except her husband saw Hanks drop her off at their house. Her husband brought her to the station to report the assault.

But by the time they came in to make a report, the woman had already taken a shower and cleaned up. There was no rape kit. No evidence to tie him to her. It would have been, "He said she said." And, like she said, she was afraid to go through and press charges. They had to let it drop.

"I wish we'd pushed that case," Melton said. "We just didn't have enough to go on."

I was thinking the same thing. If only the department had not dropped that case, if only the woman had pressed charges, maybe Dewayne George would still be alive. She was right to believe him when he said he would kill her. He proved that.

Melton went home, leaving the case to me. Watching him walk away I was struck by a realization: this was my first murder case as lead. Oh, I had assisted Melton of course but I was the drug guy. I worked narcotics. I just happened to be the investigator on call when this came in. No mistakes, Davidson, I told myself. No mistakes.

Ken brought me up to speed with a complete rundown of all that happened. I called Sabine Parish Sheriff's Office, telling their Chief Detective John Rainer we needed a warrant for Herman Hanks for the murder of Junies Dewayne George. Then I examined and photographed his body, gathering evidence, paying attention to the tedious details that make or break an investigation.

Dewayne George was smallish, at least by comparison. I'm six foot-one. I'd say Dewayne was five foot-eight. Maybe five-nine. But every ounce of him was muscle. He looked like his brothers. Dark complexion, high cheek bones. Thick black eyebrows that framed coal-black eyes. Dwayne had eyes so dark you could not discern the pupil. His collar-length hair was the same color.

Poor guy. The nurses had cleaned his bloodied body but there was no way to wipe away the battering Dewayne George had taken. He was laid out on the stainless steel table and I studied his injuries. Most of his face was purple. His right eye swollen shut. His forehead, chin, and upper lip were raw, as if he were dragged across asphalt. Similar scrapes ran along his lower back and left side. Painful injuries but a man could survive all that.

No one could survive the gaping slash in the middle of his sternum. It measured two inches vertically and three inches across. The amount of force and the kind of knife that did that likely sliced all the way into his beating heart. A medical examiner would determine that.

He had a second stab wound to his upper back, not as long but as wide. In each case the knife was probably twisted as it was pulled out, enlarging the cut. I measured and photographed all the wounds.

When the Sabine Parish Chief Deputy got to Mansfield from Many with the arrest warrant, we headed for Herman Hanks' mother's house on State Highway 509—what we called Lake Road. Sabine Chief Deputy John Rainer rode in the patrol car with me. Ken Roberts—the first man on the scene, the deputy who had tried so hard to save Dewayne George's life—followed in his own patrol car. Ken's shift was long over, but with a case like that nobody stopped working.

Though I heard of him through the would-be rape case, I'd never personally seen Herman Hanks. Melton had said the woman described him as very tall and blonde.

Nearing the Hanks' home, we passed a big, blonde,

bearded man walking down Lake Road carrying a flat tire that was still mounted on the rim. It was a big tire—a truck tire—that he carried like a book satchel. It appeared he intended to tote it all the way into town, half a mile or more, which testified to his brute strength.

Dewayne George was solid, but Hanks was half a foot taller and at least a hundred pounds heavier. Dewayne George would have been no match for Herman Hanks in a fight.

Believing we'd just passed the man we were looking for, I turned around and stopped the patrol car in front of him.

Stepping out I asked, "Are you Herman Hanks?"

"Yeah," he replied.

"You're under arrest for murder."

He didn't cut and run or even act surprised. He didn't ask who I was. He just said, "Yeah? Who'd I murder?"

"Junies D. George," I replied.

Nothing. No facial expression denoting surprise or fear. Hanks said nothing, just stood there with the tire in his huge paw as I read his Miranda Rights then he asked, "Can I go home and tell my mother where I'm going?"

"Yes," I said.

Rainer asked, "Do you want to change clothes?" Hanks was wearing cut-off blue jean shorts and a T-shirt.

"Yeah."

He folded himself and the flat tire into the back seat of my patrol car, a 1978 Chevy Impala four-door sedan. White with dark-tinted windows.

On the ride back to his mother's house, we began asking him questions.

"Where were you last night?"

"The VFW, the Weekend Liquor, and Alice's Wagon Wheel on Highway 1 in Red River Parish," he said. He'd gotten home about five or six that morning, he said.

At Gertrude Hanks' house, John Rainer went with Hanks to a bedroom where he changed his clothing. I waited in the living room with his mother, explaining what was going on. She didn't say a word, just listened.

When Hanks and Chief Deputy Rainer came out of the bedroom, I asked, "Where are the clothes you had on last night?"

"In the dirty clothes hamper," his mother said. She was a raw-boned red-headed, ruddy-faced woman.

Hanks whispered something to Rainer.

"Y'all come outside with me?" The Sabine Parish Chief Deputy motioned for Ken and me to follow the two of them.

At the patrol car, Rainer handcuffed Hanks, saying, "Repeat what you just told me to these officers."

"I stabbed him," Hanks said.

"Do you know anything about Suzette?" I asked.

"She's on Hunter Cut-Off Road."

Ken Roberts demanded, "Is she dead or alive?"

"I don't know."

We all looked at each other— Ken, Rainer and I—as Hanks continued, "I stabbed her three or four times in the chest. And I killed him because he made fun of me on the job."

"Can you show us where she is?" I asked.

"Yes."

I put Hanks' clothing in a sack in the trunk of my patrol unit. We put him, handcuffed, in the back seat of the patrol car—minus the flat tire—and he guided us to find the body of Suzette George. From that point on I did what I could to keep him talking. I didn't want him to have time to think, to change his mind and clam up. Without his help, it would be almost impossible to find Suzette. Maybe, just maybe, she had survived. People survived being stabbed. Maybe we'd get to her in time.

The four of us drove to Lula Road. Me, John Rainer, and Herman Hanks rode in my patrol car, and Ken Roberts followed in his. As we crossed Clement Creek Bridge south of US Highway 84, Hanks popped off, "That's where I threw her clothes."

"Threw her clothes," he said. He'd said he stabbed her. He didn't mention raping her. Did he rape her? The woman in March said that he'd raped her holding a knife at her throat. It crossed my mind, *Was the knife he used on Dewayne George the same knife he held at that woman's throat in March when he raped her. Did he stab Suzette George with that knife?* My hope of finding her alive dimmed but was not dead. Hope is a hard thing to let go of.

Hanks directed us down several turns, deeper and deeper into the woods, finally telling me to stop at a deeply rutted dirt logging road that intersected the narrow black-top parish road. He pointed. "She's down there."

Timber trucks are ungodly heavy, typically hauling anywhere from 80,000 to just under 90,000 pounds, legally. They routinely run heavy, which is one reason Louisiana has such strict laws on weights and measures. Over-weight timber trucks carrying pine, oak, and hickory can crack an asphalt road. Imagine what a convoy of five or ten timber trucks, each weighing forty tons or more, can do to a dirt road a day or two after a rain. That's what I was looking at. A pickup truck might maneuver those ruts, but my low riding patrol car would drag bottom, and I'd have to call a tow truck. No thanks. I'd have to walk.

Eyeing Hanks in my rear-view mirror, I asked, "How far?"

He shrugged, leaned back to rest his huge head against the back seat, and stared at the headliner. "I don't know," he muttered. "But she's down there."

"John, will you stay here and guard him?" I asked.

The chief deputy nodded. Rainer weighed about as much as Hanks only he was five-foot-nine. And he was a lot older. It was too hot. We had no idea now how far down that trail she might be. It was better for Rainer to stay in the air-conditioned car and keep an eye on Hanks. Anyway, I'd just as soon take the god-forsaken walk as sit in the car with that prick Hanks.

I told Ken to go back to headquarters. He still had to

write his report before he could finally go home. "I'll go with you," he offered. I knew he would. He was that kind of guy.

"It's okay," I said. "You've had a hell of a night and day and I'm just getting started. You got to Dewayne in time for him to tell you who did it. That's what matters."

"But I couldn't save him."

I heard and felt his regret. Ken Roberts was about the same size as Dewayne George but old enough to be his dad. He joined our department several years earlier after retiring from Shreveport P.D. That was not uncommon. Guys like him and Melton, they retired from one law enforcement agency then came to work for DeSoto Parish. Why? No one enters law enforcement for the pay or benefits. They probably needed the income to supplement their retirement.

It's a win-win arrangement: Those second-career guys drew full retirement pay from one department and earned a second paycheck working a job that was normally pretty uneventful while the people of DeSoto Parish benefitted from their vast experience.

I had no idea what Ken's experiences were with Shreveport P.D., but I was certain that during his time with DeSoto Parish, he had never dealt with any situation as intensely emotional as finding Dewayne George bleeding to death on that deserted stretch of highway.

"Nobody could have saved Dewayne," I said, certain after having seen his wounds.

As Ken drove away, I told John Rainer I would probably be a while. "I've got my radio with me. If she's down there, I'll find her."

About a quarter mile and a gallon of sweat later I did— led by that distant swarm of flies. I am retired now but I can still close my eyes and see Suzette George's body lying in the brush beneath the hideous swarm, her feet at the road's edge, almost as if she dropped off a logging truck.

Long, wavy brown hair fanned around, falling across one shoulder. Lying on her back, her head tilted back and left to expose a purple throat. That answered the first question: cause of death, strangulation. There were no ligature marks. He used his hands. Her upper left arm was purple.

Waving away the flies, I squatted for a closer examination. I couldn't do anything about the ants beginning to cover her.

There was a circle of puncture wounds between her breasts. Hanks said he stabbed her 'three or four times'? She was stabbed too many times to count. I never saw so many stab wounds concentrated in such a small space—not in decades of investigating.

That there was almost no blood around the circle of stab wounds told me this was done after she died. Most people will try to defend themselves against a knife. Had she been alive when she was stabbed, there probably would have been cuts on her hands or fingers. There were none.

Clinched fists fallen to either side of her head testified that she had fought, best she could.

Time of death? She had been here long enough for the insects to find her but not long enough for the buzzards. The hotter it is, the faster flesh decays, putting off enzymes that attract insects. As hot as it was, nearby ants and flies were on her almost immediately. Flies can detect death from as far away as a mile in one hour. Judging by the size of the swarm that led me to Suzette's body and the insects on her, it was my guess she died before her husband. Had I not found her when I did, the scavengers would have been on her before long. I could spare her that final indignation, at least.

I radioed Deputy Rainer, "She's here."

"Ten-four."

I thought of Herman Hanks, the hulk, sitting handcuffed in the backseat of my air-conditioned patrol car. He did this. He had shown no emotion about anything—no emotion when he was arrested, no emotion when he confessed. Rainer said Hanks expressed no emotion whatsoever when he heard on the radio that I found Suzette's body. It was eerie that a person who could display this amount of calm could be so explosive. So deadly. Very Jekyll and Hyde.

"Call the coroner," I radioed. "And call for someone to come guard this scene till the coroner gets here, will you? And John—tell them they need to come in trucks."

John Rainer remained with Hanks while I processed the scene, covering her body after photographing and measuring the wounds. I took photographs of everything, including the tire tracks that appeared to back up about six feet from Suzette's body. The tread marks should match the tire Hanks was carrying when we found him.

Back at the unit, I read Herman Hanks his Miranda Rights for the second time that day, this time for the murder of Suzette George.

"Do you understand your rights?"

"Yes, sir, I understand. I just want to get this off my chest."

I almost laughed. Want to get it off your chest? You would never have 'gotten it off your chest' if Dewayne George had not lived long enough to identify you.

If Ken Roberts had not gotten to Dewayne George when he did, we might never have solved two murders.

There would have been nothing to link Herman Hanks to either the stabbing of Dewayne or the disappearance of Suzette. He had not left the Rendezvous with them. James Caston would have testified Herman Hanks took him home. How could he possibly have killed the Georges?

Someone would have found Dewayne dead on the highway, but no one would have found the body of Suzette George for no-telling how long, if ever. If enough time passed before a crew came down this timber trail, the vultures would have cleaned her body. There would have been nothing left for a passerby to see. Wild dogs or hogs would have carried off the bones. She would have been just another unsolved missing persons' case.

When DeSoto Parish Sheriff's Deputy Billy Lynch arrived to secure the crime scene, we turned it over to him to wait for the coroner. Hanks directed John Ranier and me to a pond off Lula Road where he said he washed the blood off his hands, cut up her clothing, and tossed the pocketknife he used to stab Suzette. We combed the area and never found the knife. If he threw it into the pond, it was buried beneath a foot of silt. Draining the pond would not only be impossible but pointless.

From there we drove to Clements Creek Bridge where Hanks said he tossed Suzette's clothing. I climbed down the bank, photographed, and bagged the evidence. From there, we took him to the sheriff's office to get his full statement.

The DeSoto Parish Jail and Sheriff's Office were housed in a three-story brick building across the street from the courthouse, but the Criminal Investigation Division was nothing more than a portable building a block away. It was cramped with dark paneling, a fluorescent ceiling light, a couple of desks and file cabinets. We took Hanks there to get his formal statement.

He was calm and compliant as if detached from his predicament. He answered our questions but neither John Rainer nor I were satisfied he was completely forthcoming. There were too many inconsistencies and blanks in the story. But then, a lot of alcohol can blank out a lot of memories.

Outside our C.I.D. hut the sun was sinking, and no one was waiting for the Fourth to start popping firecrackers and setting off bottle rockets. There was the lonesome wail of a westbound train, an ambulance siren coming or going from DeSoto General while the Mansfield High School Marching Wolverine band was tuning up on the courthouse lawn, practicing for tomorrow's parade.

I asked Hanks, "Can you tell us now where this all began, starting from leaving the liquor store south of Mansfield on 171 early this morning? Just start there. In your own words, step by step."

"Okay. We left. They left."

"They? You're talking about George and his wife?"

"George and his wife. Dewayne and his wife Suzette. I followed them to right this side of Converse."

The veins in Rainer's thick neck were bulging. He bounced out of his chair, leaned across the desk resting his weight on his chubby knuckles so that he was eyeball to eyeball with Herman Hanks handcuffed in his chair.

"For what!" Rainer thundered. "Why did you go after them?"

It was the first time Hanks had looked either of us squarely in the face. Locking eyes with John Rainer, Hanks said, "Well, I was mad and wanting to fight, wanting to raise hell."

"What were you mad about?" Rainer barked. He needed to understand. "Him? Her?"

Another moment of silence as Rainer crouched, frozen across the desk within a foot of the big man's face until Hanks looked away. "I can't rightly say I know."

Rainer sat back down as Hanks went on with his story.

His plan to follow the Georges got detoured by his buddy James Caston, whose car would not start. Caston asked Hanks to drive him home less than a mile away toward Mansfield, which Hanks did. Then he raced to overtake the Georges who were driving about fifty miles an hour in the other direction.

"I passed them— Mr. and Mrs. George. I blowed the horn when I went by them, pulled off the shoulder of the road, and he pulled over behind me."

"Okay this was in your blue Chevrolet truck?" I asked.

"My mother's truck."

"Your mother's truck?"

"A 1975 blue Chevrolet truck."

"Okay, go ahead," I prompted.

"Dewayne got out of his car, come up to the truck. We talked a few minutes. He went back to his car and set down in his car and that's when I stabbed him."

"Where did you stab him the first time?" John Rainer asked.

"In the chest."

"And then what happened?" Rainer asked.

"And he went to kicking, trying to kick me. His wife crawled on top of him. Dewayne got out and had his knife in his hand and that's when I stabbed him again in the back. And he staggered to the front of the car and fell."

I wasn't clear. "That was with *your* pocketknife?" I asked.

"Yessir, with my pocketknife."

"After he fell, what did you do with your pocketknife?" I asked.

"My knife fell out of my hand, and it's still out there. I never could find it."

"What kind of knife was it?"

"Uh, an Old Timer."

"Is it a large knife?" I was trying to picture it.

"Yessir, it's about that long." Hanks gestured with his hands. "About eight inches long."

"When it's open?"

"Yessir, when it's open."

That meant Hanks punched a hole four inches deep into the center of Dewayne George's chest. I didn't know how he lived as long as he did.

Rainer asked, "At this time he was laying in front of his car, right?"

"Yessir. He was laying in front of his car."

"Now at that point, what did you do?"

"I got Mrs. George, put her in my truck, and drove off."

His account of what happened after that is the only version anyone will ever have. Like everything else he told us, I was not convinced it was true. But the only person who could tell us otherwise was dead.

In the blackness of that moonless night, restrained by the iron grip of a man who stabbed her husband and dragged her from her car, Suzette George froze in fear. They drove in silence into Converse then turned north on Lula Road.

"Where are we going," Suzette asked. "Where are you taking me?"

No answer.

She pleaded, "Please, don't kill me."

Still, no response.

This was the man from the club— James Caston's friend. Herman. She'd talked with him. Danced with him. He rode to work with Dewayne sometimes. How could this be happening? Was Dewayne all right? Was he dead? Would he come for her? Would anybody come for her?

Deeper and deeper into the woods they drove in silence until Hanks turned down a rutted logging road, the truck bouncing heavily in and out of the deep grooves. Finally, he stopped, backed up, and turned around so he could drive straight out. Then he turned off the truck.

With the headlights off Suzette could see nothing—not the man—not even the hand in front of her face. But she could smell and hear: the aroma of pines, the frogs croaking, the crickets, and the cicadas, the stench of stale alcohol and sweat and cigarette smoke.

Her throat tightened as she heard Hanks unzip his jeans. "Take off your clothes," he said.

She did. She removed her yellow terry-cloth top, her bra, and her jeans. He grabbed her hair, shoving her head into his lap, holding her there.

She did what she had to do to survive. When it was over, before she could reach for her clothing, Hanks grabbed her left arm again, dragging her from the truck. He pulled her screaming into utter blackness as she clawed and scratched.

"Shut up," he yelled, "Shut up!"

Grabbing her throat with one enormous hand, Hanks cut off the screams. She pulled at his hand, clawed his face, kicked, and flailed as he picked her up off the ground, ever tightening his grip on her throat. He threw her into the thick brush, his 250 pounds coming down on top of her, knocking the breath out of her as he continued squeezing her neck, choking, choking, choking until she was still. Her arms fell limp.

Then Herman Hanks got the pocketknife—her husband's pocketknife—from the dashboard of his truck and began stabbing Suzette George in his drunken rage.

He described washing the blood off his hands at the pond and hurling the pocketknife into the brush. He told how he cut up her pants for some unknown reason there at the pond, that he stopped and threw her possessions over the Clements Creek Bridge as he drove home.

"What possessed you to do this?" John Rainer asked. "What brought this on? Can you tell me what the motive was?"

"No sir, I have no idea. I don't have no idea."

Hanks was different. The interrogation room was close quarters. Suspects usually squirm. They shift around in their chair, glance around the room. Herman Hanks did none of those things. He answered our questions with the same stoicism he displayed from the start, usually staring at the desk or the corner of the room rather than looking at either of us.

I struggled to fathom the amount of hatred it took to do all he had done. Imagine the strength necessary to stab a man through the sternum, plunge a knife four inches into his chest, then pull it back out through the bone. And to stab anyone the way he stabbed Suzette? I could not conjure up the motive for what had happened that morning.

"Had you ever been with Suzette before?" I asked.

"No sir. Last night was the second time I'd met her. I'd seen her once before at the V.F.W."

I asked, "Did she know you?"

"She knowed my name. Dewayne had talked about me. I don't know what he said or nothing about me."

I continued, "But you were sitting together at the Weekend Liquor—the Rendevous—and she was talking to you?"

"Yes, sir."

"What was this conversation about?

"Just records, dancing."

"Was there something in what she had done to you or you to her that made you want to go out with her," John Rainer asked.

"No sir."

"How much did you have to drink last night," I asked. "Just guessing. What do you think?"

"About twenty-five or thirty mixed drinks."

Our interviews were all recorded so they could be transcribed by secretaries and the recordings were preserved but I also scribbled notes for my use. I stopped writing. I was— I won't say shocked, not much shocked me—but surprised by how much alcohol he said he consumed in one night and still functioned.

"Say that again?" John Rainer was surprised, too.

"I'd say maybe twenty-five to thirty mixed drinks. And some beer."

"What kind of mixed drinks?" I asked.

"Charter and Coke."

"Did you take any drugs?" I asked.

"No, sir."

"Do you use drugs?"

"No, sir. I do not."

I would have been willing to bet money he did.

"At one time you rode to work with Dewayne. Right? Did you have any misunderstandings or disagreement on the job?" I asked.

"No, we didn't work together. He worked with the electricians. I worked for the pipefitters."

I leaned in, forcing him to look me in the face. "Well, you told me that you had a misunderstanding and they picked on you."

"Calling me names: Fat boy. Asshole, everything else. Just generally picking on me."

"Was this every day?" I asked.

"Might near every day."

"Well, did this happen at the Weekend Liquor also last night?" I thought maybe that prompted the rage.

"No, sir."

"Did *not*?" I asked.

"Did not."

"It was just something in your mind?"

"Yessir."

I asked if he owed Dewayne money, or did Dewayne owe him money. Neither man owed the other money.

I had a killer who confessed and a victim who identified him. But a confession is not enough to ensure a conviction. He could always recant. We needed forensic evidence. I took Hanks to DeSoto General Hospital to collect that evidence—samples of hair and blood. Suzette had clawed him. He had scratches on both arms. Was his blood type under her fingernails?

Then John Rainer took Hanks to Many to the Sabine Parish Jail. He was booked there for the murder of Junies Dewayne George and the aggravated kidnapping of Suzette George.

In DeSoto Parish, I filed charges of capital murder for the death of Suzette George. If I had my choice, Herman Karrel Hanks would fry in the electric chair.

I impounded his truck and the Georges' Oldsmobile. There was blood all inside of both. On Hanks' truck there was blood along the driver's window, on the door handle, the seat, the dashboard. In the front seat of the Georges' car, the same thing. Blood everywhere. Most likely all the blood was Dewayne's. We fingerprinted everything.

Hanks' blue jeans I got from his mother's house—they were soaked in blood. Forensics could tell us if it was his or hers or Dewayne's. Suzette's clothing from Clements Creek would be tested for blood, hair, semen. Anything to connect him to her.

In 1981, we never imagined DNA evidence. But forensics could type blood to see if it matched any of their types. Same thing with hair and semen. With no murder weapon, we needed all the forensics we could get.

The next day Rainer and I questioned Alan Yarbrough, who said he had never seen Suzette George without her husband; Rendezvous bartenders Bruce Rogers and Lenora Lee, who overheard Dewayne and Suzette argue that night at the bar. Lenora Lee said she saw Suzette go outside with Hanks. I interviewed James Caston who admitted he wondered why Hanks peeled out after dropping him off that morning.

We took statements from the ambulance attendants and all the officers who had gone to State Highway 171 to back up Ken Roberts. Army Sgt. Pat Lanagan made her statement to the C.I.D. at Fort Polk.

After interviewing all the others, I went down to the Sabine Parish Jail to ask more questions of Hanks. That was July 6. Rainer was with me.

"I appreciate you being cooperative," I told Hanks. "But there are some discrepancies I've got to get cleared up."

Some facts became clearer with questioning, but others were never explained. There was never any explanation about what was said between Hanks and Dewayne George outside the vehicles after Dewayne was pulled over and stopped. What excuse had Hanks given for pulling Dewayne over, if any? Had they argued? We never found out.

After whatever was said, Dewayne went back to the car. Hanks followed, the eight-inch knife in hand, then stabbed Dewayne as he sat down behind the wheel.

"Did he see you coming?" I asked.

"No, sir. I don't believe he ever saw it coming. I dropped the knife right there."

"Stop right there," I said. "After you hit him the first time what did he do?"

"He just leaned over in the seat, told his wife that I had stabbed him."

"What did he say?"

"He said, 'This turkey stabbed me.'"

"What did she say?" I asked.

"She didn't say nothing, she just sort of leaned over and looked and she started crawling over him."

"What did you hit him with the second time?"

"With a knife. With his own knife, that I got from him."

"You stabbed him with your knife in the chest?" I wanted to be clear.

"Right."

"The knife stab in the back—"

"Was with his knife. I couldn't find mine, I dropped mine, lost mine."

"He was taking his out and you reached in and took it away from him or what?" I was just trying to get the scenario in my head.

"I took it away from him."

"And stabbed him in the back with it?"

"Yessir."

The Sabine Parish Chief Deputy sat in any time I questioned Hanks—and vice versa—since we were both working cases against him for the same incident. Part of it happened in Sabine Parish. Part of it in DeSoto Parish.

"What did she do?" John Rainer asked.

"She went to screaming and hollering and started crawling over him."

"Toward you?"

"Yessir. I guess to keep me off him."

"Is that when you grabbed her arm?" John Rainer asked.

"Yessir. Her left arm."

Some of it we heard two days earlier, but you ask again to see if they change their story. His was the same. He went on talking, painting the scene for us. As Hanks withdrew from the vehicle Dewayne came out behind him, holding onto the door for support, then the hood. Suzette was in the motion of crawling across the driver's seat to follow her husband when Hanks reached in and yanked her out. I could see it all. That much adrenaline—this huge man just pulled her out and across the pavement almost effortlessly. It explained her bruised arm.

"He just got out of the car and staggered to the front of it? When he fell what did you do?" John Rainer asked again.

"I got his wife and went to the truck."

We still could not explain the way Dewayne's face had been battered. The blackened eye swollen shut. The scrapes across his forehead, chin, and upper lip.

Had the two men fought, I asked again.

"No, sir."

"When you struggled in the car, did you ram his head against the steering wheel?"

He insisted no, the two men never exchanged blows.

But he had to wrestle the knife away from Dewayne. Maybe that was when he got the black eye, I suggested.

"No, sir, there wasn't no wrestling. I may have hit him in the back with my knife. All I know is my knife is right there in the car somewhere. Or there in the area because that's where I dropped it. That is where I lost it."

"You're not really sure if you used his knife to stab him in the back or not, are you?" John Rainer said.

Silence. We waited for a response. Finally, "No, sir. I'm not for sure."

We continued to try to get the picture clear but there was never a clear explanation of what the two men discussed outside the vehicles—had they argued then? Had Dewayne called him names?

"No," they just talked, he said.

"What education do you have?" I asked.

"I went to the tenth grade."

Why had he dropped out of school?

"I just quit and went to the service."

"What service were you in?" I asked.

"The United States Army."

"Where were you stationed then?"

"I was in Germany when I got out."

"Have you been to the penitentiary?" It was a standard question I asked. I'd run his background—he had no real criminal record.

"No, sir."

"Never been in jail?" John Rainer didn't seem to believe this guy had never been in trouble before.

"Once."

"Where?" the chief detective asked.

"Morgan City, for fighting."

"That's all?"

"That's all."

"No other charges?"

"When I was a little boy, stealing a bicycle."

"No, I'm talking about after you were adult age," John Rainer said.

"That was all."

"This deal in Morgan City. Was there a knife involved?" I asked.

"No, sir. It was just fist fighting."

I went back to July third. "When you went down there looking for him or trying to catch him, did you have in your mind to do something to him and take her?"

He shook his head. "No."

Why then had he killed two people? Had he just chased Dewayne George, looking for a fight?

"Did you just want to whip his butt?" I asked.

"That's what I was mainly after."

"After the stabbing took place with him, did you decide right then to take her with you?"

"Yessir."

"When you left the scene there—what did you have in mind doing with her?" John Rainer asked.

Hanks pursed his lips, answering at last, "I really don't know."

"After you got over to the woods, over around Lula Road, where we found the body, I guess at that point you decided to engage in some sort of sex?" I asked.

"Yes, sir."

"After you got through with the sex you decided to get rid of her?"

"Yes, sir."

John Rainer interjected, "What was the purpose of that Herman?"

"Of what?"

"*Of getting rid of her,*" the chief detective said.

Hanks shrugged, "It just come over me. That she could identify me and all."

John Rainer asked, "Let me ask you another question. You just answer it anyway you want to. It is going to be kind of off the top of my head and it is going to hit you pretty hard: Is sex your hang-up?"

"No, sir."

"Do women mess you up?" Rainer pressed.

"No, sir."

He never registered anger or surprise at anything we asked.

"What is it that possesses you to want a woman?" John Rainer went on. "Under these circumstances, I'm talking about."

"I couldn't really tell you," Hanks said. "I don't know."

"Is it in your mind?" Rainer asked. "Is it something you want to do? Or is it something brought on or how is it brought on? Is revenge part of it?"

"I guess it could be. I don't really know."

"Have you ever been mistreated by a woman?" I asked.

"No, sir."

I went back to the March sexual assault case.

"Just like we were talking a while ago you just come out with it if you want to," I said. "In this crime last March, you were the number one suspect. Nothing ever came of it. The case was closed because she didn't want to pursue it. We understand that. No problem there. To clear our minds, did you have sex with her?"

"No, sir. I did not. I took her straight home."

I had to ask. "Why do you think she would tell us that y'all had sex and you threatened to kill her?"

"I have no idea," he said.

I wasn't buying any of this. That woman had been scared to death and credible. God, I wished they had pushed her to file charges back then.

"Where did you meet her?"

"Out at Alan's."

"Did she approach you?"

"She asked me after her and her husband had a fight, and he left. She asked me if I'd take her home."

"That's how you got involved in it?"

"Yessir."

"Have you ever taken a girl before?" Rainer asked.

"No, sir."

He was questioned in Morgan City about a woman who was murdered after riding in his cab, he admitted, but her boyfriend killed her, he explained. The police had questioned all the cab drivers.

"Is there anything else you want to tell us," I asked. "Anything at all?"

"I've told you everything," Hanks said.

I didn't buy that and neither did Rainer. Hanks raped the woman last March and he *had* pursued Dewayne George sparring for a fight—but the deeper motive all along, I believe to this day, was the girl.

The court scheduled a sanity hearing for September,

requiring Hanks be examined by two unaffiliated clinical psychiatrists. The judge assigned Dr. Paul Ware of Shreveport and Dr. Richard Oosta of Many to examine him.

Both doctors concluded Hanks was mentally capable of aiding in his own defense, but Dr. Ware's comprehensive assessment of the accused killer gave prosecutors greater insight into his thinking and his actions.

According to Dr. Ware's report, Hanks described his parents as loving people. He told Dr. Ware his mother would give him anything he wanted and was very affectionate toward him. He described his father as a good-hearted person who would do anything for people.

Hanks told Dr. Ware he began drinking at the age of sixteen and had never stopped; that his father never knew of his drinking. He said he 'got messed up on drugs' in Germany and was given a discharge for not being able to adjust to military life.

He told Dr. Ware he often drank ten to twelve drinks a day and that he'd been drunk to the point of passing out perhaps a dozen times in his life. According to Dr. Ware's report, Hanks said he had been arrested several times for fighting, contradicting what he had told us.

Hanks' detailed account of his actions on July second, leading up to his bloody highway rendezvous with Dewayne George, helped prosecutors understand just how intoxicated he was at that time.

He said he slept until about 9 a.m. then watched television at his mother's until about 2 p.m. when he drove to his lawyer's office to pick up his disability check. He returned to his mother's house where he watched more television until about 5 p.m. Then he bathed and dressed to go out.

He said he drove first to a liquor store, where he bought a six pack of beer and headed to Alice's Wagon Wheel, a bar in Red River Parish on Highway 1. He shot pool and drank ten to twelve mixed drinks at Alice's Wagon Wheel before driving to the VFW in Mansfield around 9 p.m.

There, he continued drinking whiskey and shooting pool, estimating he had another ten to fifteen mixed drinks. Hanks admitted having trouble driving from the VFW to the Rendezvous Club. Once there, he ordered more mixed drinks. He recalled driving James Caston home and chasing down the George's car. Hanks disavowed any memory of stabbing Dewayne George though he clearly recalled pulling the knife out of his chest.

Dr. Ware wrote, "He said things were a blur and the next memory he had is standing out by his truck on a little road and looking down in front of him and seeing Dewayne's wife lying out on the ground looking like she had been stabbed. He said he then got in his truck and drove home."

Dr. Ware diagnosed Herman Hanks as an anti-social personality who suffered from chronic alcohol abuse. "He denied any confusion in thinking," the psychiatrist wrote in his report to the court, "he tends to reminisce and daydream about wishing he had lived in the Old West. He denied visual or auditory hallucinations. The patient demonstrated an excellent memory.

"As he described the events leading up to the crime, his memory became sketchier. However, he did clearly remember seeing the knife in the man's chest and pulling it out. He also talked about remembering being out on a small road and seeing the woman lying in front of his car, and there was a slip of the tongue, which suggested his memory was more intact than he stated. This kind of fluctuating sketchy memory impairment for actual events in someone drinking is very unusual and questionable.

"The patient's overall personality adaptation was that of an antisocial with poor integrated conscience formation, poor impulse control and a tendency toward acting on one's impulses rather than thinking about the consequences. He has significant denial in regard to his substance abuse and the dangerousness and seriousness of the substance abuse."

Dr. Ware concluded Hanks was mentally capable of

aiding in his own defense. "And furthermore, was able to distinguish between right and wrong at the time of the offenses."

Herman Hanks had a speedier-than-normal trial. Arrested on July 3 and charged with two counts of capital murder and one count of aggravated kidnapping, he remained in the Sabine Parish Jail without bond until his trial and conviction.

On July 15, his eight-inch Old Timer knife, which had been used to kill Dewayne George—the one he said he dropped by the car on State Highway 171—was discovered in the parking lot of an abandoned, burned-out café in Converse by an employee of the Louisiana Highway Department. The knife was handed over to Converse Police Chief Hugh Spillard, who delivered it to the 11th Judicial Court District Attorney's Office, which covered DeSoto and Sabine Parishes, where it remains in evidence lockup to this day.

In September 1981, Herman Hanks was found mentally competent to stand trial and assist in his own defense. His attorneys filed a motion to quash his indictment on grounds that he never understood his Miranda Rights when they were read. However, after a hearing and testimony, the court denied that motion and set the trial date for December of the same year.

The trial was comparatively brief and scantily attended. There was no big press coverage or public interest. Suzette George was an only child raised by a single mother who had died several years earlier. Authorities had trouble finding her estranged father in New Orleans to notify him of his daughter's death.

Junies George did not attend the trial of his son's killer although his son Joe did attend some of it, prosecutors recalled.

"For the most part it was a slam dunk," said Herman Lawson, the assistant District Attorney who was second chair in the trial. Lawson handled the sentencing phase. "One of the main reasons the jury didn't give him the death sentence was because a family member testified, Herman Hanks still wet the bed at age thirty-one," Lawson recalled.

Given the viciousness and efficiency of the attack on the Georges and the March rape report, Lawson said he could not help but wonder if Herman Hanks had not committed similar attacks somewhere in his past.

"I just don't believe this was his first rodeo," the former prosecutor said.

That made sense to me, too. Herman Hanks befriended a woman stranded in a nightclub then took her into the Big Woods where he raped her and threatened to kill her. He took Suzette George to the Big Woods to rape and kill her. That was no coincidence. He took her where he felt sure she would never be found, a quarter mile down an almost impassible logging road in the middle of nowhere. I believed he intended to rape and kill her from the moment he plunged the knife into Dewayne's chest. Maybe from the minute she walked away from him after they danced. He wanted her. How many other women had he raped and or killed? How many men, like Dewayne, had he killed? How many unsolved missing persons cases were there between Morgan City and Mansfield?

Hanks was found guilty on all charges and sentenced to life in prison for each murder charge and thirty years in prison for the aggravated kidnapping. The life sentences ran concurrently while the kidnapping charge was to run consecutively. In other words, Herman Karrel Hanks was sentenced to life plus thirty years for his murderous rampage. He died in Louisiana's State Penitentiary at Angola of a heart attack on September 29, 1988.

Dewayne and Suzette George had a double funeral, which was largely attended by people from Sabine and DeSoto Parishes. They were buried side by side in Mitchell Cemetery outside of Converse in Sabine Parish. Herman Karrel Hanks is buried a few miles away in the Beulah

Cemetery on Lula Road in DeSoto Parish.

The Georges were the first murder investigation that rested on my shoulders. It was followed by so many, but your first anything always stands out in your mind. I am satisfied that in each case I worked I did the best I could, but not unlike the regret Ken Roberts voiced so long ago, I still wish we could have saved them. I wish Dewayne George could have gotten to the hospital on time; wish someone could have saved poor Suzette.

The longer I live the more often, late at night, one case or another elbows its way into my mind as I drift off, denying me sleep. I want people to know Dewayne George died loving his wife and she was driven to her death wondering if her husband was all right. Would Dewayne come for her? How could Suzette possibly have known that being nice to a stranger would cost her and her husband their lives? That was her seemingly insignificant decision that led to two deaths and it reaffirmed what I have long believed: Drunk men and beautiful women make a deadly cocktail.

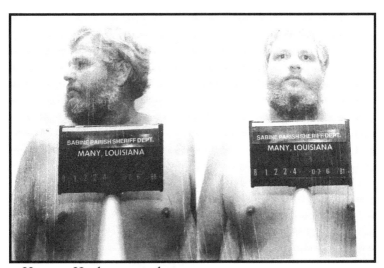

Herman Hanks arrest photo
—Courtesy DeSoto Parish Sheriff's Office

Herman Hanks' bloodied truck in DPSO impound
—Courtesy DeSoto Parish Sheriff's Office

Gangster Tales

The Crips are one of the largest, most violent street gangs in the United States with untold thousands of members operating in metropolitan areas across the nation. They are involved in drugs, drive-by shootings, robberies, and murder. Since their inception in the 1970s, violent street gangs have inspired many young men.

Their influence stretched even to the backwoods of western Louisiana.

Bare, gray treetops swayed beneath a biting wind that scattered fallen leaves. Though I was warm enough, wearing a heavy goose down jacket, I was losing feeling in my fingertips. You can't wear gloves and operate a camera. At least I never knew how.

A hushed voice from behind startled me. "You see that guy over there?"

That was Ray Sharrow. I knew his voice but moreover,

I could smell Ray's cigarette smoke before I saw him. He was a chain smoker.

"The guy talking to the reporters."

Why was Ray almost whispering? There was no one nearby. I stopped what I was doing—helping process a crime scene—to look down the street at a man encircled by a group of reporters. There wasn't much to him—a wispy little guy.

"What about him?" I asked.

With half a cigarette dangling from his lips, Ray explained, "He was burning trash in a barrel down the street when I got here. When the TV people pulled up, he hauled ass over and starts telling them how he saw a red truck with an Arkansas tag come out of here Saturday night."

We were on Hatfield Street, a narrow, barely paved lane in a part of Mansfield the city seemed to have forgotten. It cut through heavy woods that were dotted with old mattresses, discarded couches, and garbage. The roadway dead-ended near a falling down, abandoned clapboard house where the body of a missing man had been found a few hours earlier.

I'd shoved my hands in my coat pockets while we talked, so the feeling was coming back to my fingertips.

"Appreciate it, Ray," I said and went back to work, keeping an eye on Ray's person of interest. When the little guy walked away from his five minutes of fame in front of the TV cameras, I approached, showing my badge.

"I'm Detective Davidson with the DeSoto Parish Sheriff's Department," I said. "Can I talk to you a minute?"

He was a nice-enough-looking kid. Clean-cut, early twenties, maybe five-foot six or seven, thin as a blade of grass. He ambled over in no certain hurry.

"You say you saw a truck coming out of here Saturday night?"

"More like Sunday morning," he said. "Maybe around— I don't know—one or two."

"What's your name?"

"Burton," he said, offering his hand. "Cedric Burton. They call me C-2."

"C-2? Nice to meet you." I shook his hand.

"Yessir. Cedric— C-2." He smiled.

"Well, Cedric, what more can you tell me about that truck? It could be important."

"It was a red truck. I can't be sure what kind. Maybe a Mitsubishi. I saw it had Arkansas plates."

Then Cedric Burton proceeded to rattle off the tag number of this pickup truck that drove past him in the dead of night.

"Good memory," I said. "Would you mind coming down to the station and giving me a statement? About the truck? It might really help."

"Sure," he replied. "Glad to help."

As we walked to my unit, I noticed Cedric wore a scabbard knife on his side. Before he got into my car, I reached down and slipped the knife out of the holster.

"Can't ride with that in the unit," I explained.

He didn't seem to have a problem with it.

"You can get it back when you leave."

We drove across town to the DeSoto Parish Sheriff's Department Criminal Investigation Division. Sheriff Frenchie Lambert was in office in 1988, but Frenchie wasn't actually *in* the office on Sunday.

The detective division operated out of temporary offices across the street from the sheriff's department, after someone torched our wood-frame C.I.D. building almost a year before. Everyone in C.I.D. ragged me about it.

"Some druggie Robbo busted got mad, poured gasoline around the building, and set it on fire," they'd say—which *someone* did. That was long before surveillance cameras. Any possible prints were incinerated along with everything else, so no one could be certain it was someone *I* arrested who torched our offices, but, nonetheless, everybody groused that "Robbo's Fire" resulted in us being in an old, cold building that was once part of a hotel.

The police jury—the governing body of the parish, what other states call the commissioners court—had rented it for us.

The only items we salvaged from the fire were case files from inside metal cabinets. Those paper files still smelled like smoke. Any time anyone opened a file cabinet drawer, everyone would cough and carry on, recalling the night the old C.I.D. building burned.

The temporary C.I.D. building had a wide reception area with a long hall behind it, detective offices on either side. They were originally hotel rooms.

Detective Lt. Charlie Frazier's office was across the hall from mine. Frazier had been recruited in the mid-70s by former DeSoto Parish Sheriff Roy Webb, who preceded Frenchie—and I don't think Frazier ever accepted Frenchie. Charlie Frazier was never bashful about showing his feelings, and Frenchie wasn't one to be disrespected. They had, let's say, a taut relationship.

I brought Cedric Burton into my office to take his statement about the truck he said he saw that night, which might be a clue in the murder of Michael Wade Langton, a young car salesman, who was last seen Friday afternoon leaving Gulf Motors with a customer who asked to test drive a red Toyota.

The car was found Saturday night.

Langton's body was located earlier that morning, Sunday.

Frazier was our fingerprint guy. He'd dusted the stolen car for prints while the rest of us worked the crime scene. Frazier sat in on the questioning along with Mansfield Police Sgt. Curtis Shaw, since we were working the case in partnership with the city police department.

Even with a videotape, you never wanted to question anyone alone. You always wanted at least one witness.

"So, Cedric," I began, "I'm going to record all this, as part of the investigation. This is just a formality. You don't have to make a statement and if you do, anything you say can be held against you in a court of law. Do you understand that?"

"Yessir," he said. "I'm just trying to help."

I read him the Miranda Warning and slipped it across my desk. He signed it, and so did I, noting the time: 2 p.m. on Sunday, December 4, 1988.

"Well, let's start out—do you live down there, where you just were—where we came from?"

"Yessir, with my girlfriend and her kids," he replied. "She lives at 106 Hatfield. I've been staying there since November."

"Okay, so tell me about seeing this truck from Arkansas."

Burton said he and his girlfriend, Jacqueline Thomas, went to her grandmother's house in Oxford Friday evening. They got home around 9 p.m. He just happened to be outside when he noticed this truck drive by early in the morning. And he called off the tag number again.

"We'll run that number," I said. "With your help, we might be able to catch a killer."

"Well, you know I could be off a number or two," he said. "But I'm pretty sure I saw that tag real good."

"By any chance, did you go to Gulf Motors Friday?" I asked.

"Never been there," he said.

Then, without prompting, Burton goes into this long story about how a Mansfield police officer named Doug Adkinson took his car, an '85 Dodge Daytona, away from him awhile back.

"That officer said my car was stolen from a car lot in Oklahoma City," Burton said. "But it wasn't. I paid $8,000 for that car."

"Where'd you get $8,000?" Frazier asked.

"I was an assistant track coach at a high school in Oklahoma City," Burton said. "They paid me $450 a week cash, every Friday. I bought that car, yessir, I did."

He looked at his hands and shrugged.

"But I just let 'em keep it 'cause—you know—it was too much trouble to pursue fighting it and all that."

There was a rap on my office door as District Attorney Don Burkett cracked it just wide enough for me to see him.

"Got a minute?" He spoke quietly.

"I'll just be a minute," I told the others and stepped out, leaving Burton with Frazier and Shaw.

Don and I walked down the corridor.

"What've you got?" he asked.

He was not only the prosecutor on this case. Don Burkett was a personal friend of the Langtons. Michael Wade Langton's father, Elmo Langton, was the Registrar of Voters in Sabine Parish. The victim, who was known by his middle name Wade, came from a well-known, well-connected, respected family.

"I'm not sure yet." I had to be honest. "But something's not right."

Cedric Burton became a person of suspicion when he said he noticed an Arkansas license plate on a passing pickup truck, in the middle of a moonless night on a road with no streetlights. Ray Sharrow was quick to snap on that.

When he rattled off the license tag number— Cedric Burton catapulted to become a suspect. How and why would anyone remember a license tag number on a random vehicle? It wasn't public knowledge that a crime had been committed at the time he said he noticed the truck and got the license tag number.

Even if it had been public knowledge, how could anyone see or read the digits of a license plate on a moving vehicle in pitch dark?

And, that story about being a track coach, paid in cash on Fridays, paying cash for a Dodge Daytona, which was a hot car at the time, no one else was buying that, either. The kid might have run track, the way he was built, but being paid by a school district in cash every Friday? That wasn't happening.

"I don't know what all he's lying about, but he's lying,"

I said. "We need to get his prints and see if they match prints from that car."

"You know him? Has he got a record?"

"I've never seen him or heard of him. No record that I've seen but we're looking."

"Get his prints," Don said. "We'll talk later."

This was a case he took personally.

When I went back in the office, for the first time, Cedric Burton was beginning to squirm. He couldn't sit still, fidgeting with his collar, scratching his head or arms.

"Cedric, I'd like to take you over to the jail to get fingerprints. Do you mind?"

"Okay," he said.

He wasn't feeling nearly as chipper as he did when he got there but, so far, Cedric Burton had not asked for a lawyer.

Wade Langton was a lanky, good-looking, dark-haired man who was quiet and shy. I could see him stepping out of a Norman Rockwell painting, wearing a plaid flannel shirt and faded jeans, standing beside his wife with a big grin, holding his little boy in one arm and a hunting rifle in the other. The classic country man who lived by a moral code.

Faith, family, friends. That's what mattered to Michael Wade Langton.

He'd lived all his life on the same land in Mt. Zion, a crossroads between Mansfield and Many. He knew most everyone in Sabine Parish, and they knew him. No one between Many and Mansfield had anything bad to say about Wade Langton. To the contrary, they were quick to recall his good deeds.

At the age of twenty-three, he married a girl he'd known all his life, Kristi Anthony. He stayed in Many, working in the body shop of the local Chevy dealership after high school while she went off to college. When Kristi came home, they married. They had a special kind of love and a son, Blake, who was a year old at that time.

"Wade adored his child," Kristi recalled. "Every day, when he came home from work, he tucked a sucker in his shirt pocket, making sure it stuck out just enough for the baby to see. The baby would squeal, and Wade would make a big show of presenting Blake with his sucker."

The only thing wrong with their picture was his job.

When the dealership closed their body shops, Wade began selling cars. It didn't suit him. His talent was in working with his hands, taking apart a wrecked vehicle and putting it back together. To rebuild what had been broken. At the age of twenty-five, Wade Langton made up his mind to quit selling cars for someone else and open his own body shop in Mt. Zion where he lived.

Kristi, who is now the Registrar of Voters for Sabine Parish, remembers December 2, 1988 in technicolor.

"The bank stayed open until six o'clock on Fridays," she recalled. "After work, I went to the grocery store, so it was seven o'clock or after when I got home. Wade always got home about six or so, so when I got home after seven and the house was dark, he wasn't home— I knew something was wrong. Wade always came straight home. I dropped the groceries and called his parents."

Then she called Wade's boss.

"He said, 'I think he took a car to show your brother,'" she recalled. "Well, that was crazy. My brother lived in High Island, Texas. So, we just started looking and looking and looking."

The manager of Gulf Motors called DeSoto Parish Sheriff's Department to report the stolen car and missing salesman. Since the car lot was in town, the supervisor on duty told sheriff's department dispatch to give the case to Mansfield PD. That was 9:45 p.m. Friday.

At 11:10 p.m. Sabine Parish Sheriff Alfice Brumley called DeSoto Parish Sheriff's Office expressing concern for Wade Langton's safety, urging this case be given real priority. All city and parish patrol units were put on alert.

In the meantime, Wade Langton's family and friends continued calling around, searching, driving.

Wade and Kristi had a lot of friends.

"We just had no clue what happened to him," Kristi said. "We could not imagine. One of the cops from Mansfield asked Wade's daddy, 'Is there any chance he ran off with some woman?' and his dad said, 'I can assure you he did not.' But I don't think the man believed him."

Friday night and Saturday, law enforcement patrol and the Langtons' family and friends searched DeSoto and Sabine parishes with no luck. It was not until late Saturday that a Mansfield patrolman spotted the stolen red Toyota at Ravine Ridge Apartments.

It was towed to the sheriff's department garage, stored for fingerprinting and processing.

Early Sunday, we were all back at Ravine Ridge Apartments, knocking doors, talking to people who lived there. A man who lived across the street from the apartment complex told officers his son was playing football in the yard Friday afternoon. The child said he noticed a black man park the car and walk away.

Charlie Frazier and Curtis Shaw went back to headquarters to dust the car and check fingerprints of possible suspects while Reserve Deputy Jim McLamb followed his gut, driving slowly through the neighborhood, cruising alleys, peering into back yards, until he eventually came to Hatfield Street.

Driving slowly down the remote lane, visually inspecting the roadside, McLamb reached the dead end at the abandoned house. Pulling into the overgrown drive to turn around, he saw a man's body concealed in heavy brush.

The man had been shot three times.

His ankles bound with a pink cord.

His wallet and wedding band were missing.

McLamb called it in.

Dispatch notified all area law enforcement agencies: "All units be advised: body found. One-hundred block

Hatfield Street. Mansfield."

Shreveport television and newspaper reporters, who monitored law enforcement radio traffic, raced to Mansfield.

The Langtons and their friends were gathered at Gulf Motors, which had served as their search headquarters.

"I don't know who told us," Kristi said. "I just remember my brother and Don Burkett caught me as I was running out of the dealership. I just started running when I heard Wade was gone. I don't know where I was running; I just started running. From that point on, I just don't remember a lot."

The serious questioning of Cedric Burton came after Charlie Frazier matched Cedric Burton's fingerprints to those inside and outside the stolen car. It was 3:55 p.m. Sunday, December 4.

After the formalities and new Miranda Warnings were given, acknowledged, dated, and signed, Frazier led this questioning in his gravelly voice. "What would you say if I told you, your prints are on the door handle of the passenger side of the car?"

Charlie Frazier is a bulldog of a man in both form and temperament. He's shorter than some but built like—well, like a bulldog. Thick. Stout. Strong. The last thing anyone wanted was for Frazier to be on their ass. He'd grab on like a pit bull and never let go.

Cedric Burton hadn't figured that out yet.

"I forgot to tell y'all, myself and a buddy of mine, we went to the Chevy place about a week ago and looked at this Toyota," Burton explained. "But it was locked."

They had peered in windows and he probably put his hands on the doors, windows, car hood and trunk, he said, explaining his prints on the car.

Frazier walked out of the room.

We waited in silence—me, Burton, Shaw, and Detective Judson Rives, who had joined us. Burton's gaze darted from one officer to another.

He shifted in his chair. But he did not ask for a lawyer.

Frazier returned in a few minutes.

"What if I found your prints *inside* the vehicle?" Frazier growled.

Burton didn't skip a beat. "Oh, well. I forgot to tell you, a salesman came out and unlocked it for us."

Frazier stood, staring Cedric Burton square in the eye, in silence.

Not a word.

Just Charlie Frazier and Cedric Burton, eyes locked like horns. I think Burton read Frazier's eyes the same way I did. He started singing.

"Well, it was Friday. Friday afternoon. These guys came up in my yard—uh, which their names were Dennis Washington, Keith Robinson, and Larry—he's sixteen. Okay, what they was— I asked—there was a drug bust in Oklahoma City about a year ago. And these guys found out that I was the one that told on them—so they, evidently, found out where I stayed in Mansfield, so they came up to the house Friday and asked me where they could go—to a car lot, and I just showed them a car lot," he said.

It was Larry (who had no last name), he said, who went to the car lot while the others remained in the car a block away.

"A salesman came out. A white male. Larry got in the car and the salesman got in the car, so we followed them in a black Maxima with Oklahoma license plates. Okay, Dennis gave me a gun. Larry had a gun. Larry and the salesman, they went off into this old vacant house, uh, right off Hatfield, in some woods and I was in the car with the others and I got out and told 'em, 'Look man, don't hurt nobody. Please don't. Just don't hurt him.' And one of the guys hit me in the back of the head with a gun, and they got back in the car. They told me to get back in the car and be quiet.

"I put my head between my legs, and I heard a gunshot,

in the house, and Larry come out and said he was hurt, because the salesman tried to—he said, 'The stupid cracker tried to wrestle with me, and I shot him.'

"Keith told him to go back in the house and drag the salesman out of the house. He had tied the salesman's legs and dragged him into the woods and at that time my gun was already missing—that they gave me—and they used my gun to kill the salesman.

"I remember when the window was down, I heard the salesman say, 'Please don't shoot me,' and I said, 'Man, don't hurt him!' and that's when they hit me again. They put the gun in my ribs, right here," he pointed at his side, "and I put my head back down and the next thing I know, I heard two more shots and I don't know where he shot him, but he shot him. And they told me, 'You're going with us,' and I said, 'What you want from me now?'"

Burton said he and the others were members of the Crips gang in Oklahoma City. After Langton was murdered, he said, the others forced him to drive the car to Ravine Ridge Apartments, threatening to kill him if he didn't.

"I said, 'Look, I've got twins on the way and I don't need to get hurt behind this kind of mess.' So I parked the car, and Larry and them had took his identification off of him. They took his wallet, and they took his license or something out of it, and they kept his money—"

Frazier interrupted, "How much money was in the wallet?"

"Eight dollars," Burton replied and went on, "I said, 'Look, I just want to go.' When I got out and they saw me locking the car, Larry jumped in the black car and I ran home. And I told my wife about it. I told Jackie, I said, 'Jackie, they shot him.'"

Curtis Shaw picked up his Stetson, which he always politely took off in the office, put it on and walked out of the room. No one seemed to notice. Burton still had the floor.

"Saturday night, about midnight, me and my little boy was walking to the store and Dennis and Keith was in a truck—that I had seen earlier—that I told the reporters about, that I'd seen, and Keith looked at me and said, 'If you say a damned thing, I'll kill you.' He said, 'We'll be here for a while. If you say anything, if we hear anything about it, your ass is as good as gone and don't worry about coming back for your wife because she won't be here either.'"

He had a captive audience, until Frazier interrupted.

"Hold up. Let's back up now. We're going to talk about— I'm going to ask you some specific questions. You said these guys came to your house. You made a statement to them, 'How did you find me.' Why were they looking for a car lot?"

"To find a car to take back with them for Larry," he said.

"To take back to *where*?"

"Oklahoma City," Burton said.

Frazier was leaning over the desk, his weight on his knuckles, making him appear more like a bulldog than ever. All he needed was some drool.

"Why did they come all the way from Oklahoma City to Mansfield, Louisiana—to get a car?"

"That I don't know," Burton said. "All I know is, when he come to my house, he made a bunch of threats to me and my kids and wife."

I took over the questioning as Curtis Shaw came back to the room.

"Mainly because you squealed on a dope deal in Oklahoma City. Right?"

"Yes," Burton said. "And I believe two are still in jail and they are the only ones that got out."

"How many people were arrested on the snitching deal?" I asked.

"Two, two—"

"No, you said two are in jail and two are out?"

He mumbled something like, "Keith and Ronnie didn't go. Larry was supposed to be a new guy taking my place."

"You ran with these people?" I asked.

"Yes, in Oklahoma."

"On narcotics?"

"Yeah, they would come to the house a lot and it would be me and my ex-wife and her brother-in-law, and we'd sit around, and we'd sell the stuff from the house."

I excused myself as Frazier resumed the questioning. Frazier was focused on the car. My mind had moved on.

"So, they came here looking for a car to carry back to Oklahoma?" Frazier re-directed.

"Yes," Burton insisted. "And the reason for that is because they was supposed to rob some mini-bank and they was going to park the car on the side of the road and when the police found them actually, run it back through here."

Curtis Shaw asked, "Did you know anything about them robbing any place in Mansfield?"

"No, they didn't mention it to me. But they plan to rob some place Friday," he said.

Shaw asked, "You mean Friday? The day they stole the car?"

"No, this Friday, coming up."

Frazier said, "Okay. What did they say to you *exactly* about going to find a car?"

"Well, he just told me 'How's it going,' I said, 'Look, I don't want anything else to do with it,' after they already threatened me and told me what they was there for. They said, 'Look, man, this is my last time telling you. Get in the car with us and we'll explain to you on the way and they told me that they wanted the car to take back there so they could do a job—for Larry to do the job—and quite naturally, they was going to kill Larry anyway."

While Larry was at Gulf Motors, Burton and the others waited in the black Maxima. During that time, he said, the Oklahoma gangsters bragged about robbing two convenience stores, including the Shop-A-Lot in Mansfield. And, they said, they killed a man in Leesville, near Ft. Polk.

Meanwhile, I'd walked across the hall, using Frazier's office to call the Oklahoma City Police Department, speaking first to the supervisor on duty in the Narcotics Division and then the Gang Unit supervisor. That was 1988. Street gangs, born in the inner-city ghettos of Los Angeles during the 1970s, had migrated east. By the mid-80s the Bloods and Crips were establishing themselves in metropolitan areas across the country, including Oklahoma City. The gangs owned the drug business in one inner-city after another, waging war on each other and others for control. Human life didn't seem to hold a lot of value to gangsters.

Narcotics and gang units worked hand-in-hand in every city where they operated.

Who in Oklahoma City had used Cedric Burton as a confidential informant?

After the better part of an hour, I found out.

No one.

Not one officer in the Oklahoma City Police Department's narcotics unit knew the name Cedric Burton. He was not listed on any roles as a paid confidential informant. No one in the gang unit had heard of Burton or the others he named— Dennis Washington or Keith Robinson.

Cedric Burton—aka C-2—was a *wannabe* gangster.

There was no truth in his story about the death of Wade Langton, which came as no surprise, really, except for the fact that he told it so convincingly, with such detail and feign sincerity. Evil doesn't always look evil.

In the meantime, having been notified of Burton's statements about the killing of a man in Leesville, Vernon Parish Sheriff's Department sent their detectives to join the questioning.

"Deputy Mike Martin and Deputy Larry Smith advised me after the interview that Cedric Burton was not involved in their homicide," Frazier wrote in his official report. "I went back in to talk to Burton and he stated he lied in giving his first statement."

They started over again.

Burton still had not asked for a lawyer.

This time, Burton said that he and a friend named Ronnie Titsworth kidnapped Langton, carried him and the car to the old house. While Titsworth was tying up Langton, Burton said, the two men started wrestling. Titsworth was shot in the shoulder so Burton shot Langton three times, he said.

Burton said Titsworth checked in at Brown's Motel in Mansfield. Also, he added, Titsworth worked on the loading docks of the Post Office in Oklahoma City.

It was now 8 p.m.

I called the Postal Inspector's Office in Oklahoma City, explaining the situation. The supervisor on duty returned my call, verifying Ronnie Titsworth worked there. As a matter of fact, he said, Titsworth was on duty.

"I'm looking at him right now," said postal supervisor Demetrius Williams. "He's physically fine. He's not hurt."

"Was he at work Friday?" I asked.

"Lemme see," the man said. "Hold on. I'll check the timecards."

In a few minutes, the supervisor was back on the line. "Ronnie Titsworth clocked into work at 9:45 p.m. Friday, Dec. 2, 1988."

Another Cedric Burton gangster tale.

How did we finally get to the truth?

The girlfriend.

When Mansfield Police Sgt. Curtis Shaw slipped out of the interrogation room earlier, he'd asked two city police officers to go question Jacqueline Thomas. She lived in a little white frame bungalow on Hatfield Street.

Mansfield Police Lt. Curtis McCoy wrote in his case report that Jacqueline Thomas said Friday afternoon, her boyfriend went to meet some of his friends at the Best Western who were there from Oklahoma City. She didn't know all their names but had once met one of Cedric's friends, whose name was Ronnie.

She said one of the men from Oklahoma pretended he

wanted to test drive one of the cars (at Gulf Motors). They drove the car dealer to the abandoned house on Hatfield, scuffled, ended up shooting and killing the car dealer.

"After one of the guys from Oklahoma shot Michael Wade Langton, what took place?" McCoy asked the woman.

"He told him to rest in peace," she said.

"When he told him to rest in peace, did Cedric come home at that time?"

"Yeah. When he came home, he was shaking and crying and nervous and he say he had killed a man and uh, later on I started questioning him and I asked him, where did he shoot him? And he told me he shot him in the leg. And I asked him, how could he kill him then, if he shot him in the leg? And he say that he had been thinking about it, but he wasn't the one that *killed* him that the dude from Oklahoma that shot him in the head had killed him."

"Okay, what did Cedric do with the gun that he used?"

"He hid it in the brick under the junk house."

"What did he hide in the brick under the junk house?" McCoy asked.

"The gun and bullet and keys to the car."

The officer asked, "The driver's license from the car salesman was missing. What did your husband do with the driver's license?"

"Uh, he told me—somebody—after they shot the man, they had got two identifications off of him, and he say, 'I think they left the picture of the little boy or something in the man's pocket, and they say before they killed the man they had made him take his wallet and they put it in the trunk of the car they had supposed to be test driving.'"

"The people from Oklahoma, did they come down here to kill anyone in particular at first?" McCoy asked.

"Well, they had a meeting and he was supposed to be going to Best Western where the boys was staying at six o'clock and he say they had told him that they had been to the courthouse and had paid two women about some information on Doug Adkinson and say they rode around looking for him the day that they killed the dude," Jackie said.

"What were they looking for Doug Adkinson for?"

"Because of the car he had taken from Cedric and sold," she said.

"Were they going to *kill* Doug Adkinson?"

"Yeah. I believe that was their intentions."

"The car they got from the car lot, was Cedric going to drive this car to Oklahoma?" McCoy asked.

"Yeah," she said.

"What changed his mind?"

"My grandmother had died, and I had talked him into staying with me," she said.

While Burton spun his tales to Frazier and Shaw, we got a search warrant for Jacqueline Thomas' residence.

Officers were sent to every motel in two parishes looking for cars from Oklahoma, talking to desk clerks, checking guest registries.

I confirmed that Oklahoma PD had never worked with Cedric Burton as a confidential informant, that none of the names he gave were known Crips' members. After meeting with Curtis McCoy to find out about the .22 derringer hidden beneath the brick, I called Frazier out of the questioning room to fill him in.

"Ronnie Titsworth is at work right now in Oklahoma City," I said. "He was at work Friday, too. I talked to his supervisor."

Frazier's face turned a color I hoped to never see again. Kind of a watermelon-eggplant blend. I was afraid he might have a stroke.

"Any idiot can listen to what he's telling and know he's making it up as he goes," Frazier said. "But it's odd. He's not messed up. He's not drunk. He's not drugged up. He seems sane and sober."

It was true. Often, the suspects we dealt with were

doped up, weirded out. Some people kill when they're out of their heads on drugs or alcohol. They do things they'd never do sober, but Cedric Burton could not use that as an excuse.

"One more thing, Charlie. PD got the gun and car keys. He hid them under a brick in what his girlfriend called the 'junk house'."

Frazier walked back in the office. Detective Pat Cobbs was there then, along with Cedric Burton, Shaw, and Rives.

"Cedric," Frazier said. "You told us you wanted to help."

"Yessir, that's what I've been doing," he replied.

"No. You've wasted a lot of time lying," Frazier said. "Your fingerprints are all over the inside of that stolen car. Oklahoma PD doesn't know anything about you ever being a confidential informant and the gang unit up there never heard of you or any of your 'friends.' There is no one from Oklahoma registered at any motel in Mansfield or Many and Leesville detectives said you're full of shit."

Frazier leaned in real close again.

"We got a search warrant for your girlfriend's house, Cedric. We know you hid the gun in a brick along with the stolen car keys. We've got enough to charge you with kidnapping, robbery, and murder right now. Cooperate and you might catch a break. Or not."

It wasn't long until Frazier stuck his head out the door. "He's confessing!"

Burton said he was ready to give a full and truthful statement of all that happened—that he alone killed Michael Wade Langton—but, according to Frazier's case report, "It was 10 p.m. Myself and Rives agreed, it could wait until morning. Everyone was tired. Burton was told of this and he agreed to give us a taped statement the next day and even go to the scene and show us everything."

The true story was more chilling than the gangster tales.

Cedric Burton wanted his car back. He'd boosted the Daytona off a car lot in Oklahoma City and driven it home to Mansfield so he figured he could do it again. Get a car off the lot in Mansfield and go back to Oklahoma City.

He bought a gun—a two-shot .22 derringer that would fit in his pants—for that purpose. He was lurking around Gulf Motors Friday afternoon, trying to decide which car he wanted when Wade Langton walked out.

"Can I help you?" Wade asked.

Burton—who, we had learned, was a very convincing liar—told Wade he had an '85 Monte Carlo he wanted to trade in on the new Toyota. Could he take a test drive?

Of course, Wade said, but he would have to ride along.

Wade went inside, came out with keys to the Toyota, handed them to Burton, and got into the passenger side of the front seat, as he did with prospective customers every day.

Driving through Mansfield, Burton was his chatty self. "I want my wife to see it," he told the salesman. Then he drove to Hatfield Street, parking in the overgrown drive to the abandoned house.

Looking around, Wade asked, "Where's your wife?"

Stepping out of the vehicle Burton answered, "She's next door. I'm going to get her. I'll be right back."

Wade slipped behind the wheel, turned the car around to drive out, when Burton jerked open the door and put the gun in his face.

"Get out," Burton ordered. "We're going inside."

Wade handed him his billfold saying, "Here, you can have it. Just leave me alone. You can take the car."

Burton snatched the wallet but kept the gun pointed at Wade.

"Get inside." Holding the gun on Wade, Burton instructed him to take a high-backed chair into the bathroom. He ordered Wade to sit in the chair, bent down to tie Wade's feet—when Wade lunged at him, grabbing Burton around the neck, throwing him back.

The two men wrestled to the floor, Wade getting the better of Burton, when Burton fired the derringer at point blank range into Wade's thigh. The bullet struck the bone. Wade was stunned.

That gave Burton time to grab Wade's arms and tie them behind his back. Then he tied his feet together and ran out of the house, jumped into the Toyota, and sped down Hatfield Road.

With Burton gone, Wade somehow crawled and inch-wormed out of the house, across the stoop, back to the edge of Hatfield Street. He was yelling for help when Burton appeared over him. Burton had parked the car at Ravine Ridge Apartments then run back to finish what he started.

"What're you doing, man!" Burton cried out.

"Leave me alone," Wade yelled. "Just leave me alone!"

Burton jerked Wade to his feet, which were still hobbled by the cord. His leg still bleeding, his hands still tied behind his back— Wade could not walk. He collapsed.

Burton untied Wade's hands, grabbed his belt at the back of his trousers, and dragged him into the brush, where he shot him again—this time in the stomach.

Burton ejected two shells. He was out of bullets and the salesman wasn't dead.

He left Wade Langton again—wounded with a bullet that ripped through his abdomen and another stuck in his leg. He just left him lying there while he ran to his girlfriend's house for more bullets.

When Burton returned, Wade was lying on his side in a fetal position.

"Get up!" the gunman ordered. "Get up on your knees. Put your fist in your mouth so you won't make noise."

Wade would not.

"You the only one who knows me," Burton told him. "I can't let you go. You'll tell on me."

"No," Wade said. "Just leave me alone."

Instead, wannabe gangster Cedric Burton fired a bullet into the back of Wade Langton's head. Then he walked to a warm house to eat dinner with Jacqueline Thomas while Michael Wade Langton died alone in cold, trashy woods in a God-forsaken part of Mansfield.

He had a picture of his baby boy in his shirt pocket.

Monday morning, Burton kept his word to Frazier.

He had finally understood, Charlie Frazier wasn't going to let go of his ass until he told the unvarnished truth about what happened to Michael Wade Langton.

"On December 5, 1988, Cedric Burton was taken from the DeSoto Jail by myself, Judson Rives, and Curtis Shaw," Frazier wrote in his official case report. "Burton was carried back to 106 Hatfield Street where he went through all his steps of the homicide scene and at his house after his incident. Burton gave us verbal permission to go in his house, where he produced a .22 magnum spent hull from a shelf in his bedroom."

"This is the hull of the bullet I shot the salesman in the head with." Burton held it up for the three officers.

"Why would you keep this and eject the others?" Frazier asked.

Burton shrugged. "I don't know."

Cedric Burton had saved the hull of the fatal bullet as if it were a trophy.

He led the officers to the burning barrel where he was standing when Ray Sharrow saw him Sunday.

"I burned his driver's license in there," Burton said. "And the wedding ring is in Mr. Robbo's car."

Frazier called me.

I ran to my unit. Sure enough— Cedric Burton had slipped Wade Langton's wedding ring underneath the passenger seat of my patrol unit on the drive to C.I.D. Lesson learned: The next time you give a suspect a free ride in the unit, go back and check to see if he stashed evidence.

Burton led Frazier, Shaw, and Rives to the old house, showed the chair where he'd tried to tie up Wade Langton, where they wrestled, blood on the floor. Burton walked the officers through the crime, step by step. He was taken back to jail and charged with armed robbery, kidnapping and capital murder.

Michael Wade Langton was laid to rest on December seventh—what would have been his twenty-sixth birthday—in the cemetery of Friendship Baptist Church in Mt. Zion, where he attended church all his life.

It was not only Wade's birthday and the day of his funeral— December seventh was the day Kristi's mother died in a car wreck a few years earlier.

"Every year, I try to get through the first part of December and move on," she said. "But honestly, early December is just hard. Still."

So many people came to pay their final respects to Wade Langton on that cold December day that there was not even standing room left inside Friendship Baptist Church. People sat or stood outside in the cold, listening to the service over loudspeakers.

One person after another volunteered their personal recollections of Wade's random acts of kindness throughout his life. Tenna Salter Cook, who went through twelve years of school with Wade, recalled one year their class drew names to exchange Christmas presents.

When all the gifts were given out, "I didn't have one," she said. "Someone had got mine, we guessed. For whatever reason, I did not have a present."

That evening, Wade talked his mother into taking him to a store to buy a bracelet for Tenna. He could not stand the idea that she was the only person in class who did not get a Christmas present.

Wade Langton was an unusually good man with an innate sense of fairness and empathy whose life was stolen, just like the car.

Wade's son has already outlived him. When Blake

turned twenty-one, his mother made a quilt for him out of his father's clothing.

"It had pockets," Kristi said. "In each pocket, I put something from our lives—our wedding set, his sucker, his dad's wedding ring.

"Wade loved Blake so much," she continued. "Everyone says Blake looks just like his daddy. And he does. He was such a good, handsome man."

I flew to Oklahoma City to meet with officers of the Narcotics and Gang units, just to verify, face to face, everything I'd learned over the telephone.

I got Ronnie Titsworth's employment records and copies of his timecards proving he was at work at the US Postal Service on the days in question. I ran Titsworth's criminal history: two speeding tickets. Titsworth was clean as far as Oklahoma law was concerned.

Pat Cobbs—who was also a part-time Baptist preacher—and DeSoto Parish Sheriff's Office Capt. Marvin Melton re-interviewed Jacqueline Thomas a few months later.

There was a lingering question: was Burton's girlfriend an accessory?

She provided more detail about their relationship and the day of the murder.

"When Cedric first came to stay with you, did he have a car?" Cobbs asked.

"Yes, sir."

"Do you know what happened to that car?" Melton asked.

"When they picked him up for—for some hot checks he wrote—they towed it off. They picked it up. The police."

Melton went on, "When Cedric told you this story about the shooting of the salesman in the leg—you said he was nervous? Upset?"

"Yes, sir," she said.

"Did he ever tell you a different story?"

"That's the only time he told me the story," she said. "Because they picked him up that Sunday."

"Okay, and in reference to the incident, he only told you about it one time and he first said he killed a man and then he said he shot him in the leg, and you asked—how could you kill him by shooting him in the leg?"

"Yes," she said.

"I think that's good," Melton said. "One last thing, Jackie. You have two children?"

"Four," she said.

"Four? How old are you?"

"Me?" she asked. "Twenty-seven."

Jacqueline Thomas was not charged with any crime.

Cedric Burton claimed his confession was coerced.

There were pre-trial motions and hearings to quash the confession, all of which were denied. There had been too many signed, dated, and timed Miranda warnings, video recorders, and people in the room every step of the way for it to be one man's word against another's.

While awaiting trial, Burton and Jacqueline Thomas got married.

The *Mansfield Enterprise*, *Shreveport Times* and all three Shreveport TV news stations covered the "Jailhouse Wedding." The story was carried on the Associated Press wires nationwide. This is part of a story carried by the Associated Press April 28, 1989:

"Cedric Burton is in jail, accused of a slaying. Jacqueline Jonet Thomas was a potential witness against him. Wednesday, they got married, and now she cannot be forced to testify against him. The couple held hands through jail bars during the ceremony. Thomas got a marriage license Tuesday. The couple said their vows before a Baptist clergyman, and two jailers served as witnesses. Burton is charged with first-degree murder in the death of a car

salesman. DeSoto Parish District Attorney Don Burkett had tried to get the courts to forbid the ceremony until after the trial. The marriage of the witness will have absolutely no effect on the case going forward, Burkett said. It is fixed for trial on June 26, and it will go to trial. He said Thomas was living with Burton when Michael Wade Langton was slain, and her testimony could have destroyed Burton's alibi."

Indicted on charges of first-degree murder, armed robbery, and aggravated kidnapping, Cedric Burton was brought to trial November 1989. He faced the death penalty.

Even without Jacqueline Thomas-Burton's testimony, the prosecution had the murder weapon with Burton's fingerprints, ballistics matching bullets from the derringer with those that killed Wade Langton. Prosecutors had Burton's handwritten confession—which he wrote on a notepad in his cell that Sunday night. They had Burton's prints inside and outside of the stolen car.

Three officers testified about Burton holding up the bullet shell hidden in his bedroom, saying, "This is the bullet I used to shoot the salesman in the head," and the officers' testified how Burton took them through the murder step by step.

His mother, Lulah Burton, testified Cedric was active in church as a child. He had been a track star in high school with US Olympics aspirations, but a knee injury destroyed those hopes. She said he'd been especially close to his father, who was murdered when Cedric was nine.

Jackie cried on the witness stand.

"I married him because I loved him," she told the jurors. "I couldn't believe he killed a man. I still don't believe it."

Cedric Burton took the stand, voicing regret for his actions.

"It hurts me a great deal," Burton told the courtroom, "because when I was coming up my father was killed. I know exactly how the (Langton) family feels."

Steve Thomas, his court-appointed attorney asked,

"Are you ashamed?"

"Yes," Burton replied.

"Do you deserve to be punished?"

Burton bowed his head. "Yes."

Don Burkett followed, "You're asking the jury to show you mercy you didn't show Michael Wade Langton."

The jury returned a verdict of life in prison without parole. Cedric Burton remains in Angola Prison to this day. While there, Burton learned CPR, achieved certification as a CPR instructor, and was credited with helping save the life of a seveny-seven-year-old inmate who suffered a heart attack on July 31, 2019. Burton's quick action was noted in the January/February 2020 edition of the prison magazine, *The Angolite.*

On those nights when my ghosts of DeSoto Parish come calling, when I wake to the remembrance of one victim or another, I often seize upon the single seemingly insignificant step each person took that led to his demise. To open the door to a stranger, to trust the wrong person, on and on.

When it comes to Wade Langton, I'm not sure he made a mistake. He was the salesman on duty. He gave a customer a test drive like he did every day. It was impossible for him to know *that* customer was a killer who bought a gun with the intent of getting a car, one way or another.

Wade tackled Burton *knowing* he had a gun. Had the bullet not struck bone, had it gone clean through flesh, Wade probably would have prevailed in the struggle. But there's just not a lot a man can do with a bullet in his leg.

I think of his tremendous will to live—to get back to his wife and son—of his horrific crawl back to Hatfield Street with his hands tied behind his back, his feet hobbled, his face in the dirt. I can't help but cringe thinking of the mind-numbing terror he must have experienced when he saw Cedric Burton standing over him again. Wade Langton did everything any man could—but evil prevailed.

We can scream, *why, why, why* for the rest of our lives and have no definitive answer.

In my mind, Wade Langton was a victim of gang violence. Cedric Burton wanted to be a gangster. He admired their violent lifestyle. Maybe he thought killing the car salesman would earn him respect—some 'cred', credibility—with gang members when he got back to Oklahoma City.

Maybe, with blood on his hands, he would be a *real* gangster.

Published Memorial
—Courtesy Mansfield
Enterprise

Michael Wade Langton photo
—Courtesy of Kristi McCormick

DPSO Det. Robert Davidson & Mansfield Police Officer Ray Sharrow escort Cedric Burton from crime scene for questioning.

—Courtesy Mansfield Enterprise

Nov 5, 1989 Mansfield, LA. DPSO Deputy Pat Jones escorts Cedric Burton back for another session at Mansfield court.
CREDIT: © Mike Silva—USA TODAY NETWORK

Jeff's Friends

A cloudless dome the color of glacier water hung above a forest that was beginning to burst into color the way a peacock unfurls its tailfeathers to attract attention—forest and fowl telling the world *Ta-da! Look at me!* Tourists flock to the Adirondacks and Smokey Mountains to ooh and aah at the glory of fall oblivious to the autumn splendor of the Deep South, where dainty yellow leaves of honey locust and elm dance in the breeze beside heavy hanging scarlet foliage of sweet gum, red oak, orange maple, crimson Cypress, and the ever-present evergreen pines laden with cones. Chattering squirrels and chipmunks scurried along the carpet of pine straw, snatching up acorns for the coming winter, while migrating thrashers, flycatchers, painted buntings, and yellow warblers carried on a concert on their way to the coastal marshes.

It is ironic that on such a rarely perfect day, I would be pulled into one of the most hideous cases of my career, beginning with an early afternoon phone call. As detective on duty, I'd spent the weekend close to home watching football on TV and monitoring DeSoto Parish Sheriff's Department radio traffic, overhearing the back and forth as one crew then another was dispatched to Stonewall at the urging of a Shreveport couple who believed their adult son was held there against his will. After each visit, deputies reported no sign of the man, no evidence of foul play.

No one imagined what would come to light on Sunday.

"Robbo, they found the ID of the missing man," the dispatcher said. "Can you meet Bobby Simone on Richardson Road in Stonewall?"

"On my way," I said. "Tell Simone it will take me about thirty minutes."

Stonewall was, then, a tiny farming crossroads at the northern tip of DeSoto Parish, closer to Shreveport than the parish seat of Mansfield. Heading west on US Highway 84 into Mansfield then another twenty miles north on Louisiana Highway 171, I arrived to find narrow, Richardson Road almost impassible, lined with mud-crusted trucks and all-terrain vehicles. Two dozen or more men milled in front of a ramshackle, singlewide trailer typical of the area. Three of four men were arguing on the porch while a plump, middle-aged woman with short curly hair sat sobbing on a concrete bench in front of them, her pudgy little hands covering her face. A boy with curly, long, dark hair raised one hand from her trembling shoulders long enough to point my attention to a handcuffed man locked inside Bobby Simone's patrol unit. The man held his head down, as if to hide his face. A second man stood handcuffed at the rear of the unit while Simone was scuffling with a third man, shackling him to a lawn chair. A separate group clustered around two young men, restraining the larger, older of the two, who appeared about to explode.

It was a sure bet, every man among them was armed with something—a knife or pistol in his pocket, handguns and or rifles in his truck.

"Get the suspects out of here," I told the deputy who

had pulled up beside me. "I mean pronto, before bullets start flying."

Several hours later, I began interviewing suspects in my office in Mansfield, starting with the teenager who had been handcuffed inside the patrol unit. Speaking softly, staring at the floor, he matter-of-factly laid out a hair-raising account of what transpired in Stonewall early Saturday. He talked, answered my questions, for at least an hour. A jailer took him back to his cell, preparing to escort the second suspect in, when I called a time out.

"Give me a few minutes," I said. "I need to stretch my legs."

My knees would lock up if I didn't move ever so often but the knees were just an excuse to leave that room. Walking outside, drawing in a deep breath of cool, pine-scented air, I struggled to reconcile the ugliness of what I just heard with the beauty on display—sinking below the tree line, the dying sun illuminated the western sky, glowing in shades of peach, pumpkin, and saffron, thin clouds of violet, turquoise, and magenta swirling throughout. I have since given up trying to explain to myself, much less anyone else, how the world can be breath-takingly beautiful and horrifyingly ugly at the same time. It is what it is. There is no peace in the knowledge that evil often triumphs over good. It is the eternal struggle—good versus evil, positive and negative, yin and yang—poles of two magnets constantly pushing against each other. I am convinced there is a war on this earth for the souls of men. My work had me walking in at the end of battles evil won.

Headlights from a passing car drew my attention for a moment and when I looked back the western sky had faded to gray, its beauty gone, never to be seen exactly the same way again. Every sunset is unique—as is every life.

All are fleeting and all are destined to dissolve into a memory.

Chapter One

It was football Friday night: September 23, 1994.

Jeff Rodgers had not bothered trying to contain his excitement when asked if he wanted to go to an Evangel Christian Academy football game. The Evangel Eagles were the top-ranked high school football team in the state. But more than the opportunity to see the champions play, Jeff's eagerness was rooted in the invitation itself—to go to a football game with friends. Where they were going was not as important as the fact that he was invited out with friends, something Jeff Rodgers had wanted for so very long. Yes, tonight Jeff would be one of the guys.

Jeff was virtually a child, diagnosed as educable mentally impaired or EMI. It is a scholastic term for people capable of achieving about a fifth-grade academic level and mentality. His deprivation of oxygen during a prolonged labor had been tantamount to a brain injury. Jeff went through special education and graduated with his certificate of completion from Shreveport's Southwood High School.

At the age of twenty-seven, intellectually and emotionally Jeff Rodgers still functioned as a nine-or ten-year-old boy. And of course, at that age, few things are as important as fitting in, being accepted, being one of the guys.

He was a nice-looking, dark-haired man, tall and slim with a broad smile accentuated by a deep dimple in his left cheek. But this was a child in the body of a man. Naïve. Wide-eyed. Trusting. Gullible. Forgiving.

He was proud of his job as a busboy at Crescent Landing Catfish Restaurant, located on Pines Road in southwest Shreveport, a short walk across a small city park behind the Rodgers family home.

During his years working at Crescent Landing, when his shift ended, he would walk home through the park, check in with his parents, and get a few dollars from his mother (who managed his money). After changing out of his work uniform, most nights he would walk to a nearby Circle K to visit. Jeff made himself useful there sweeping and stocking. He liked feeling productive. He needed to be needed and in turn the store employees relished his presence. Not only did he help, but he was also pleasant and polite. A man's presence made the female cashiers feel safer on their late-night shifts.

There, Jeff met Gary, an eighteen-year-old who lived in an apartment nearby. The two became acquainted at the store and that night, Gary suggested they go to the Evangel football game.

"You got your ID and some money?" Gary asked.

Jeff shook his head. "No."

"Well, how do you expect to get into the ball game? You've got to have money to get in the game," Gary said.

"I got paid tonight. But my paycheck is at home."

"Hop in." Gary motioned for Jeff to get in his car. "I'll take you back home to get your billfold and ID. We can get something to drink before the game. It'll be fun."

Gary Barber was one of those kids who would not stay out of trouble. He dropped out of North DeSoto High School the year before, after having been suspended repeatedly for disciplinary problems. He had the same issues functioning in the real world that he had in school. Barber was fired after working a brief stint as a security guard, then hired on as a handy man for an elderly Shreveport woman.

In January, Barber had been arrested and charged with assault for attacking his ex-girlfriend's younger brother. In that incident, Barber brandished a handgun. He would not comply with the terms of his probation, which had been scheduled for revocation October sixth.

One of Barber's distant cousins, Tracy Williams recalled that a week earlier, Gary Barber had suggested, "Let's go make some money."

"How?" Tracy asked.

"I know some people we can rob," Barber replied, then he opened the trunk of his car to show Tracy a stash of guns and rifles.

"Get lost, fool," Tracy said. "I ain't robbing nobody."

Gary Barber was a predator and though he may not have been the quickest study, it had not taken him long to recognize what a tender target he had in Jeff Rodgers, who saw nothing but the good in people. In his childlike innocence, Jeff Rodgers was incapable of conceiving of, much less recognizing a fiend posing as a friend.

In a parallel journey, Tracy Williams' younger brother Stacy was having his own trouble with the law. Stacy Williams graduated from North DeSoto High School that May. By September he had been arrested three times: for assault and battery, destruction of property, and arson.

Williams was a special-education student himself, though socially he functioned on a more age-appropriate level than Jeff. After receiving his certificate of completion from North DeSoto High School, Stacy drove to the U.S.

Army recruiting office in Shreveport, eager to enlist. To his great disappointment, Stacy Williams failed the Army entrance exam. It was just one more of a long string of disappointments.

Raised at the edge of poverty, Stacy and his three brothers bounced around as their parents moved from town to town looking for better jobs. Though his father owned a tree service in 1994, when the boys were younger, Stacy said, his parents worked in bars. The boys attended any number of schools in Louisiana and Tennessee, he said.

"I was always having to start over," Williams recalled.

He was a standout in high school football—even had scouts looking at him in his final game against Logansport— but with his academic struggles, Stacy Williams was not bound for college. By the time he turned eighteen, Stacy was a bitter, brooding young man who resented his plight. Out of school, with no job and too much time on his hands in the summer of '94, drinking and fighting became his pastime.

"If I drank, I got mad," Stacy recalled. "We fought a lot—all of us—with other kids. We used to have a rivalry with kids from Shreveport. Seemed like we were always drinking and that's what would happen. We'd fight."

Though Williams and Barber were related—their mothers were distant cousins—and both had lived in Stonewall, neither was well-acquainted with the other, nor had they spent any significant amount of time together until that ill-fated night.

Chapter Two

Gary Barber left home around ten o'clock Friday night, about the same time Jeff Rodgers got off duty at Crescent Landing, where he had received his paycheck. One hundred seventy-three dollars was not much money for two weeks' work, but the busboy's earnings was an amount of money that high school drop-out, wannabe robber-handyman Gary Barber could use. And an amount he figured he could get if he could intercept Jeff before he handed his paycheck over to his mother for deposit, which was another of Jeff's habits. Barber had strategically cultivated a friendship with Jeff for just such a purpose.

Rather than walking home that night, Jeff caught a ride with his longtime friend and coworker Brett Rogers, who dropped him off at the family home on Fox Chase Trail, in a comfortable if not affluent neighborhood in southwest Shreveport. Catching the ride instead of walking, Jeff was a little earlier than normal arriving home. Inside, his parents George and Loretta were in their bedroom. When Jeff knocked on their door to ask for his nightly allowance, Loretta slid two dollars under the door without seeing her son. She was dressing for bed when her son knocked, she later explained, which was the reason she did not open the door.

Not long after hearing Jeff slam the front door to leave, Loretta recalled, she and her husband heard him return and go into his bedroom. At the time, if anything, they thought he probably forgot his cigarettes and they assumed he'd come back to retrieve them. After hearing Jeff slam the front door as he left a second time, George and Loretta turned out the lights and drifted off to sleep, believing their oldest son was going about his regular routine.

They had no idea Gary Barber was parked in front of their house and had directed their son to go back inside to get his paycheck and ID so that Jeff, who was of legal age, could buy him some alcohol.

The waning moon was bright on that clear night, enabling Linda Sanchez, the Rodgers' next-door neighbor to clearly see Jeff squatted down by the drivers' door of a light-colored car, talking to the driver about 10:30 p.m.

More often than not, George and Loretta Rodgers are described as 'the salt of the earth' —hard-working, kind-hearted people who raised their three sons to be good men.

Married while both were in their teens, George had told his young wife, "I will work hard, and I'll make you a living. You take care of this," indicating with his gesture their home and family. He did. She did.

"My boys all attended church for nine months before they were born," George was proud to say.

When Loretta delivered their first-born child in a small north Louisiana hospital, the baby was breach. George held her through an arduous twenty-seven-hour labor, which resulted in the birth of a beautiful boy. It was determined when Jeff entered school that his brain had been deprived of oxygen during the lengthy labor, permanently restricting his ability to learn. Neither of their other two sons had any impairment.

George Rodgers started his own construction company, which he built into a successful business. Every year for three decades George Rodgers Construction built a house that was auctioned to benefit St. Jude's Children's Hospital. As general contractor, George persuaded sub-contractors to donate their services—framers, roofers, painters, plumbers, electricians, landscapers. For an outlay of about $40,000, these men built a house that auctioned for up to half a million dollars, all of which benefited the children's hospital. Since George's retirement, his son Phillip, who took over the construction business, continues that family tradition. The Rodgers are known across northern Louisiana for their character, sense of community, and charity.

Early that Saturday, George and Loretta were awakened by the ringing of the telephone. Looking at his clock radio, George made a mental note. It was 3:10 a.m.

"When somebody calls in the middle of the night," George said, "you know you are expecting bad news. To myself I said, 'Who would be calling at this time unless something happened?'"

As George reached for the telephone, Loretta was already sitting up in bed, reaching to turn on the bedside lamp.

It was Jeff.

"Daddy," he said. "Come get me. I'm scared."

George Rodgers' blood ran cold at the fear he heard in his son's voice. He sat up. Loretta was already standing before him, to better hear their son.

"Come get you where, Jeff? Where are you, son?" George asked.

"I'm in Stonewall."

"Where in Stonewall?"

"I don't know for sure. By the rodeo arena. We were going to go to a ballgame, Daddy, to see Evangel play, but we came down here instead."

"How did you get to Stonewall, Jeff?"

"With my friends."

"Who are your friends?"

"Gary."

"Gary who?"

"Gary Barber."

"Where does Gary live, Jeff?"

"He lives in Huntington Apartments."

George's mind was racing. Jeff was in Stonewall. Where in Stonewall? He didn't have any idea and Jeff couldn't tell him.

"Hold on, son," George said. "Stay on the line. I'm giving the phone to your mother and I'll be right back."

Covering the receiver with his hand, George whispered to his wife, "Keep him on the phone. Don't let him hang up."

Handing the receiver to Loretta, George strode to the dining room where he had an office and a telephone with two lines as well as a mobile phone. Along the way he pounded Phillip's bedroom door.

"Wake up, Phillip! Wake up! I need you to get up. Get up and get dressed and meet me in the dining room."

As George got back on the telephone, he heard Jeff crying, telling his mother, "They hurt me, Mommy. They hurt me. Please, come get me. Come get me. I want to go home."

George interrupted. "Which rodeo arena did you pass, Jeff? Which rodeo arena?"

"A & R."

"A & R?"

As Phillip entered the office, George handed him his mobile phone.

"Go to the rodeo arena in Stonewall," he told his youngest son. "We've got to find Jeff. He's down there. Someone has hurt him."

No questions asked, seventeen-year-old Phillip Rodgers took his father's mobile phone, got into his pickup truck, and headed south to Stonewall, which was, at best, a twenty-five to thirty-minute drive, while his parents continued talking to Jeff on the phone.

"Daddy, they hit me in the same place as those boys did the other day," Jeff said.

The incident Jeff referred to occurred at a different Circle K in southwest Shreveport earlier that month. There, two boys jumped Jeff in the parking lot after he refused to buy beer for them, blacking his eye and bruising his ribs. The Rodgers had made a police report and Jeff had been treated at the hospital.

"Phillip is on his way, Jeff," George reassured his son. "Can you describe how to get there?"

"Turn left on the first dirt road past the rodeo arena. I'm in a trailer house."

George and Loretta each continued to talk, to keep their oldest son on the telephone while their youngest drove to Stonewall, connected to his parents through his father's mobile phone for instructions and directions.

Loretta had an idea. "Jeff! See if there is some mail laying around. Try to find some mail that would have a name and address on it."

On the kitchen bar of the mobile home, Jeff found a telephone bill.

"Jeff, you know on our phone bill where the name is?"

"Yes, ma'am."

"Well, look, and tell me the name on the phone bill."

Jeff found it. He could not read well but he could spell.

"Spell the name for me," she said.

"B-O-N-N-I-E-S F-I-R-E-W-O-O-D."

Then Jeff spelled aloud the address.

George wrote the letters as Jeff spelled aloud.

Then Jeff read out the telephone number.

As George kept Jeff on the phone, he directed Loretta to use the other phone line to call Shreveport Police.

Her son was an adult, Loretta was told. He had not been missing long enough to file a missing person's report.

As Phillip drove to Stonewall, one or both of his parents kept Jeff talking on the home telephone. Alternately, George or Loretta used the other line to call various law enforcement agencies: Shreveport Police, Caddo Parish Sheriff's Department finally DeSoto Parish Sheriff's Office, each time being told their son had not been missing long enough to file a missing person's report or "that's not our jurisdiction."

Exasperated, George called his friend, retired Colonel Marlin Flores, who worked with the Department of Public Safety. Col. Flores called DeSoto Parish Sheriff's Department on the Rodgers' behalf. DeSoto Parish telephoned George to say they had dispatched an officer to Stonewall on a welfare concern.

"Tell your son (Phillip) to stand down," George was told. "Do not go to the trailer until the deputy arrives."

Despite his wife's increasing angst as time passed, George remained confident Phillip would find Jeff and bring him home. He intended to keep Jeff talking on the phone until Phillip and the deputy arrived.

After talking more than an hour, Jeff told his father, "There's somebody at the door, Daddy. I hear somebody."

"Don't hang up the telephone, Jeff!" George directed his son. "Do not hang up the phone! Just lay it down and go to the door and whoever is there tell them to come to the telephone. But don't hang up!"

The telephone receiver clattered, followed by silence. Straining to hear, George detected no voices in the background, no whispers, no footsteps. There was no sound for what seemed several minutes. Then, ever so quietly, he heard the faintest "click" as the telephone receiver was placed back on its base.

The phone line went dead. George Rodgers noted it was 4:20 a.m.

The bewildered father stared at his telephone, dazed, as minutes ticked by. His wife was horrified. Their only connection to Jeff was gone.

What to do? What could they do?

George dialed the number that Jeff had just read to his mother. The phone on the other end rang ten to fifteen times. No one answered.

"Maybe they're in the backyard." He spoke his thoughts as he hung up the telephone.

He paced. He waited several minutes then dialed the telephone number again.

"Hello?"

"Who are you?" George demanded.

"I'm Stacy Williams."

"Are you the man of the house?"

"No, my father and mother own the house. I'm staying here while they are out of town. Uh, it's awful late to be calling somebody, isn't it?"

"Well, ordinarily it would be awful late to call somebody," George replied. "But I just talked to my son there a little bit ago and I'm wondering where he's at. I want to know where he's at."

"I don't know. I don't know nothing about him. I don't know what you're talking about."

Click. The phone connection was gone again.

<hr />

DeSoto Parish Sheriff's Deputy Sgt. J.R. Thomas met Phillip Rodgers at the J & M Grocery on Linwood Avenue in Stonewall about 5:30 a.m. After a brief discussion, Sgt. Thomas led the way to the Williams' trailer on Richardson Road with Phillip following in his own truck. They arrived there at 5:36 a.m., Thomas noted in his report. Lights were on inside the trailer, but no vehicles were parked in front or under the carport.

The officer knocked on the front door. No answer.

He walked to the carport, spotting a side entrance from it. Peering through the carport door, seeing no one, Sgt. Thomas then pounded on that door. No answer.

"At that point I went back to my unit and advised the

dispatcher that there were lights on and it seemed like nobody was answering," he said later. "So, I radioed the dispatcher to call the telephone number given her by Loretta Rodgers."

Standing at the side door, the deputy heard the telephone ringing, ringing, ringing.

Minutes later the dispatcher radioed back what he already knew: there was no answer on the call to Bonnie's Tree Service.

"After that I went to the back of the house," Sgt. Thomas reported, "where I saw a red Chevrolet truck with 'Bonnie's Tree Service' written on the side of the truck bed. There was a blue Ford truck there also."

Thomas walked around an outbuilding as well as a travel trailer in the back yard.

"It seemed no one was there," he noted.

The clock neared 6 a.m. and Thomas' shift was ending.

"I went 10-98 and advised the dispatcher that I was going to stay in the area and look some more," Sgt. Thomas said. "I also went to Stonewall-Preston Road looking for Gary Barber. I was unsuccessful in locating him. I also advised Phillip that I was going off shift and I would pass the information on to the next shift coming on so they could be on the lookout for Jeff."

As the officer drove away, with no one at the Williams' residence, young Phillip Rodgers felt as helpless as his parents who were pacing at home. What else could he do?

He drove home.

Phillip did not realize he'd seen something the deputy had missed. Something important. There in the Williams' backyard, parked in the shadows away from the area illuminated by the flood light and patrol car headlights— Phillip had seen a small, light-colored sedan.

In Shreveport, the Rodgers were persistent. They wanted answers. They wanted their son home. George called

DeSoto Sheriff's Office a second time, insisting more be done. By law enforcement standards, because Jeffrey Scott Rodgers was an adult, he had not been missing long enough to launch an official investigation. If he was a child, it would be different. Law enforcement departments frequently received calls like George Rodgers', family members concerned about adult loved ones who were overdue, who almost always came home safely from somewhere they should not have been. Still, Sgt. Larry Boyd was dispatched to Richardson Road along with patrol deputy Bobby Simone on a second welfare check for Jeff Rodgers.

They pulled up at the Williams' trailer at 9 a.m., and, this time, there were signs of life.

Seeing the patrol car, a young woman walked over from the trailer house next door. Sgt. Larry Boyd told her they needed to speak with whoever was at this house. She entered the Williams' residence through the unlocked carport door, stepped out minutes later, and motioned for the deputies to come inside.

Two men were asleep in the living room, one on the couch and the other in a recliner.

It was Stacy Williams on the couch. The officers awoke him.

"I talked to Stacy Williams," Sgt. Boyd reported. "Williams appeared to be under the influence of something. Another subject was asleep in a chair. I asked Williams who that was, and he stated that was Gary Barber. I asked him if he knew a Jeffery Rodgers and he said that he did not. I explained to him Rodgers' condition and told him that his father was concerned about him. I asked him again if he knew anything about this matter. He said he did not. I advised Williams of the consequences of filing or telling a false report. He still said that he did not know anything about this matter. Deputy Bobby Simone was present during the time."

Boyd and Simone went back on patrol.

George and Loretta's middle son, Christopher Shane, was twenty-three years old at the time. When Chris Rodgers entered junior high school, he met any number of girls who were also named Chris, so he took his middle name, introducing himself as Shane Rodgers. To this day, the man known publicly as Shane Rodgers is Chris to his family.

In 1994, Shane had moved out of the family home and was working as a waiter at El Chico's—an early step on a winding journey that led him to obtain two master's degrees from Louisiana State University before he eventually established "Shane's Seafood & Bar-B-Que" chain in Shreveport and Bossier.

George Rodgers called Shane that Saturday morning, bringing him up to date on the events of the morning. George continued to display calmness for the good of his wife and sons but inside, his certainty that Jeff would be found unharmed was waning. Still, he believed, his son was alive, perhaps injured and traumatized but George swore to himself he would get Jeff home. He had to find him.

The original fear gripping Loretta Rodgers had only intensified. The normally protective mother was terrified for her son. She wanted him home, safe.

I have heard a lot of jokes about 'women's intuition' but over the years I observed many women who seemed to possess a sixth sense, an innate intuition, particularly about their children and danger. Men may feel that same dread but, like George Rodgers, they refuse to accept it, for in doing so one accepts defeat. George vowed to bring his son home. He called several friends asking if they would help him find Jeff. He told Shane to enlist his friends.

Stonewall is part of the Shreveport-Bossier Metropolitan area. The past decade it has mushroomed into an upscale bedroom community of young professionals who work in either Shreveport or Mansfield but in 1994, Stonewall, named after Confederate General Stonewall Jackson, didn't have a single street light. It was a crossroads community dotted with single-wide trailer houses sitting at the end of winding, rutted dirt lanes. One manufactured home after another was tucked beneath towering trees, separated by pastures, cultivated crops, or thickets. Stonewall was a place where T-shirts, mullets, and mudding trucks proliferated alongside Southern Baptist churches. Most folks there liked rodeos, football, fishing, hunting, sweet tea, or beer.

That morning George Rodgers, his sons and several friends drove up and down the roads into, out of, and within Stonewall, hoping to find Jeff wandering around. They knocked on doors, asking anyone they encountered, had they seen Jeff? Twenty-seven, dark hair, six feet four inches tall. Thin.

One person after another shook their heads, apologetically. No, they'd seen no one like that. But one after another offered to help any way they could.

Driving slowly up and down Richardson Road, trying to determine which was the place Jeff called from, George finally spotted a young man working outside a trailer that he thought might be the Williams'. The man approached, curious to know why George was driving back and forth in front of the trailer house.

It was Stacy's oldest brother, Bobby Williams, who listened sympathetically to George's story. Bobby was of medium height, slightly built with long, dark hair. He seemed genuine. Like everyone else his answer was, sorry—he did not know Jeff and had no idea where he might be. He didn't live there, Bobby explained, he was there chopping wood for his dad. His parents were out of town but his youngest brother, James, had spent the night next door. Calling James outside from the neighbors' house, Bobby asked, had anyone spent the night at their parents' house? The boy shrugged. He didn't know, but he had noticed a small silver-looking car parked over there.

Who did that car belong to, George asked?

"Gary Barber."

Bobby Williams bristled. What was Gary Barber doing with Stacy?

George asked James Williams, where did Gary Barber live?

In Shreveport. In the Huntington Apartments, the boy said.

Shane Rodgers headed to the Huntington Apartments on Industrial Boulevard in southwest Shreveport, Phillip following.

Shane knocked random doors until someone pointed him to the Barber's apartment, where Shane spoke with David Barber, Gary's older brother. David Barber appeared irritated by Shane's questions and inferences, but he finally brought Shane inside to speak with Gary, who had come in late and was just exiting the shower.

"Do you know where my brother is," Shane asked. "Where is Jeff?"

Gary Barber shrugged. "Hadn't seen him in two or three weeks."

"I know you're lying!" Shane got in Barber's face. At his age he had not yet cultivated his father's calm demeanor. "Where is my brother?"

"I don't know, man. I don't have any idea. I haven't seen him."

Jeff had told their parents he was with Gary Barber and Shane knew his older brother did not know how to lie.

"I guess he didn't want his brother to know he had seen Jeff," Shane recalled. "For some reason he was scared of his brother so after his brother went outside, I kept asking and Gary finally admitted he had seen Jeff, that they bought some beer the night before. He said they got into a fight about 1:30 a.m. at the Charter Station on Mansfield Highway and he left Jeff there and that was the last time he saw him."

Now Shane was stumped, feeling as Phillip had when the deputy drove away from the Williams' trailer. Shane didn't know what more he could do. He was preparing to leave when Gary Barber made an irreversible blunder, blurting out, "I spent the night at Stacy Williams' house."

Wait a minute, Shane thought. Stacy Williams' house? Jeff called his parents, crying, terrified, from Stacy Williams' house and now, Gary Barber admitted he spent the night there?

"Liar!" Shane yelled. "Liar! My brother called my parents from Stacy Williams' house!"

Barber became nervous. Fidgety. He backtracked, his gaze darting around the room. "Well," he stammered, "I'm not sure what time I got there. I was drunk. If Jeff was there, I didn't know it. I was drunk and asleep."

"Okay," Shane said. "Will you come with me to my house and tell this to my father?"

Reluctantly, Gary Barber agreed. It was mid-afternoon Saturday.

Loretta called George to say Linda Sanchez just told her she saw Jeff talking to someone in a silver car parked at the curb in front of their house, about ten-thirty the night before. James Williams had just told George a car like that was parked overnight at the Williams' and Phillip had seen a car fitting that description at the Williams' residence. James Williams said that car belonged to Gary Barber. Jeff said he was with Gary Barber.

On the advice of Col. Flores, George called Shreveport Police to make a missing person's report based on this new information, telling them about Gary Barber, who lived at the Huntington Apartments. Find Gary Barber, George believed, and you would find Jeff. Shreveport police said they would dispatch an officer.

Finally, George thought. They were getting

somewhere.

When George got home from Stonewall, Shane was waiting in the living room with a bedraggled Gary Barber in tow. Barber was taller than Shane but not as tall as Jeff. He probably stood over six feet. He was thin with a shock of brown hair.

"Gary," George said, "I know you picked Jeff up last night and I know you went down to the trailer house. Now, tell me where Jeff's at. That's all I want to know. Just tell me where Jeff's at and you can go home."

"I don't know," Barber said. "I, I picked Jeff up and we—we bought a lot of beer and a lot of liquor; and we was drinking, and we went down to Stonewall, and we was riding four-wheelers and the deputy sheriff come down there and told us all to go home. And, uh, me and Jeff got mad at each other and got into an argument and we were coming up Mansfield Road and I let Jeff out at the Charter Station about one-thirty."

"What happened after that?" George asked.

"I went back to the trailer house and went to bed. I hadn't seen Jeff since."

George leaned forward, looking squarely in Barber's eyes. "I know that Jeff was in that trailer house from 3:10 to 4:20 because I had him on the telephone. He read me the address off the phone bill. He had to be there."

"Well, Jeff might have walked through the woods," Barber offered.

"Jeff's not going through those woods and it's dark," George scoffed. "And he could not have found the trailer house cutting through those woods— I mean he couldn't have found it; and he wasn't going through those dark woods anyway."

"Well, maybe somebody picked him up and brought him over there. I don't know," Barber insisted. "We were all drinking and, you know, we was all pretty drunk. If Jeff was in the trailer house, I didn't know it."

The Rodgers' telephone rang, interrupting the

conversation. George excused himself.

It was Vicki Halverson, Jeff's supervisor at Crescent Landing.

"George, did you know Jeff got his paycheck Friday night?" she asked.

Vicki knew, as did everyone who knew Jeff, that he could not handle money. Jeff did not comprehend its value. One time, Shane recalled, Jeff bought a hundred dollars' worth of bubble gum and passed it out to the entire neighborhood. If Jeff paid for a pack of cigarettes with a twenty-dollar bill and the clerk handed back fifty cents in change, Jeff would put it in his pocket and ask no questions.

Eyeing Barber across the room, George replied, "No, I didn't know that. Thank you for calling."

Turning to Barber he asked, "Did Jeff have any money on him?"

"Yeah," Barber replied. "He had lots of money."

"What do you mean by 'lots of money'?"

"Well, he was pulling it out and showing us his money. Lots of money."

"You mean two dollars? Five dollars?"

"No, no. More than that. Lots of money."

"Gary," George asked. "Did y'all go get his paycheck cashed?"

Barber's eyes widened as he threw his hands up. "I didn't know he had a check."

"Gary, you had to get his check cashed if he had any money because we gave him two dollars when he left here," George insisted.

"No. No," Barber said. "I didn't know nothing about his check."

"I just knew he was lying," Shane recalled. He jerked Barber up and out of the chair and shoved him toward the front door. As Barber fumbled to open it and flee, Shane hit him in the back of his head, grabbed him, and threw him outside onto the front lawn. Then Shane pounced on top of Gary Barber, pounding him with his fists.

George and Phillip scrambled outside, both grabbing Shane's flailing arms.

"Stop it!" George hollered, pulling his son away from Barber. "You know this is not the answer. This is not the way to find out something. Maybe the boy is lying. I don't know. But you're not going to accomplish anything doing this."

"I had to pull Chris off of him," George remembered. "I thought he was going to kill him. I said, 'Chris, if you kill him you will go to jail.'"

George was ushering Shane inside the house as a Shreveport Police unit pulled up. George brought the officer and Barber back into the living room where George told the officer everything he knew.

Looking at Barber, he nodded. "Okay, Gary, you tell him what you know."

Barber recited his story to the policeman, who listened intently, but George could not help but notice the officer took no notes. He did not ask for names, addresses, or times, or fill out any forms. He was not, to George's mounting frustration, initiating a missing person's investigation.

At last the officer said, "I patrol this area. I know Jeff. I know what he looks like and I know where he goes." He stood to leave, "I'm going to ride around to all the places that I know I've seen Jeff. I'll see if he's probably around in one of the places."

That was it. There was no missing person's report taken.

The officer left and George instructed Phillip to drive Barber back to his apartment.

"I was afraid Chris would take him down the road and jump on him again," George said. But before Gary left the room the frustrated father thought to ask, "Who was at the Charter station when you left Jeff there?"

"Some lady," Gary replied. "I bought a Coke from her."

George nodded. "Phillip, take Gary home."

Shane drove to the Charter gas station north of Stonewall on the Mansfield Highway, hoping to speak with the woman who had been on duty the night before. What he learned deepened his suspicions: there had been no woman on duty. Michael Arnold went on duty at 10 p.m. Friday and worked until 6 a.m. Saturday. He had done a turn-around, arriving back at work shortly before Shane arrived. No one matching Jeff's description had been in the store at any time during Arnold's shift the night before, he said.

Saturday was slipping away and there was no sign of Jeff. In Shane Rodgers' mind, he was, indeed, his brother's keeper. He fought back a growing fear for his brother's welfare, summoning up his father's optimism that they would find Jeff lost and wandering around somewhere near Stonewall and bring him home.

Leaving the gas station, Shane drove back to the Williams' trailer where, for the first time, he encountered Stacy Williams. Introducing himself, Shane asked Stacy what he knew about Jeff's disappearance.

He heard a different story from the one Gary Barber had told. Stacy said he had seen Jeff late Friday or early Saturday at the end of Pond Road where they had all ridden three-wheelers.

"What time was that?"

Stacy shrugged. "I don't know," he said. "I was drunk."

Now that was an answer Shane Rodgers was tired of hearing.

After leaving Pond Road, Stacy said, he spent the night with his girlfriend and had not gone to his parents' home until around six-thirty that morning. He had no idea where Jeff went after he left Ponds Road.

Driving back to his parents' house, Shane stopped at every liquor store and grocery store along the route from Stonewall and southwest Shreveport.

At the Liquor Shoppe on Mansfield Road in

Shreveport, the owner told Shane a man matching Jeff's description had been in late Friday with another fellow and they had tried to cash a check for $173. The owner said he refused to cash it. Someone else must have, he said, because the two men returned with cash and bought liquor at 11:30 p.m.

Shane called his father.

The pieces were coming together.

Gary and Stacy or just Gary or maybe even others—whoever was involved—had used Jeff to buy liquor because they were too young. Gary Barber had lied. They had cashed Jeff's paycheck.

There was no doubt in Shane Rodgers' mind that Gary Barber was behind his brother's disappearance, that Stacy was involved, also, and that money was the motive.

Hearing from Shane, George called the DeSoto Parish Sheriff's Office a third time, relaying this new information. The dispatcher took his information and promised to pass it on.

Hanging up the telephone, George Rodgers wanted to scream. He wanted to pound something in anger and frustration. His son was gone. Law enforcement was lollygagging. They refused to launch an organized manhunt. They had not dragged Williams or Barber in for questioning. Shane, not the cops, had hunted down and questioned Gary Barber. Shane questioned Williams, the convenience store clerk, the liquor store owner. The police had not done any of that. And the Shreveport cop? He just listened. He had not made a report.

Williams and Barber—they knew the truth; George Rodgers was certain. Linda Sanchez saw Jeff talking to someone in a silver car; Phillip and James Williams saw a silver car parked at the Williams' trailer; the liquor store owner said Jeff tried to cash his paycheck and came back with cash to buy liquor; Gary Barber lied when he said he had no idea Jeff got his paycheck, and he lied about buying a Coke from a woman working at the Charter gas station.

Jeff said he was with Gary Barber. Jeff had called home from the Williams' trailer. A certain rage welled inside George as he recalled the fear in Jeff's voice. He heard his son all over again pleading, "Daddy, come get me. They hurt me."

In the morning, he resolved, they would take an army to Stonewall. He called more friends, asking if they would join him and maybe they'd enlist other friends. "Of course," each person promised, they would help find Jeff.

George said to his wife and two sons, "We're going to find Jeff. He may be out there. They may have left him out in those woods, and he's lost, and he can't find his way out."

Each member of the Rodgers family went to bed Saturday night, clinging to the hope that Jeff would be found and would be home with them this time tomorrow night.

Chapter Three

Neither George nor Loretta Rodgers slept. Their minds wandered to places they did not want to go as Jeff's words reverberated.

"Daddy come get me. I'm afraid."

"Mommy, they hurt me."

"They hit me where those other boys hit me."

"Daddy, somebody is coming."

What had they done to Jeff? Where was he? Was Jeff lost in the woods, huddled at the base of a tree somewhere? Was he hurt?

George fought an overwhelming sense of dread, burying his fear beneath a reassuring demeanor. Through tears, Loretta fought a suffocating terror.

George had intended to search Stonewall with his sons on Sunday, but when it came time, he could not leave Loretta to face this day alone. He remained home at her side, telephone in hand, as Chris and Phillip joined search volunteers in Stonewall.

The Williams' trailer house served as a staging area. They would fan out from there, this time working methodically covering a grid.

Among the volunteers was George's good friend, a former Caddo Parish sheriff's deputy Dennis Berry. The Rodgers and Berrys had been neighbors for nine years prior to the Rodgers moving to Fox Chase Trail. Dennis Berry watched Jeff Rodgers and his brothers grow up, playing with his own children.

The older, more experienced former deputy assumed the role of coordinator. What had not been searched yesterday, he wanted to know. They pointed southwest. Missile Base Road.

Berry instructed the group to scour Missile Base Road. Look in the ditches and in culverts. Look under bridges, he told them. Walk creek beds.

Go down every pig trail off Missile Base Road, he instructed them. "Be thorough."

In the meantime, Shane confronted Stacy again.

Stacy repeated his story from the evening before—that he had seen Jeff at the end of Pond Road where they all rode three-wheelers. He was drunk, so he went to his girlfriend's house to spend the night, but this time Stacy added a new twist. He said he went home at 5 a.m. where he found Gary Barber asleep in the living room chair. So, Stacy said, he went to sleep there on the couch.

This idiot didn't know Phillip and the DeSoto Parish sheriff's deputy had been at his house at five-thirty, Shane thought.

"You're lying," he said. "My little brother was here with a deputy at five-thirty Saturday morning. You weren't here and neither was Gary. No one was here."

Stacy tweaked his explanation, saying he just came home to check on Gary at five o'clock but left and went back to his girlfriend's house.

"If you were just checking on Gary, why drive back over here from your girlfriend's house? Why didn't you just call?" Shane asked.

"Because it's just a little way here," Stacy replied.

"A little way from where?"

"From Homalot."

"Homalot? That must be at least ten miles away!" Shane said.

"It's just a little way," Stacy repeated.

Shane was certain Stacy Williams and Gary Barber were lying. They were lying about everything. The question was, what were they covering up?

Sgt. Sandra May was the dispatcher on duty at DeSoto Parish SO that Sunday afternoon. About 12:30 p.m. she answered a call from a man identifying himself as Chad Evers. Evers, she said, told her he was calling to make police aware that he gave a ride to a man matching Jeff Rodgers' description the day before. The man was walking along the Old Mansfield Highway in Stonewall.

"He asked me to take him to the rodeo arena," Evers told the dispatcher.

"What time was this?" Sgt. May asked.

"About 5 a.m."

"5 a.m.?"

"Yes," he said. "I was on my way to see my girlfriend. She lives in Stonewall."

"Okay, can you describe this man?"

"He was real tall and skinny," Evers replied. "He asked me to take him to the rodeo arena and someone was supposed to pick him up there. The guy acted real retarded."

Evers hung up without giving a return phone number or address.

Through Sunday morning the crowd continued to grow around the Williams' trailer. Stacy's parents had returned

Saturday night from their trip out of town. Bonnie and Sue Williams were filled in on the events and the search. Stacy's brothers, Bobby and James, were there along with various Stonewall residents who had heard of the search for the missing man.

Then there were the volunteers from Shreveport and Bossier, friends of the Rodgers and friends of friends of the Rodgers, on three-wheelers and four-wheelers, in trucks and on foot. Richardson Road had never been so congested, with vehicles parked all along the narrow, two-lane dirt road, even in some yards. All the while, there was the incessant buzz of all-terrain vehicles coming and going.

For hours, dozens of people combed north DeSoto Parish looking for Jeff Rodgers, stooping to peer inside concrete culverts, picking up and inspecting trash that might lend a clue, wading through ditches and pastures of knee-high grass.

The September sun was high in the clear sky when Dennis Berry came to a wooden bridge over a creek that crossed Missile Base Road. Stopping his truck, the former lawman walked to the bridge railing, visually examining that side of the creek bed. The banks were thick with waist-high nandina, holly, and privet tied together by saw briars, poison ivy, and Virginia creeper. Nothing caught his eye.

Rick Van Huss, Berry's neighbor and search partner, climbed down the bank of the creek on the other side. Berry watched from the bridge. He saw the smallest patch of white caught in the brush. Whatever it was, it did not belong there.

"Rick!" Berry yelled. "Come back this way! What is that?"

Pointing, Berry directed Van Huss to the speck of white caught in the vines. There it was!

Van Huss picked up a small card, examining both sides.

Looking up to the bridge, Van Huss hollered back, "Dennis! This is Jeff Rodgers' ID card!"

Berry rushed down the bank to see for himself.

The two men began combing through thick brush,

looking for more evidence that might have been left along the creek bank when Berry was struck by a realization.

"I've got to go call George," he said. "He has to know this now."

Several miles away, about the same time Berry discovered the ID card, two teenage boys were walking to their favorite fishing hole off Rambin Road. Fifteen-year-old Ryan Greco and Jeremy Sweet were making the hike through the woods to Dew Pond, a prime fishing spot familiar to locals, which was accessible only by walking through Jeremy's family's land or from a rutted, winding deer trail off Rambin Road.

Rounding a bend in the trail, as the pond came into view, both boys stopped in their tracks. Jeremy first, drawing in his breath with Ryan a second behind him.

"Look!" Jeremy pointed. "Look!"

They sprinted around the bend to the clearing at the pond's dam, where they could see more clearly. They stopped again—stunned. Horrified, the two boys turned and ran back to Jeremy's house.

On Missile Base Road, Dennis trudged up the creek bank to get to his truck, so that he could call his friend.

"George," he said. "I found Jeff's ID. You need to contact the sheriff's department and get somebody out here right now. We are starting to find some evidence."

George's heart sank and his eyes filled with tears. The fear he had been stuffing inside welled into George's throat. He could not speak. He choked back the need to sob.

After a long pause Dennis offered, "Do you want me to call the sheriff's office, George?"

"No," George replied. "I will do it."

Word spread quickly through the staging area that Dennis Berry found Jeff's identification card. Shane Rodgers got two friends and started to head to Shreveport to get Gary Barber, but he needn't have. Sue Williams had already called Gary Barber, ordering him to come to her house to explain what had happened there overnight.

In the meantime, after receiving George Rodgers' call, dispatch sent Sheriff's Deputy Bobby Simone to retrieve the ID card from Dennis Berry and called me. As I drove to Stonewall, things were exploding on Richardson Road. From various witness statements and later court testimony, no two people remembered what happened there at the Williams' trailer the same way.

What was certain was that, in Stonewall, patrol deputy Bobby Simone—who had been sent to retrieve Jeff Rodgers' ID—was met by what he considered a mob. Less than two years on the job, the young deputy was intimidated by the size of the crowd congregated at the Williams' and the apparent tension filling the air. Volunteers had stopped searching and hung around waiting for Berry to bring the ID to the deputy. Stonewall residents had gathered, drawn by rumors of the missing man and all the commotion. Stacy Williams, Bobby and James were there as were Gary Barber, Shane and Phillip Rodgers, and a host of their family friends.

The accused and the accusers were all there. Simone sensed the slightest misstep could set off a melee.

Seeing the deputy's patrol car pull up at his house, Bonnie Williams took the initiative, meeting Deputy Simone at his patrol car. Bonnie Williams, a small, muscular man like his son Bobby, introduced himself.

"Mr. Williams are you aware of what's going on?" Deputy Simone asked.

"A little," Bonnie Williams said.

The deputy explained that he'd been sent to retrieve an ID that had been found.

That man wasn't back yet, Simone was told.

The deputy briefed Bonnie Williams on the Rodgers'

report that Jeff had called them from their house in the middle of the night, of their welfare check on Jeff Rodgers there the morning before when Stacy denied any knowledge of Jeff Rodgers' whereabouts, and that Stacy had been warned about the consequences of making false statements.

Bonnie Williams shouted at a tall young man standing nearby, "Tell him the truth!"

"Okay," the tall young man said. "Jeff was here but we took him to the Circle K and left him there about one-thirty."

Believing it was Stacy Williams who spoke, Simone slapped handcuffs on the young man, saying, "I'm going to have to arrest you for criminal mischief for making a false report to authorities."

As Simone read the Miranda warning to his suspect, Bonnie Williams cried out, "That's not Stacy. That's not my son. That's Gary. That's Gary Barber!"

This was the boy who had been asleep in the chair yesterday morning, Simone realized. Now he recognized him. "Okay," the deputy said. "You stay right where you are. You're not under arrest right now but I don't want you going anywhere." He left Barber by the patrol car, handcuffed.

Bonnie Williams ushered the deputy, his wife, and Stacy inside the trailer where Bonnie Williams repeated, "Tell this man the truth, Stacy. Tell him what happened."

Before Stacy could say anything, Simone handcuffed him. "We warned you about making false statements to police," Simone said. He placed Stacy under arrest on a charge of criminal mischief, read him the Miranda Warning, then escorted him to the back seat of the patrol car.

"Stay there," Simone told Stacy, slamming shut the back door of the patrol car, which could not be opened from the inside.

Dennis Berry arrived, handing Jeff Rodgers' ID card to the deputy just as Bonnie Williams yelled from the carport, waving his arms for Simone to come there. He and Bobby were standing at the tailgate of a brown Ford truck parked beside the carport maybe fifteen feet in front of the patrol unit where Stacy was sitting.

The deputy saw what Bobby and Bonnie Williams were looking at, what appeared to be blood.

Bonnie Williams cried out, "Oh, God, Stacy! What have you done? What have you done?"

Handcuffed in the back seat of the patrol car, seeing his father and the deputy spot the bloodied truck bed, his father railing out of control—as Bobby Simone opened the front door to his patrol unit intending to call for more backup— Stacy Williams erupted in the back seat, blurting out, "We did it! We did it! We beat him up and threw him in the pond!"

Caught off-guard, Simone was momentarily dumbfounded. Had everyone—anyone—heard what Williams just said?

"Don't say another word, Stacy. Don't say another word!" Simone warned. "I'm not an investigator."

Simone turned on the patrol car video camera, which was installed on the dashboard to video drunk drivers and their sobriety tests. It was mounted aimed out the front windshield and could not be turned around. Still, it picked up audio well.

Simone read the Miranda rights card again and called headquarters. "This subject wants to make a statement. Do I take his statement or not? I'm not an investigator. I don't want to take it without permission."

A moment later dispatch came back.

"Take his statement."

The recorder running, Simone prompted Stacy. "Okay you can make your statement."

"We did it," Stacy said again, this time with a calm resignation. "We beat him up and threw him in the pond."

Nearby, Bonnie Williams lost control. In the words of Bobby Simone, Williams "nutted up."

Still screaming, "What have you done? What have you done!" he charged at the handcuffed Gary Barber, threatening, "I'm going to hurt you!"

Several men wrestled and subdued Bonnie Williams. Simone was handcuffing him to a lawn chair as I pulled up in the yard along with Simone's supervisor, Sgt. Larry Boyd, and DPSO Chief Deputy Andy Anderson.

And then dispatch came over the car radios, echoing across from Simone's patrol car, my unit, Anderson's, and Boyd's: "All units be advised. Caller reports finding a deceased person in a pond off Rambin Road."

In a moment of silence, as everyone absorbed what they heard, the hackles rose on the back of my neck. It was the spark that could ignite a bloodbath. We stuffed the handcuffed suspects into patrol cars and got them out of there before the crowd could react.

"I wanted to kill him (Barber)," Shane Rodgers admitted. "I even thought about it. It crossed my mind. I had a pistol in the truck. But I kept hearing my father's words 'You will go to jail.'"

It was late afternoon and Dennis Berry felt the burden of responsibility to tell this final truth to his friend. He made the call.

"George," Dennis said. "I'm so sorry to tell you…." He couldn't bring himself to say it.

"What," George said. "Just tell me."

"George—they found Jeff. They found Jeff's body—in a pond."

That was more than twenty-five years ago, and George Rodgers remembers it like it was this morning. He will carry it to his grave.

"You are never the same," he said. "Nothing would ever be the same. You fall to your knees and you hit the ground and you stay there. You stay there a very long time."

Sunday evening approached. The guessing was over. George Rodgers had learned the truth. Now, he had to tell his wife.

Chapter Four

Before leaving the Williams' trailer, I impounded Barber's silver car and Bonnie Williams' pickup with the bloody bed. I would gather evidence from them, from the Missile Base creek bridge, and the Williams' trailer later. The suspects were being booked into jail. I needed to get to the pond where Jeff Rodgers' body was discovered before I did anything else.

It was tucked away in deep woods, seven or eight miles away. The pond was not visible from the road and only accessible by walking a winding path, once a deer trail, which, it appeared, had been rutted by an ATV after the last rain. Arriving at the dam, I surveilled the serene scene, a three-acre pond fringed by the autumn-palleted forest, which swallowed up any wind, leaving the water clear and still. Cattails and sedges grew along the far bank with milkweed and cardinal flowers not far from Jeff's body. It could have been a landscape painting, the kind of place people seek for peace and quiet. What a paradox that it became a place to kill.

Jeff Rodgers was unrecognizable after being submerged face-down in the pond more than twenty-four hours. His feet were at the bank's edge. Rigor mortis had set in. Looking at death is something you learn to endure but certain images never go away. We needed to turn the body, but as flesh decays, especially in warm water, the skin becomes a putrid mush that slides away as you try to hold onto and move it. Pulling a body from a pond in order to examine it is not a simple or swift task.

"These people were sick." I turned to see DPSO Chief Deputy Andy Anderson coming up behind me. Anderson was a retired sergeant major in the Army, and I had asked him to give me a hand at the crime scene. "What the hell did they do to that boy?"

I couldn't be sure if Andy was thinking out loud or if he expected an answer as he went on, "Why would anyone do that to another human being? For that matter why would you do that to an animal?"

"I have no idea why anyone would do this to anyone else," I said, but then I'd said that before, looking at victims. This was about as bad as it gets. Jeff Rodgers' face was crushed like someone smashed a pumpkin with a baseball bat.

Some people put mentholatum under their nose to overpower natural odors at crime scenes, but I taught myself not to breathe, to draw in air through the mouth sparingly during times like that. I took photographs of the victim, wide shots to show the way his body was found and tight shots to show his wounds. I photographed the entire area to aid the prosecutor in painting a picture for the jury. I took pictures of three sets of footprints, bloody pine straw, drag marks through pine straw.

I measured everything—the individual shoe prints: could each be identified to Rodgers, Barber, and Williams? The drag marks, how far was the victim dragged from where he collapsed on the ground to the water? How far was it from where the trail opened onto the clearing to the spot where Jeff Rodgers fell, to the first bloody matting of pine straw?

With plastic gloves, I collected any number of samples for forensic analysis while Anderson oversaw several deputies cordoning off the crime scene.

Using tweezers, I took samples of bloody pine needles from various places, putting each into a plastic bag and giving each a unique ID. Would each match Jeff Rodgers' blood type? I collected soil samples—would pathologists be able to determine that exact soil was on Gary Barber's shoes? Stacy Williams' shoes?

The care and handling of any crime scene can make or break a case, and anyone could contaminate it. Every deputy called to help had to be careful not to step on evidence. We told them, "Keep your hands in your pockets. Don't touch anything."

Preservation of the crime scene is the reason the public and media are kept away. It's not because we're trying to hide something. We are trying to preserve the crime scene in order to exact justice for the victims. Television cop shows, the news media, and even people who write crime fiction often fail to detail just how tedious and important it is that the crime scene be processed precisely.

At last, I left the pond in the hands of Andy Anderson to await the coroner. I headed to Mansfield to get some truth out of two suspects.

I got my first look at Stacy Williams and Gary Barber in my office late that afternoon. Offices in the Detective Division of the DeSoto Parish Sheriff's Department were small. They still are. There is room enough for a desk, filing cabinet, and a couple of chairs. Close quarters, to say the least. We recorded statements from suspects with a video camera set up on a tripod in a corner of the room, and we started recording before the suspect entered the room, so we could see them walk in and sit down. The camera was aimed at the chair in which the suspect would sit, directly across the desk in front of us. The videotaped questions and answers were transcribed so that a video and written record of all statements were permanently preserved.

I don't believe they were designed for this purpose, but because the offices were so small, as an investigator, you were near enough to get a good read on your suspect. You can smell them. You can see them sweat, catch the widening and narrowing of their pupils as they react to questions. You can watch their body language. Are their fists clenched? Do they drum their fingers? Do they tap their feet on the floor? Do they fidget in the chair? Do their gazes dart around the room? Do they pull at their hair, their clothing? We are trained to observe and read body language.

Both men— Gary Barber and Stacy Williams—were tall. Each was slender built with brown hair, and being related, had generally similar features. It was clear to see how Bobby Simone confused the two earlier at the Williams' trailer.

Deputy Simone and Sgt. Boyd were in the room with me during the interrogations. We did that so, even with the video, there could never be just the detective's word against the suspect's. I did the questioning. Boyd and Simone were there as observers.

I interviewed Stacy first. He was handcuffed and shackled. His head hung low, as it had the first time I saw him in the patrol car, his shoulders still slumped. The teenager, who had always been a daddy's boy, had witnessed his father's hysterical reaction learning what happened. Bonnie Williams' breakdown had clearly shaken Stacy to the core and prompted his abrupt admission in the patrol car.

"Okay, Stacy," I said, "in your own words what happened to Jeffery Scott Rodgers?"

Staring at the floor, avoiding the camera or eye contact, Stacy began to talk slowly, haltingly.

"Well, uh, him and Gary Barber come to my house to spend the night with me and, uh, we—we got into—he told me he was mentally retarded, and we started picking on him about it. Me and Gary did."

"Who told you that?" I asked.

"Gary Barber told me that boy was kind of mentally retarded, so we started picking on him and stuff. Like I said, we was real drunk. We went to, you know, pushing on him and stuff."

"Who was drinking?"

"Me and Gary and that boy was also."

"What were you drinking?"

"I was drinking Budweiser and they was drinking— Maddog or something like that."

"Okay, go ahead."

"And, uh, we got to my house and we started picking on him. We come outside into the back yard and we started hitting on him and stuff. We left and went down to the pond where he was at."

"Both of y'all were hitting on him?"

"Yes, sir."

"With your fist or some kind of weapon?"

"With our fists."

"Just because you were drinking?"

"Yes, sir. We knew he was retarded so we started picking on him."

Stacy described the beating of Jeff Rodgers, which took place in several locations over a period of hours. I had not been made aware that Jeff Rodgers had the mental capacity of a ten-year-old, but listening to Stacy detail the beatings, I think all of us in the room— Bobby Simone, Larry Boyd, and I—were stunned at the matter-of-fact way in which he spoke of their cruelty. I believe we all struggled to understand how such savagery was meted out, motivated, this teenager explained, because Jeff was mentally impaired.

The deputies took Stacy out and I took that break, when I watched that unforgettable sunset on the heels of having seen and heard what happened to Jeff Rodgers. I had seen suspects feign regret, asking for forgiveness. That's not what just happened. It was clear Stacy Williams was living in a hell of his own making. He would live in it the rest of his life.

With the sun gone, I went inside to meet Gary Barber. Those two might have been distantly related and looked similar but their demeanors could not have been more different. There was no light in the eyes of Gary Barber. I had seen eyes like that before. He did not hang his head. He glared and sneered.

While I explained to him the Miranda Warning he said, "Apparently, you've already found me guilty."

At that point I had not learned about his criminal background, that he had been through this before.

"No, let me read—really explain this to you," I said, the video camera rolling. "I'm going to read this all over again, okay? Before we ask you any questions, you must understand your rights. You have the right to remain silent. Anything you say can be used against you in court. You have the right to talk to a lawyer for advice before any questions, have him present during questioning. If you cannot afford an attorney one will be appointed to represent you free. If you desire to answer questions now without a lawyer present, you will still have the right to stop answering any time."

"Okay," he said.

"You also have the right to stop answering at any time until you talk to an attorney and then what this is, it is a waiver."

"Okay," he said. "I was just reading."

"Gary, you know why you're here, involving Jeffery Scott Rodgers. His disappearance. I don't know what you know or if you know what we know but I'm going to be straightforward with you. I'm not going to lie to you, try to trick you, or anything else. You're in lots of trouble. The other guy that came in with us that is currently back in the DeSoto Parish Jail— Stacy Williams. He has been charged. We found the body in the pond. The coroner is up there, the crime scene crew is up at the pond, we have a statement from

Mr. Williams on what happened and what happened in the trailer house, at the bridge, going to the pond, and coming back. And I just— I would like for you to give me a statement on the facts that happened, your part of it, because I don't know your part."

"My part is, I took him to the Charter and dropped him off," Barber replied. "I mean, I went back to Stacy's house and went to sleep. What happened I don't know—and it's got me— Jeff was my friend. I wouldn't kill no goddamned body."

"Where did you first see Jeffery Scott Rodgers?"

"At a Circle K in Shreveport."

"What time was that?"

"I'd say ten-thirty or eleven."

"What day?"

"Friday night."

"Ten-thirty or eleven o'clock Friday night he was at the Circle K with who?"

"By hisself."

"Did he go with you or—"

"Yes. He left with me."

"He left the Circle K with you?"

"Right."

"And you came where?"

"Out here. To DeSoto Parish. To Stonewall, you know, where the Pond Road—"

"Pines Road?" I was not familiar with their hangout.

"*Pond* Road," he repeated.

"I guess I don't know," I replied. "Wright Road, I guess? Whose house did y'all go to when you got to Stonewall?"

"We went out there. We rode three-wheelers. And then we left and, uh, went to Stacy's house, and wasn't nobody there, 'cause I was very—we was both intoxicated and—"

"You and Rodgers both?"

"Yeah. We were both intoxicated. And I told him to stay there while I went and looked for Stacy. So apparently at that time he called his parents or some crap like that. And so, I came back and picked him up and we got into an argument. I left him at the Charter, and I went back to Stacy's house and I went to sleep in the chair till the next morning."

"Well. At this time, you are charged with murder, robbery, and kidnapping."

I told him about the forensic evidence we were collecting, hoping he would talk more. I was getting nowhere. Finally, I said, "If you want to sit and play hardball and be the one to take the heat—"

"I'm not taking no heat," he said. "I'm telling you what I know."

"And you were never—you were not involved in any way with his death?"

"No."

"Never hit the man? You're saying Stacy Williams is lying about everything?"

"I don't know what he said, all right? I'm through with this. Just take me back to where I got to go." He stood to leave; his face contorted by hatred. It was an 'I'd like to reach across the desk and rip out your throat' look. It wasn't the first time someone looked at me that way.

"Suit yourself," I said. "I tried."

My interview with Gary Barber ended eight minutes after it began, and half of that time was spent getting him to sign the form acknowledging that I explained to him his rights.

The obvious question became—which one was telling the truth? It was the same question a jury would eventually grapple with since the two continued to tell very different versions of the events surrounding Jeff Rodgers' death. They continue to do so to this day. But some facts are indisputable.

Chapter Five

Jeff never made it into the Circle K that night. The clerk said he never came inside. Barber was waiting for him on the parking lot. No one can know the conversation between the two, but we know Jeff Rodgers told his parents, "We were going to the Evangel football game. But we came down here, to Stonewall."

We know Jeff got his paycheck that night. We know longtime friend and co-worker Brett Rogers took Jeff home from work after 10 p.m. His parents heard him leave the house shortly afterward with his two dollars that Loretta slid to him under her bedroom door. And Linda Sanchez saw Jeff squatted down at the curbside, talking to someone in a car matching the description of Gary Barber's car.

His parents heard him come back inside the house, go into his bedroom, then they heard him leave again.

"If we had had any idea Gary Barber was out there at the curb, we'd never have let him go," George told me.

From the Rodgers' house—with Jeff's paycheck now

in hand— Barber drove to the Liquor Shoppe on Mansfield Highway, five miles away. The owner told me he refused to cash Jeff's paycheck, so they left.

Barber drove to Thrifty Liquor #5, about a mile away on Bert Kouns Road, where the clerk, Pam Brenner, cashed Jeff's payroll check from Crescent Landing. She wrote Jeff's ID number on the back of the check. She said Jeff bought a fifth of Kentucky Deluxe Whiskey. Brenner said Jeff was not alone, but she could not remember who else was with him or how many other people were with him.

From Thrifty Liquor #5, they went back to the Liquor Shoppe where they bought beer, and possibly more liquor. They paid in cash.

Loaded up now with liquor and beer, which he never could have afforded on his own, Barber drove south to Stonewall. If Jeff asked why they weren't going to the football game, it makes sense that Barber might have explained the game was over and they could ride ATVs in Stonewall. But we will never know that for sure. We know it was not Jeff's nature to argue with anyone. Besides, he was invited out with friends.

Pond Road was the late-night place to be in Stonewall, where kids got drunk and drove their all-terrain vehicles, a remote hideout where locals brawled with each other and their Shreveport rivals. The narrow lane off Wright Road cut through pastures of tall grass, ending near a shallow basin, the perimeter of which they had turned into a racetrack.

Stacy Williams went to Pond Road sometime between 12:30 and 1 a.m. Saturday, specifically to fight. With his parents out of town, Stacy had been riding three-wheelers and drinking beer with Bobby since early afternoon. After midnight, a friend, James "Booger" Evans, came to Bobby's trailer.

"James said some boys from Southwood was down there [at Pond Road] and they were trying to jump on him," Stacy said. "So, I got in my truck and we loaded the three-wheeler in the back of my truck and my brother got in the truck with him, so we went down there. Gary and the other boy was the only ones there."

Whoever had threatened or insulted Evans was gone. To Stacy's drunken disappointment, there would be no fight. Still stinging over his recent rejection by the Army, Stacy was spoiling for a fight. Bobby left with Evans to go home, but Stacy stayed on at Pond Road to ride the three-wheeler.

The early-morning noise awoke people who lived nearby. One of them complained to the sheriff's office that a car and a three-wheeler were racing on Wright Road. At 1:37 a.m. dispatch sent DeSoto Parish Sheriff's Deputy Raymond Burr to Pond Road.

At some point, Stacy let Gary take a turn on the three-wheeler, which ended when Barber flipped it. Jeff made the mistake of laughing.

"I got it back over and I was trying to put the gas line on it," Stacy told us. "And he (Jeff) was sitting there on the hood of Gary's car, Rodgers was, and Gary looked over at him and said, 'Man, you're retarded' or something like that. And he hit him in the nose."

It was the first blow.

Jeff began to cry, Stacy said. He was holding his nose, leaning against the hood of the car when Deputy Burr arrived at 2:10 a.m. Burr radioed in the license plate of a car he saw parked about fifty feet away from where he stopped. He saw two white men sitting on the hood of that vehicle, their backs to Burr, and another man kneeling beside a three-wheeler.

As Burr stepped out of his patrol car, Stacy stopped working on the ATV and approached. Burr knew Stacy Williams. He arrested him a few months before for beating up a guy—some girl's boyfriend.

"What are you doing down here, Stacy?" he asked.

"We were riding three-wheelers, but the gas line came off. We're just trying to fix it."

"How did you get that three-wheeler down here?"

"In the back of my truck."

"Well, get it back in that truck and go home!" the

deputy barked.

Stacy obeyed. He went and got his truck, which was parked out of the deputy's sight farther down Pond Road.

"They then loaded the three-wheeler in the back of this red Ford truck," the deputy wrote. "While they were loading it, I radioed the dispatcher for a 10-28 back on the vehicle. She advised me it came back to a '79 Honda, four-door, gray, which it was belonging to Gary Barber."

Just before 2:20 a.m., Stacy Williams drove off in the red Ford pickup, the deputy noted, and the other two subjects drove off in the gray Honda.

The deputy never got a look at Jeff Rodgers. If he had, he might have seen Jeff's bloodied nose and asked more questions.

When Burr ordered Stacy to load up and go home, Stacy quoted Gary Barber as saying he didn't want to go home. "So, I said my parents are out of town. You can come down there if you want."

By the time Stacy got to his parents' trailer, he said, Barber and Jeff were already there.

At 3:06 a.m., sixteen-year-old Candace Berry was wakened by a phone call from Stacy Williams. Candace said she spoke a minute with Stacy, then with Gary Barber. Candace told me Gary said he had a guy there, and he would pay her a hundred dollars if she would talk to him for a while. He handed the phone over.

Candace asked, "What is your name?"

He answered, "Jeff Rodgers."

She said something like, "Well, Jeff. It's really late and I need to get off the phone."

"Okay," he said. And they both hung up.

During the time Jeff was speaking with Candace, Stacy and Gary Barber went outside.

Left alone at three in the morning in a strange place, having already been punched in the nose by Barber at least once, Jeff called his parents. That was 3:10 a.m., according to George Rodgers.

Jeff was frightened and asked his parents to come get him.

"They hit me," he had said.

Jeff was alone in the trailer for the hour that his parents kept him on the telephone. Stacy said Gary sat in his car listening to the radio while he spent that time working on the three-wheeler.

"I knew I was going to be in trouble, because it was my dad's," he said.

At 4:20 a.m. Jeff told his parents someone was there. Minutes later the phone line went dead.

While Phillip Rodgers was racing to Stonewall, while George and Loretta desperately called one law enforcement agency after another asking for help— Jeff Rodgers was taking his first beating by two angry drunks—his so-called 'friends'.

Stacy recalled, "We wanted to go somewhere. But Gary didn't want Jeff to go. He told Jeff to stay there, but Jeff didn't want to. He followed us outside."

Angered that Jeff tagged along, Barber hauled off and slugged him, Stacy said.

"Gary had him on the ground hitting him," Stacy recalled. Stacy joined in—both pounding on the meek man who never attempted to fight back. Like a child, Jeff cowered and cried, trying to shield himself from the blows.

"Stop!" he cried. "Stop!"

Finally, they did.

"Okay. You can go," Stacy recalled Barber telling Jeff. "But you have to ride in the back of the truck."

Stacy and Barber got into the cab of Stacy's father's truck. Bleeding, holding his ribs, Jeff climbed into the truck bed like an obedient child. They drove down Missile Base Road and Stacy stopped his father's truck on a wooden bridge. It was one of his favorite spots to shoot snakes in the creek below. He had brought along his 12-guage shotgun and a flashlight for just such a purpose. He got out and went to the railing to peer below, using the flashlight to illuminate the creek bed. He fired off a shot.

He said Barber got out of the truck, also, but he went to the back of the truck and began picking on Jeff again. Stacy said he heard the two arguing. He said he heard Barber yell, "Give it to me!" then, he heard Jeff crying, "No, no. I'm not going to give it to you…I'm not!"

Barber began hitting Jeff again, grabbed his billfold, and jerked it away from him, Stacy said.

Back in the cab of the truck, Stacy said, Barber threw some money on the seat saying, "Here. This will help pay for the three-wheeler."

Stacy drove south, Jeff now lying down in the bed of the truck. On Rambin Road, he said, Barber asked, "Have you ever been fishing in that pond?"

"I said, 'No,' and he said, 'Pull over, I'll show you how to get back there,' and he told Jeff that he'd show him a place to fish."

Jeff followed. These were his friends.

Using the flashlight, the three made their way through the forest down the darkened deer trail, dappled by moonlight. As they came out of the woods into a clearing near the pond, "Gary just started hitting on him," Stacy said. "For whatever reason, I got in on it."

Both men pounded Jeff Rodgers, hitting him in the face, the arms, chest, abdomen, and legs. Again, Jeff used his arms to shield himself from their blows. Gary grabbed a stick and struck Jeff with it. Stacy used his shotgun like a bat, striking Jeff with the steel barrel. When Barber's stick broke, Stacy said, Barber grabbed the shotgun and started hitting Jeff with it while Stacy resorted to kicking the man who had crumbled to the ground.

Eventually, Jeff lay motionless in a fetal position.

"That's enough," Stacy said at last. "That's enough."

He said he turned to walk back to the truck, but realized Barber was not behind him. Turning around, he said, he saw Barber dragging Jeff to the pond where he dropped him, his face in water at the pond's edge.

Then, Stacy said, he saw Gary Barber put his foot on Jeff Rodger's head and hold it underwater. He recalled Jeff's head was turned to the side.

"What were you doing at that time?" I asked.

"Standing there watching."

"What happened then?"

"We left."

"What did Gary say after he held his head underwater?"

"When we got ready to—when we was leaving, he said, 'I hope he ain't dead' and I said, 'Well, me too.' And we left and went back to my house."

"Okay, did y'all leave him in the pond?"

"Yes, sir."

"How long did he keep his foot on his head?"

"Long enough to kill him."

George Rodgers family—back row: Shane, Jeff, Phillip
Front row—George and Loretta
—Courtesy Rodgers family

Stacy Williams, left, and Gary Barber, center,
escorted into court by DPSO deputies Jerry Lowe, left
and Huey Speights, right.
Photo by Vickie Welborn,
—Courtesy Mansfield Enterprise

Chapter Six

Jeff Rodgers' body was found on Sunday and his funeral was held Wednesday in Shreveport. He was buried in Forest Grove Cemetery in Taylor, Arkansas near his mother's family. Instead of flowers, the Rodgers' asked that donations be made in Jeffery's name to two different banks, the money from which would be donated to help handicapped children in the area.

Heartache is not a figure of speech. It is not just an emotion. Grieving, the human heart can literally ache just like any other muscle. A few weeks after burying his oldest son, George Rodgers suffered a massive heart attack that was brought on, his doctors said, by the intense trauma of the disappearance and loss of his son. He underwent triple bypass surgery and struggles with heart issues to this day.

Because of the heinous nature of the crime and because George Rodgers was so well-known throughout the Shreveport-Bossier area, the news media was all over the story of his son's abduction and murder.

Jeff Rodger's case dominated news in print and on television. The headlines screamed, "Teens arrested for murder," "Victim sought friendship," "Teens indicted," and on and on and on. After being indicted by a grand jury, both men pleaded not guilty to the charges of capital murder, kidnapping and armed robbery. News reporters, photographers, and TV cameras were on hand any time the pair went into or out of court.

Vickie Welborn, who is now an investigative producer for television news, was working as a reporter for the *Mansfield Enterprise* at the time. On October 13, 1994, she covered a pre-trial motion to separate the trials of the two teens, observing, "neither [Williams or Barber] offered audible pleas, their attorneys speaking for them. Williams stood with his eyes downcast during the reading of the indictments, but Barber gently shook his head back and forth."

Her observation of the two suspects' behavior encapsulated the difference in how Williams and Barber faced the aftermath of Jeff Rodgers' death: one hung his head in shame while the other remained defiant.

Stacy was assigned a court-appointed attorney, Steve Thomas of Mansfield.

The Barbers hired Peter Flowers, who for decades before his death in 2018, was one of Louisiana's most-respected, high-profile criminal-defense attorneys. But in 1994, Flowers had never defended a capital murder case. He enlisted the assistance of his mentor, Daryl Gold, who was even more seasoned and equally regarded.

Sitting at an enormous conference table in his posh downtown Shreveport law offices a stone's throw from the Red River, Gold looked back on the long-ago case that brought him and Peter Flowers together.

"This was Peter's first capital case," Gold recalled, "and I had handled several. Pete had already done all the work. He just wanted me there in case it went to a penalty phase. Peter was a very good attorney and very impassioned." Peters and Gold would go on to form a partnership that lasted until Gold's semi-retirement. He still takes a limited number of cases.

At the time, DeSoto Parish was part of the 11th Judicial District, which also included Sabine Parish. District Attorney Don Burkett announced he would seek the death penalty against both teens. Now the longest-serving district attorney in Louisiana, Burkett has successfully prosecuted dozens of capital cases, sending fifty-three people to prison for life for their crimes. Three are on death row. But in 1994, Burkett had his hands full prosecuting eight other murder cases pending in the two parishes. Recognizing his plate was overloaded and learning what a formidable defense team the Barbers hired, Burkett brought in his own hired gun—Clifford Strider—to present the case, naming Strider an Assistant DA for the purpose of the Barber trial.

During his eight years with the Orleans Parish prosecutor's office in New Orleans, Cliff Strider had made a name for himself as an expert in prosecuting capital cases and violent crimes. He rose to the position of Chief of the Trial Division in Orleans Parish before moving to Alexandria. While there, he began assisting small jurisdictions across the state prosecuting capital and corruption cases. Strider worked with fourteen Louisiana parishes at one time, prosecuting dozens of capital cases during his long career.

"I went to law school at LSU with the idea of being a prosecutor," Strider said. "I never once thought about being any other kind of attorney."

Two tragic life events precipitated Strider's decision to devote his life to prosecuting criminals: his younger brother was a murder victim, and he had a dear friend who was raped and brutally beaten. Strider's empathy for victims and the families of victims is, to this day, immeasurable.

Driven by his devotion to seek justice for victims, Cliff Strider is extremely thorough. He left nothing to chance. Before he put anyone on the witness stand, the witness knew every question he was going to be asked, and Strider knew the answer. Strider went over every aspect of every case he tried meticulously. He walked the crime scene and in the Rodgers' trial, after eight hours of courtroom testimony, we would go back to his office where we spent hours preparing for the next day. He and Don Burkett met each night.

"When you look at a capital case, you look at two things," Strider explained. "The defendant—what kind of defendant do we have? Is he a career criminal? Someone with a violent past? And we look at the victim—the nature of the victim; the egregiousness of the crime itself.

"In the Rodgers case, we had two individuals who did not have real criminal histories but a very sympathetic victim and a completely unnecessary murder. It was almost a thrill killing, it appeared. The sheer viciousness of the crime merited special attention."

For two years following Jeff Rodgers' death, the 11th Judicial District Court heard a myriad of pre-trial motions filed by Thomas and/or Flowers.

The Chad Evers episode was a goose chase. We searched databases, school enrollment records in Caddo and DeSoto parishes, driver's license numbers. Convinced that 'Chad Evers' who made that call was really Gary Barber trying to put us off the scent, I had Sgt. May, who had been the dispatcher on duty that Sunday, listen to the recorded statement Barber made in my office. She believed it was the same voice, but the court ruled in favor of Barber's defense that May's identification of the voice would not be allowed in court.

Williams and Barber would be tried separately, the court ruled.

Burkett would seek the death penalty for each.

In May 1996, Stacy Williams agreed to plead guilty to life without parole and Burkett agreed not to seek the death penalty in his case. Williams would testify against Barber, whose trial was set for that September.

"Stacy was absolutely remorseful," Thomas recalled of his client. "I've seen fake remorse a million times. I know what it looks like and that's not what this was. I felt bad that that young man was going to Angola and spend the rest of his life, and Bonnie Williams felt like I didn't do right by Stacy in the plea agreement. Bonnie served time in Angola when he was young, and he couldn't stand the thought of his son going there for life. But he didn't realize I did everything I could just to save his son's life."

11th Judicial District Judge Elizabeth Pickett would preside over the trial.

At the time, to an outsider, Elizabeth Pickett might have seemed an unlikely judge for such a high-profile, closely watched capital murder trial. After all, she was in her early thirties. She was tiny. She ruled from the bench over men who were much larger, older, and who had many more years in practice than she. Between them Strider, Burkett, Flowers, and Gold had decades of experience.

A 1984 graduate of Tulane Law School, Elizabeth ran a private law practice then worked as an assistant district attorney in Sabine Parish before being elected judge in 1990, making Louisiana history as the youngest judge ever, male or female, elected to the district bench.

She became the third-generation Pickett to hold that office, following in the footsteps of her father John S. Pickett, Jr. and grandfather, John Samuel Pickett, Sr. The only reason John S. or Samuel retired was because they turned seventy. It was mandatory. One Pickett or another had held the post since 1959. Serving on the bench was in Elizabeth's blood.

She will also go down in history as the first female district judge ever elected to office in Northwest Louisiana. Judge Pickett never let her age, gender, or size keep her from commanding the courtroom.

"The role of a trial judge is to maintain order in the courtroom," she said, recalling the Barber trial as a "high-stress case, from everybody's end."

"No judge could be more 'veteran," recalled retired 11th Circuit Court Senior Bailiff, Lt. Rick Pharris of Judge Pickett. "She was a third-generation judge. She could do it in her sleep. She commanded that courtroom, and no one questioned her ability or authority. Not the prosecutors or defense attorneys or anyone else. I loved working with her."

Gary Barber's trial would be the last major case over which Judge Elizabeth Pickett would preside before being elected to Louisiana's Third Circuit Court of Appeals, where she serves today.

It is still the longest-running trial in DeSoto Parish history.

Chapter Seven

The jury pool for the capital murder trial of Gary Barber was selected by random computer drawing and jury selection began September 16, 1996 in Louisiana's 11th District Court in Mansfield—one week shy of two years after the date of the murder of Jeffery Scott Rodgers. Judge Elizabeth Pickett presided.

Flowers quickly filed a motion for mistrial, asking that the jury pool be dismissed after learning one prospective juror worked with Loretta Rodgers years before she retired, and failed to make that known during questioning.

As it turned out, Loretta Rodgers had told someone in District Attorney Don Burkett's office she knew the woman when the list of potential jurors was first published. Prosecutors failed to notify the defense beforehand but made them aware during the *voir dire*.

Judge Pickett dismissed the potential juror and overruled Flowers' motion to dismiss the entire pool. Flowers argued it was a reversible error, alleging the prosecutor in charge, Clifford Strider, acted unethically by failing to inform the defense beforehand. The bitter accusations and fight over that potential juror set the tone for the entire trial.

Flowers and Strider were vehemently combative throughout the lengthy proceedings—it became personal—each man equally passionate for his client, Cliff Strider's client being the Rodgers family and state, Flowers' client being Gary Barber and his family.

After days of *voir dire*, the jury was empaneled. Nine men and three women, with two female alternates, would determine Gary Barber's fate. A single juror, a man, was African American. Once the jury was agreed upon, they were sequestered. When the trial started with opening arguments, it continued daily, through weekends. Jurors were housed in the Best Western Motel in Mansfield and 11th Circuit Court Senior Bailiff, Lt. Rick Pharris was at their 'beck and call.'

"The jurors could not discuss this case or any case that has any particulars that this one did," the retired bailiff said. "They could talk about whatever they wanted to, focus on their families and their lives. But I worked to keep them from focusing on what they had to do when they weren't sitting in the jury box."

All witnesses were put under the rule of sequestration. None of us, including the detectives, could hear testimony of any other witness nor could we discuss anything about the trial with any other witness. We were to refrain from reading about it or listening to any news about the trial.

Since Cliff Strider had subpoenaed every single person who had anything to do with anything about the case, and Flowers had his own long list of witnesses, most every office in the courthouse had subpoenaed witnesses just sitting around, waiting to be called, unable to discuss much of anything but the latest football game and the weather, which was hot.

The DeSoto Parish Courthouse was not equipped with

air conditioning when it was built in 1911. Like other structures of its time, the brick courthouse was built with high ceilings and enormous arched windows designed to allow for free flow of air. The second-floor courtroom was large, by any standards, measuring fifty feet wide and forty feet deep, with twelve-foot ceilings at the time.

Decades before, the DeSoto Parish commissioners voted to install air conditioning in the courthouse but by 1994, the system was antiquated and inefficient at best. At times it dripped condensation on people sitting in the jury box.

"The blowers were in the back of the room," the bailiff, Lt. Rick Pharris recalled. "They [the blowers] were huge, maybe eight feet wide and sixteen feet long. They were so loud that it was not uncommon for me to have to turn one or the other or both off when evidence was being presented. They could be a major distraction, and you can't have distractions during testimony."

Not long into the Barber trial, Judge Pickett recalled, Assistant District Attorney James Calhoun spoke up. "Does it concern anyone other than me that there is smoke coming out of the vents?" he asked.

The air conditioning was turned off.

"We had to open the windows and the doors," Lt. Pharris remembered. "All of a sudden we had street noise pouring into the courtroom. You could literally hear people talking outside on the courthouse lawn. You had road noise and sirens. But we had no choice. We had to have some air circulation."

The overhead ceiling fans were turned on, scattering work papers on the defense and prosecution tables, defense attorney Daryl Gold recalled.

"It was unbearably hot," Gold said, "I finally had to say, 'Judge, I have to remove my jacket.'"

Prosecuting attorney, Cliff Strider had the opposite reaction.

"I refused to take off my suit," he recalled, "Because I

wouldn't let them see me sweat."

Portable room air conditioners were brought in, helping cool the room somewhat, but the noisy units made poor acoustics even worse.

"The evidence is so crucial to trial. The judge, the jury, the court reporter, the prosecutors, and defense—everyone must be able to hear," the bailiff said. "You need to have it where you can hear a pin drop."

The court recessed and overnight, workmen were brought in to repair the air conditioning, the retired bailiff said.

George and Loretta Rodgers' never missed a day of the trial, but since they were called as state witnesses, no member of the Rodgers family was allowed to hear the testimony of others, which was, I thought, a blessing. They were spared hearing details of their son's suffering.

Strider laid the foundation of the state's case with his opening statement delivered directly to the jury.

"September 24, 1994 was the last day on earth for Jeffery Rodgers," he began. "Jeffery Rodgers was a young man, twenty-seven years old. He was mentally handicapped. He was mentally retarded. He had an IQ in the mid-fifties.

"If you were to meet Jeffery Rodgers on the street you would think he was a normal human being just like everybody else. He looked normal. He was tall, and he was slender, he was easy going—he was a good guy. He never met somebody he didn't like. That, ladies and gentlemen, is one of the reasons that Jeffery Rodgers is no longer among us.

"Jeffery Rodgers comes from a family that we dream about," Strider continued. His opening remarks were impassioned, explaining Jeff's inability to understand money, his need for friendship and approval, and the state's theory of what happened that deadly night.

Every trial is about assigning guilt. Flowers' opening statement outlined their defense of Gary Barber, shifting guilt from their client to the state's chief witness.

"There is no question but that a very awful, terrible thing has occurred," Flowers told the jury. "That a man, a sweet, mildly mentally handicapped young man, an outgoing, friendly fellow, was beat up and drowned in that pond. There is no question about it. It's a terrible, terrible thing. That's not what this case is about. The case is about who's responsible. The direct evidence that will be presented by the State is—guess what— Stacy Williams, the guy that Mr. Strider says is the convicted murderer. The rest of the State's case is circumstantial. The State will provide no motive for Gary Barber to hurt Jeff Rodgers, no reason. The state will have no physical evidence to connect Mr. Barber to the crime scene. What the state has is an accusation from a convicted murderer, a man who is deflecting blame."

Vicki Halverson, the manager of Crescent Landing and Jeffery's boss, was Strider's first witness. She was followed by Brett Rogers, Jeff's friend and co-worker who took him home from work; Vicki Sanchez, the neighbor who saw Jeff talking to someone in a light-colored sedan. He went through everyone who saw Jeff that night—the liquor store clerk who cashed his paycheck. Every member of the Rodgers family was called to testify, detailing their frantic, frustrated efforts to find Jeff once he called them early that Saturday morning. Strider would eventually call every person who saw Jeff that night, every law enforcement officer who responded to the Rodgers' calls, as well as people who participated in the search and those who found the ID card and Jeff Rodgers' body.

Strider called me as lead investigator to present the foundation of the state's forensic case and to introduce evidence we seized: blood samples from the Williams' pickup truck and Barber's car, from the bridge, Pond Road and Dew Pond, evidence seized in search warrants at the Williams' trailer and the apartment where Gary lived with his brother, as well as the statements from Stacy Williams and Gary Barber.

On cross examination, Peter Flowers went for the

jugular, knowing his case hinged on discrediting me and the evidence we pulled together for the Northwest Crime Lab forensics team.

"The very first thing you tell Gary Barber is, I'm not going to lie to you, try to trick you, or anything else. I'm going to be straightforward, —that's what you told him, right?" Flowers said.

"That's correct," I answered.

"Then you tell him basically, 'You better wise up, Buster, because we have the crime scene unit down there,' right?"

"Basically."

"But you don't have a 'crime unit,'" Flowers said. "In fact, the people that were down there—they couldn't even investigate the scene until you got there, from what I understand, is that right?"

"I didn't say they couldn't investigate. They were to stand by and secure the scene, but they are capable of seizing anything they see that needs seized," I said.

It was my use of the term 'crime scene unit' that Flowers considered trickery.

"Detective Davidson, when Mr. Barber refused to confess you told him, 'Well if you want to play hardball you can take all the heat,' right?"

"I did say that."

"Why?"

"Why?"

"Yes—was it because you weren't hearing what you wanted to hear? Why would you tell him that he if he doesn't change his story that he's going to take all the heat?"

I could see Gary Barber sitting in my office, sneering.

"I told him that because I had a man in my office prior who had given me lots of details of a brutal homicide. Then Mr. Barber is in my office—who, his friend had just been murdered—and I felt he had been uncooperative. I felt he had a bad attitude. I knew he was lying to me and I was trying to instill in him that we had lots of evidence connecting him to this crime, and we had the ability or would probably seize more evidence and he should talk to me more, tell me more about what he knows."

"You were trying to instill in him that you had more evidence, but you really didn't, did you!" Flowers thundered.

"At that point we had evidence that hadn't been collected," I explained. "We were going to be in the process of collecting it, and we had evidence already connecting him to the crime."

"Stacy Williams, right?"

"Stacy Williams what?"

"That was your evidence connecting him with the crime at that point, right?"

"Not necessarily. Not all of it."

"You are suggesting my client had a bad attitude and was uncooperative." He pointed at Barber sitting there in a new dark blue suit. "We just saw the videotape. What part of it did he not cooperate with?"

"Well," I answered, "if your best friend or your friend that you were out with a day or two earlier had just been found murdered—to my opinion—you would be a little more, ah, not so cocky or want to talk or help the investigator solve this crime."

Flowers hammered on, knowing his client's future depended, to a great degree, on discrediting me. That was all right. We both understood our jobs.

Northwest Crime Lab Forensic Pathologist Dr. Brenda Reames proved to be one of the prosecution's most powerful witnesses. Dr. Rheames testified Jeff Rodgers would almost certainly have died from his physical injuries had he not been dragged to the pond and his head held underwater.

Either of two blows to his head would have killed him, she determined. One blow to his temple was so powerful it caved in his skull and ruptured his eyeball. The other wicked blow, most likely from the shotgun barrel, caught right under Jeff Rodgers' nose, breaking away the bone that held his upper teeth from the rest of his face. Either of the head wounds would most likely have rendered him unconscious, she said, but having suffered two such extreme blows indicated Jeff Rodgers was certainly unconscious when he was drowned.

Jeff Rodgers suffered numerous broken ribs and a broken bone in his neck. The death certificate, Dr. Rheames said, read blunt trauma of the head and drowning.

Court bailiff Lt. Rick Pharris, who retired in 2019, recalled jurors wincing, closing their eyes, turning their heads at the graphic evidence.

"I was always taught security and decorum were everything in the courtroom," Lt. Pharris said. "The jurors were instructed not to show emotion but with a trial like this there was the gamut of emotions. I always let the jurors know when I took them back, we had to be professional, compose ourselves and do what we needed to do. The minute they got out of sight of the courtroom, sometimes, it would erupt; and I'd have to find out if they were good to go on."

Jeff Rodgers' blood alcohol level was negligible at .03 percent; no more than what the body would have produced, Dr. Reames testified, during the decomposition that occurred in the thirty-six hours his body was in water. The chemical process is called postmortem fermentation. If a body is not kept cool, as it decomposes, there can be a false positive blood alcohol level of up to two and a half times the legal limit.

At the time of his autopsy, Jeff Rodgers had a blood alcohol level one third the legal limit of intoxication. "I don't think—in this case, I don't think that it was present before his death. But I can't rule it out."

Dr. Rheames' testimony refuted statements by Stacy Williams and Gary Barber that Jeff was drunk. It made sense to me. They were so drunk they did not recognize he was not. Jeff paid for the alcohol, he might even have consumed some, but Jeff Rodgers was sober when he was beaten to death by his 'friends.'

The foundation of Flowers' defense was built on Gary Barber's adherence to his claim that he picked Jeff up at the Circle K, they bought alcohol, they went to Pond Road, to Stacy's trailer, they argued so Barber dropped Jeff off at the Charter Station and he went back to Stacy's to sleep. Any harm that came to Jeff Rodgers was carried out by Stacy Williams, Gary swore.

The Williams' next-door neighbor Charles Sersch proved to be an influential witness, identifying Gary Barber as the person he saw getting out of Bonnie Williams' pickup truck with Stacy about 6:30 a.m. that Saturday, at the time Barber swore he was asleep inside.

Sersch testified the sun had just come up when he heard a truck door shut and looked out his bathroom window to see Stacy Williams, carrying a shotgun, getting out of his father's truck. And he identified Gary Barber as the person he saw getting out of the passenger side of the truck. Serscsh said he was curious when he heard the truck doors slam, because he knew Stacy was not supposed to drive his father's truck while Bonnie and Sue Williams were out of town.

Sersch told the jury he had seen Gary Barber before and knew it was he who followed Stacy into the Williams' trailer and not Bobby, who had long hair and a beard.

When the defense questioned the accuracy of Sersch's eyesight at daybreak, Cliff Strider took a scene right out of a famous movie.

"In the trial I took a tape measurer, a big round one like they use at track meets. I had the witness hold one end of it and I walked off fifty feet. I couldn't believe that courtroom was fifty feet, actually. Then I held up my fingers and asked him to tell me how many he saw," Strider recalled the testimony. It was a scene straight out of *My Cousin Vinny*.

For his defense, Peter Flowers argued that Stacy Williams was homophobic; that because Jeff was "different," Stacy 'got it in his head' that Jeff must have been gay and that his hatred of gay people provoked the gross over-kill. Defense attorneys often work to dirty the image of the victim, any way they can. In this case Stacy gave him the opening when, during one statement, he said Jeff blurted out, "I'm a faggot," which prompted a beating.

Asked later why he said that Stacy shrugged. "I made it up. They wanted a reason and that popped into my mind. But no, he never said that."

Gary Barber took the stand in his own defense telling the jury he and Jeff had gone out together on several occasions prior to September 24.

When asked by Flowers to characterize his relationship with Jeff Rodgers, Barber said, "I thought we was best friends and I know he thought I was his best friend."

"What makes you think that?" Flower asked.

"He has told plenty of people that," Barber replied.

Gary's mother, Anne Barber testified Gary was a heavy sleeper and well could have slept through the telephone ringing and a deputy pounding on the Williams' door at five-thirty that Saturday morning. She also testified Gary, her youngest son, had been physically abused by his older brother David, most of his life. Anne Barber testified David had a drinking problem and when he got drunk, he often beat Gary, perhaps explaining Shane Rodgers' perception that Gary Barber was afraid of his older brother.

Blood found on a shirt in Barber's car was linked to Jeff Rodgers.

There was blood in the bed and cab of Bonnie Williams truck and on the shotgun and Stacy's left boot. In 1994, forensics could only prove the blood was or was not the same type as the victim's or suspect's blood. That was a pre-DNA era. But it was conclusive that blood on and in Barber's car matched Jeff Rodgers' blood type.

Because the Williams' pickup truck had been washed, no tests were conclusive other than that the samples taken were blood. It could not be type matched.

Blood of the victim's type was found in pine straw at

the Dew Pond.

In the end, it was not the forensic evidence that convinced the jurors so much as it was the inconsistencies in Gary Barber's explanation of the facts. The jury did not believe Barber's explanation that he dropped Jeff off at the Charter gas station, especially after Michael Arnold, the manager on duty that night, testified he knew Jeff Rodgers because they had both attended Southwood High School in Shreveport, and Jeff never came in the store that night. Arnold also testified he was the only person operating the cash register that night. Gary could not have "bought a Coke" from a woman because the only woman who had been there was another manager working in a back office. She never came up front.

George and Loretta Rodgers' testimony about their conversation with Jeff— Loretta's presence of mind to have Jeff read the name and number on the phone bill, and George's presence of mind to note the times that the conversation began and ended—made the 'dropping off Jeff at the Charter gas station' explanation implausible. Their son had most certainly been inside the Williams' trailer from 3:10 a.m. to 4:20 a.m.

The jury gave more credence to Stacy's testimony than to Gary Barber's, just as I had from their initial interviews. Stacy Williams walked into my office hanging his head in shame and voiced remorse, telling me, "I would like to apologize to his family if I could."

The closest thing to remorse I ever heard from Gary Barber was, "Jeff was my friend. I wouldn't kill no goddamned body."

On October 6, 1996, at the end of the twentieth day of trial, the case went to the jury at 6:38 p.m. They deliberated for three hours to reach a verdict: Guilty of capital murder.

Having attended to more juries than he can recall, bailiff Lt. Pharris said, "That's a quick verdict, as verdicts, go. Three hours is not much time at all in a trial like that."

The next day, Daryl Gold presented the defense in the

penalty phase of the trial, arguing to spare his clients' life.

"It did not serve justice for the state to let that guy [Stacy Williams] get life because he testifies against my guy," Gold said. "Jail personnel said Barber was a model prisoner. He did not appear to be a bad guy. Obviously, he was involved in a bad thing. But he was a youthful offender. That was a mitigating factor."

It took the jury one hour to unanimously agree with Gold that Gary Barber's life would be spared. He would be sentenced to life in prison.

On October 28, 1996, Gary Barber was sentenced by Judge Elizabeth Pickett to be held in the custody of the Louisiana Department of Public Safety and Corrections at hard labor, for life, without the benefit of probation, parole, or suspension of sentence. He remains in Angola State Prison in West Feliciana Parish.

As with all capital murder convictions, both Stacy Williams and Gary Barbers' sentences were automatically appealed. Their cases have been in the Louisiana Appellate Court system for the past twenty-five years, most recently with both men seeking release on good behavior.

The case had long-lasting effects on most of us involved.

Looking back over his long career in prosecution, Don Burkett said, "I've handled a lot of horrible cases. I'd have to place Jeff Rodgers' murder in the top three or four. His parents' desperation is just so moving. He's on the phone with his parents and the parents are on the phone with his brother—they were so close to getting him and they missed. A few minutes and maybe this crime wouldn't have happened."

I met with Stacy Williams in David Wade Correctional Center outside Homer in putting this story together and he reminded me, he has lived in prison longer than he lived before prison. The man I met at David Wade no longer held his head in shame, though he again expressed his regrets.

"Why, why, why did I do it?" He shook his head. "I've

asked it a million times. Just meanness, I guess. I was just a bitter kid."

During his decades in prison, Stacy said, he had gone through the Twelve-Step program and Anger Management classes.

Stacy recalled testifying for the state against Gary Barber in 1996. When he finished testifying and walked out of the courtroom, he said, "Some of Jeff's family was in the lobby of the courthouse. His mom was there. I said, 'Ma'am. I'm sorry for what I done,' and one of them— I think it was her—hugged my neck. And we all cried."

While serving time in Angola, Stacy became active in the rodeo, as he had yearned for as a child. In Angola, he won the title of "Best All-Around Cowboy" in 2003-2004, competing in Bull Riding, Bareback, and Bull Dogging.

I asked him, looking back, was there any advice he could give kids that they might learn from his mistakes.

"Stay busy," he answered quickly. "People here come from low-income families. I never met anyone in prison who was involved in 4 H or FFA."

While in Angola, Stacy said, he started going to church. "But I never felt comfortable," he said. "The relationship you have with God is between you and God."

"Do you have a relationship with God now?" I asked.

"Yes," he replied. "I do."

Stacy lost both parents and his youngest brother, James, during the time he has been in prison.

"Mom and Dad both died of cancer," he said. "James died in a car wreck. What I did – it hurt them so bad. I'm so sorry I hurt them so bad."

Then he shared a story about an incident that occurred not long after his father died in 2007, when he was being transported somewhere in a prison van. He didn't recall where they were going but what happened along the way.

"We crossed a bridge. It was early morning and there was fog coming off the river. As we crossed the bridge, I looked, and I saw a man in a little boat—and he looked up, raised his arm, and waved to me. I swore it was my father," he said. "I looked back, and he was gone. To this day I believe, I saw my father doing what he loved: fishing."

In a twist of fate, District Attorney Don Burkett recalled his father was hospitalized, down the hall from Bonnie Williams, when Williams died.

"One bizarre thing about the case," he said, "several years later my father was diagnosed with stage-four lymphoma. They put him in Christus and told us…he wouldn't make it. He was very ill. It turned out, Stacy's father was a few doors down, dying of cancer. I ran into his brother, and we talked in the hall. How ironic that the prosecutor and defendant both had fathers hospitalized near each other at the same time."

Burkett's father escaped death. He survived stage-four lymphoma and is more than ninety years old.

George and Loretta Rodgers never celebrated Christmas after burying their oldest son. "We go to Chris and Phillip's houses and celebrate with their families but Loretta and I—we do not celebrate Christmas anymore," George said.

Ironically, Cliff Strider shared an uncannily similar story.

"Everybody talked about what a sweet young man he was—not a mean bone in his body," Strider said. "Those people were the salt of the earth. Generous, easy-going, loving people. The depth to which it affected them was clearly obvious."

Every Christmas morning, Cliff said, he gets up early, before anyone else in this family, and sits in the dark in front of the Christmas tree, thinking of all the families of the victims he has represented. He thinks of the Rodgers first, he said. "I think about how this day is going to be for them. The Rodgers family is the first I think about to this day."

I visited with Tracy and Bobby Williams and I was stricken by the overwhelming effects their brothers' crime had on their family.

"Back then," Tracy said, "Mom and Dad were going to a little church here in Stonewall. After Stacy's arrest they got a letter that read, *Murderers are not welcome in this church.* To this day," he went on, "I think about it every day. Every single day. But it's not about us. It's about the Rodgers. They lost their son and brother forever. We can at least go see Stacy."

Epilogue

Advances in forensic technology have radically changed criminal investigations since 1994. DNA evidence has become standard practice, and instead of just being able to say a blood spatter was the same type blood as that of the victim or suspect, today they can determine conclusively that it is or is not the victim's or suspect's blood or hair or body fluid.

Convenience stores like the Circle K and Charter gas station now have twenty-four-hour surveillance cameras. Investigators could go to the store, ask to see the footage, and subpoena it if the owner is not cooperative, to know exactly what time Jeff got into the car and with whom. Surveillance video could have identified the boys who beat Jeff at the first Circle K the month earlier and it could prove conclusively if Gary Barber had dropped Jeff off at the gas station—or not.

Today, voice-identification technology exists that could prove that "Chad Evers" was really Gary Barber—or prove it was not. There would be no guessing about it.

Most notably, GPS tracking technology that exists today could help prevent such a tragedy from ever happening again. Imagine, if Jeff Rodgers had been wearing a Fitbit or other GPS tracking device. If his family was connected with Life360 or some other smartphone tracking software, George and Loretta could have driven straight to get him when he called, or they could have given exact directions to Phillip or the DeSoto Parish Sheriff's Office.

If law enforcement agencies had a database of impaired persons equipped with GPS tracking devices linked to a mapping system, think of the lives that could be saved.

Louisiana joined Texas and other states in enacting Amber Alerts, named after nine-year-old Amber Hagerman who was abducted and murdered in 1996 in Dallas, Texas. Louisiana adopted a statewide Amber Alert system in 2002. It is a cohesive effort between law enforcement and broadcasters, the goal of which is to safely locate an abducted child within the critical two-to-three-hour time period following an abduction. If that law could be expanded to include people like Jeff who are mentally impaired, who function as children, lives might be saved, especially if it was used in combination with GPS tracking devices and software.

It is my hope the State of Louisiana will consider funding for Adult Protective Services to equip mentally impaired individuals with GPS tracking devices if they or their families request it and or cannot afford it, and to coordinate with law enforcement to develop a database and companion computer software program that can locate any mentally impaired person immediately upon the family's report that they are missing. Two state lawmakers, District 7 State Representative Larry Bagley and District 38 State Senator Barry Milligan have committed to researching such a program, and if found financially feasible, to co-sponsor a bill entitled "Jeff's Law."

Time is everything in a missing person's case. George

Rodgers told me he believed, had Phillip not been told to 'stand down' that perhaps he could have saved his brother's life. Sadly, that is something of which we can never be certain. But we can take steps to make sure such a tragedy does not befall another family. Passage of Jeff's Law would be a giant step.

Judge Elizabeth Pickett, Louisiana
Third Circuit Court of Appeals
Former Louisiana District Judge

Don Burkett

Cliff Strider

Peter Flowers

Daryl Gold

Voodoo Confession

Sheriff Frenchie Lambert called me into his office, nodded at one of two curved-back chairs in front of his over-sized desk, indicating for me to sit down. As I walked through the door the sheriff said, "Shut the door, Robbo."

Damn it, why did I come in this way? If you parked in front, you had to walk right past Sheriff Lambert's office; his desk strategically placed in the center of the big room offering the old Cajun a view of anyone who walked down the main hall. Two walls of Frenchie's office were lined in massive mahogany bookshelves filled with plaques and pictures of him with one influential Louisiana lawmaker or another. The dark shelves continued along the bottom half of the wall behind his desk with ceiling-high windows above—but no one ever caught Sheriff Frenchie Lambert looking out the windows. That would put his back to the door.

He preferred monitoring who came and went from the department. We got called into his office sometimes, to be briefed on one thing or another but when Frenchie said, "Shut the door," it was either top secret or your ass was in a bind.

My ass was in a bind.

Frenchie's real name was Floyd Lambert but because of his coonass ancestry and accent—he hailed from south of Baton Rouge—he'd been called Frenchie since childhood. Straight-backed, no-nonsense retired Louisiana State Police. Tall, black hair, dark skin, black eyes. He didn't have an ounce of a sense of humor, but he'd been in office more than a decade and we all knew, deputies served at the sheriff's pleasure. Everybody was afraid of Frenchie to one degree or another.

"Robbo," Frenchie growled as I sat down, "I want to ask you something." He leaned across his big mahogany desk, squinting those black eyes as if trying to peer into my soul. "I get more complaints on you than anyone in the department. Now, why do you suppose that is?"

I'd been warned this might be coming. I met his gaze straight on. It was the only way with Frenchie. I said, "Maybe, Sheriff, it's because, of the sixty-one people in your jail, I put forty-three of them in there."

Frenchie paused, leaned back in his swivel chair, plunked his cowboy boots up on the desk, chunked his pen on the ink blotter, and waved me away with his arm. "Get out of my office."

Nobody complains when you make an arrest on a homicide or robbery but rounding up people for using or selling drugs could be very unpopular, sometimes with very influential people. You arrest the son or daughter of a well-to-do businessman on drug charges and the sheriff hears about it. You do that over and over again and the sheriff begins to hear about it a lot.

Most of the inmates I booked in the DeSoto Parish jail at any given time were there on drug charges and a large percentage of those who lived in the Big Woods practiced what they called voodoo or hoodoo—some personalized, impure blend of black magic. They kept talismans in their pockets or wallets to ward off what they called the *haints*—angry spirits.

Black magic was brought to Louisiana on slave ships more than 300 years ago.

French invaders slaughtered thousands of Chitimacha men, enslaving the women and children, imposing themselves on the petite, raven-haired, almond-eyed native women. The African slaves belonging to the French intermarried with native and mixed-race slaves. The comingling of the indigenous American people with African slaves and French conquerors created the Creole people of southern Louisiana, the vast majority of whom are practicing Catholics or Protestants like Frenchie. A lot of people call those with native American and African blood Creoles, and those with native American and French blood Cajuns.

But then—even all that gets all mixed together.

The merging of the religions— African Vodun, French Catholicism, and the worship of Chitimacha deities—melded into what Louisianans call hoodoo or voodoo, this blended belief that holds that spirits of the dead live on among us, that everything on earth has a spirit—rivers, trees, animals—and those spirits can be summoned up to protect people or haunt enemies depending on the rituals practiced. It is observed primarily by low-income, uneducated blacks or Creoles, but you can also find very well-to-do people, particularly Creoles, in an around New Orleans, who hold onto voodoo and hoodoo traditions and practices to one degree or another.

Through my years of interacting with people who believed in the dark arts—regardless of how ridiculous I thought it was—it became clear to me that they put as much faith in their religious beliefs as I did in mine. That knowledge came in handy during a murder investigation I worked years after Frenchie left office.

It was in 1995, I was in the thick of the Jeff Rodgers' murder investigation preparing for court appearances on one defendant or another, consolidating results of forensic tests and conducting follow-up interviews with witnesses, when I was asked by then-Sheriff Hugh Bennett to help out with another murder investigation, one that involved several suspects, all of whom were hard-core druggies.

Hazel Mosley was a fixture in Logansport, which is to say everyone living in the lazy little town on the banks of the Sabine River knew her by name or by sight. In her younger years she was the wife of the revered Reverend Ernest Mosley. After his passing, Hazel carried on serving her Lord, teaching Sunday school and acting as treasurer of St. Luke's Baptist Church, Logansport's largest black congregation.

She was a stout, straight-backed woman with neatly coiffed short white hair who walked wherever she went with a purse, chosen for the occasion or the season, swinging on her arm. She never failed to offer a wave and a smile for anyone who passed by as she walked to her destination be it the grocery store or the bank or to visit one of her many friends in town.

Logansport lies at the headwaters of Toledo Bend Reservoir and despite the South's largest lake being ringed by multi-million-dollar vacation castles, the old town itself is quiet, quaint, and poor. Having lived there all her seventy-nine years, it was no surprise Hazel Mosley was a familiar name and face. A person can be well-known but not well-respected. Hazel was both. She was a bedrock of the Christian community, beloved by townspeople, both black and white.

She spent her childhood in the Roaring '20s, which had not roared at all for Southern blacks like her parents, Deorsie and Carrie Harris. Coming of age during the Great Depression, Hazel Harris Mosley knew the value of a dime. She lived humbly in a small wood-frame house beneath a canopy of towering oaks a stone's throw from the railroad tracks in Japan Quarters.

To my knowledge, no one alive can tell you when or why the part of Logansport that lies north of US Highway 84 and east of Louisiana Highway 5 became Japan Quarters. ("Jay-pan" Quarters or just "the Quarters" to those who live there.) There are no Japanese people living there. It is a low income, primarily black part of town on either side of the railroad tracks, dotted with churches and their congregants who lived in modest houses or mobile homes and, in 1995, drug addicts who would sell their souls for a rock of crack cocaine.

Hazel Mosley did not seem to fret about the influx of crack into the community. She was not afraid of these kids. She had taught many of them in Sunday school. She knew their parents and grandparents. Hazel viewed this drug craze as a fad.

"This, too, shall pass," she would often say.

January '95 was colder and wetter than normal, and in all her walking about town, Hazel had gotten chilled to the bone. She felt feverish, she confided in some girlfriends, but going to the doctor wasn't much of an option for a poor woman with no car living in rural Logansport.

Saturday, January 21, she decided to stay inside, either in bed or sitting near one of her old open-faced space heaters. She could visit with her friends, like Lula Barnes, on the telephone. After a chat about church business that morning, Hazel promised to put one of Lula's relatives on the church prayer list. Midafternoon, Ricky Shepherd said, she waved to him from her screened-in porch as he drove by. Around four o'clock Beulah Markham called Hazel. Hazel again mentioned her miserable bad cold and they gossiped as women do about church goings-on. Beulah promised to check back on her friend later that evening but got sidetracked and did not call back until about ten-thirty that night. When she did call, there was no answer.

"I wondered, now where would Hazel be at this hour of the night?" Beulah said, but she went to bed not overly concerned.

The last person known to speak with Hazel Mosley was her friend Sharletta Duncan. They spoke most every day and on January 21, 1995 just after 5:30 p.m., Mrs. Duncan was certain, because she remembered the news was on her television set during their conversation. Other than her bad cold, Hazel wasn't worried about anything, Sharletta said, nothing out of the ordinary except that, feeling as poorly as she did, there was the possibility Hazel might not make it to church in the morning.

Now that would be unusual.

Hazel raised her brother's son, Reginald. Reggie, as she called him, was an infant when he lost both parents in California. He was brought to Hazel's mother Carrie, but when Reggie was a toddler Carrie died. He came to live with Hazel and Ernest. He refers to them as his mama and daddy.

"She was my aunt, really—but she was the only mother I ever knew," he explained. "Hazel was there for me every step of the way."

When Reggie was young Hazel operated a food stand right next to their house. "She cooked and served hot food— fried chicken, sweet potatoes, sweet potato pie. And she made a pretty good living at it," he added.

Through the years, she worked as domestic help for several of the more prominent white families of the town.

"She was all about work, let me tell you," her son said. "We were poor, but we didn't know it. We never went hungry. We didn't have any money to spend but there never was a day we didn't have food.

"She never let me hang with the boys who smoked and drank. I played basketball from the ninth grade all the way through and Mama was at every basketball game. She would walk there, to the high school and then she and I would walk home together afterward, when my daddy (Rev. Ernest) didn't go."

He said his mother walked wherever she went simply because she preferred it. "She didn't know how to drive," he said. "She didn't care anything about riding. She just liked to walk."

In 1978, Reginald left for college, attending Northwestern State University in Natchitoches. From there, he moved on to Houston. He checked in with his mother regularly, and when she did not answer the telephone that Saturday night or Sunday morning, he became concerned. He called Vera Beck, the woman who lived across the street from Hazel. Reggie had known Vera all his life. She was working at Goldens Truck Stop on US Highway 84 when she got the call from Reggie asking her to check on his mother.

Leaving work, Vera hurried to Hazel's house a few minutes away. Everything looked normal. The doors and windows were closed and locked. The *Mansfield Enterprise* Sunday newspaper was still in Hazel's front yard. Knocking on the door, calling out her name, Vera could not raise Hazel. She walked home and called Logansport Police. Could they come help? She was concerned for her friend's welfare.

Logansport Police Officer Anthony Wilson met Vera at Hazel's house and when the officer could not raise a response either, Wilson called for backup. Officer Norm Garner joined him at the tidy cream-colored house with the screened-in porch by the railroad tracks.

With two police cars in Hazel's front yard on Sunday morning, neighbors began to gather. The crowd grew exponentially as members of St. Luke's Baptist Church next door began to pour out of the church doors.

"When Miss Hazel didn't show up to church, and she hadn't told anybody she wasn't going to be there, everyone got worried," recalled Tameka Mays, who was a senior at Logansport High School that year. Hazel had been her Sunday School teacher. "Everyone knew something wasn't right. I'll remember that day the rest of my life."

The two police officers checked the doors and windows of Hazel's house. Everything was locked from the inside except for a bedroom window slightly opened. It did not appear to be disturbed. The screen was intact.

There was no sound inside or out. Peering as best they could through the curtained windows, the officers detected neither movement nor a glimpse of Hazel. They needed to get inside. At last, Officer Garner pried open the kitchen window and crawled inside. It was a small room with old linoleum flooring, a small kitchen counter with an old-fashioned pie safe holding Hazel's dishes. She had a small, square table with a red-checkered tablecloth against the wall beside the pie safe, across from the free-standing gas stove.

Despite having felt poorly because of her bad cold, Hazel had baked a chocolate cake for Sunday lunch, still sitting on the stovetop waiting for its icing. The officer noted a large-embroidered banner of the Twenty-Third Psalm hanging on the door to the living room and a small painting of Aunt Jemima on the wall above the table, with a list of telephone numbers tacked beneath it. The cake on the stove and the painting above the table were about the only items in the house undisturbed.

Garner drew in his breath and rushed to the kitchen door, unlocking the deadbolt from the inside. "Wilson!" He yelled. "Call the police chief! And call the coroner!"

Hazel's neighbor Linda Austin watched it all unfold from her house nearby. She had become concerned about her elderly neighbor before Vera or any members of St. Luke's congregation arrived.

"Miss Hazel didn't like to be cold, and she always goes to church," Austin told the *Mansfield Enterprise* reporter who drove to Logansport to cover the parish's first murder of 1995. Early that morning, Linda Austin said, she had walked to the church to light the furnace so the building would be warm when Hazel and other members arrived. Along the way, she noticed the rolled-up newspaper in Hazel's yard, thinking how peculiar that was. Hazel was an early riser, and she was never too sick to pick up her morning paper.

Austin shook her head in disbelief.

"It's a mean world now-a-days," she said. "Miss Hazel did harm to no one."

A certain element of despair exists among impoverished people living in rural Louisiana towns like Logansport. The more fortunate leave for college or a trade school. Those who stay and go to work straight out of high school have few options. The well-connected hire on with the parish or the school district, maybe the power plant in Mansfield or International Paper. In 1995, the Louisiana Pacific Lumber Company was still operating but has since closed. Tyson Poultry in Center, Texas some twenty miles west is the area's largest employer. If you worked at Tyson, you could ride the company bus to and from work. Otherwise, no public transit exists in rural Louisiana. A person needed a car to drive to work. And many of the rural poor did not have the means with which to buy a car.

The region of western Louisiana and deep East Texas known as the Big Woods is one of the poorest in the nation, with a poverty rate near forty percent. A large percentage of people live in either rundown trailer houses on a patch of family land or in government housing projects in town, subsisting on one form of welfare or another.

Not surprisingly, cheap drink or drugs help alleviate some of that hopelessness, if only for a short while (a matter of minutes as in the case of crack cocaine). In 1995, you could buy a small rock of crack (maybe half the size of a man's fingernail) for as little as five dollars. Fifty dollars would buy a rock the size of a buckeye.

The euphoria that almost instantly envelopes the crack user is quickly followed by a crash of agonizing physical pain, driving the addict to do whatever it takes to ease the pain. It is an endless cycle that never has a good outcome.

DeSoto Parish Sheriff's Department investigators worked twelve murders in the two years before 1995, all of which were related in one way or another to the drug trade.

During the first four years of the 1990s, members of the DeSoto Parish Drug Task Force made more than a thousand drug arrests, probably a third of which were right there inside little Logansport.

The town was founded in 1830 by a Dr. Logan, who came to the frontier to practice medicine on both sides of the Sabine River when Texas was still a part of Mexico. The only international border marker in the United States is located there in Logansport. In order to practice on both sides of the river, the good doctor put in a ferry. "Logan's Ferry" quickly grew into an operating port, ferrying timber and agricultural products to the Gulf of Mexico, which was a faster and more financially efficient method of transport than carrying goods by wagon.

When a post office was established in 1848, the town became Logan's Port. But when the railroad came through forty years later, the ferry business went the way of the stagecoach and so did the booming 'port'.

Fast-forward to 1995. Logansport had evolved into a very different kind of port—a point of entry for illegal drugs into Louisiana and on to the eastern United States. US Highway 59, which runs from Laredo, Texas to the Canadian border, is a four-lane drug corridor funneling untold tons of marijuana, cocaine, heroin, methamphetamine, and now opioids through the heartland of America. It is fifteen miles from Logansport.

A hard right in Tenaha, Texas onto US Highway 84 and in just a few minutes the drug runner was across the Sabine River at Logansport and onto the quiet backroads of Louisiana. It became the route of choice for eastbound drug traffickers back in those days after one particular Texas Department of Public Safety trooper became notorious for busting drug runners north of Tenaha, between Carthage and Marshall.

The word was out. "Get off Highway 59 in Tenaha."

We got wise to it. There is no way of knowing how many tons of illegal drugs slipped through Logansport in cars and trucks, but the bus station we had staked out. It was right across the street from the Logansport Police Department. The bus from Houston arrived at four o'clock each morning, stopping right in front of the police station to let passengers get off or on and to let those travelling on to stretch their legs and use the restroom. Members of the DeSoto Drug Task Force would routinely be waiting to board the bus with drug dogs.

In one thirty-day period around that time, we confiscated ten pounds of cocaine and 400 pounds of marijuana at the Logansport bus station. We confiscated so many drugs and drug runners there that a superior officer let it be known the Drug Task Force should leave the Logansport bus station alone. The rationale was that most of those drugs were not going to stay in DeSoto Parish, so we were needlessly clogging up the local jail and court system with someone else's offenders. We didn't let that stop us. We had all signed on to serve when there was a "War on Drugs," and as law enforcement officers, we had a close look at what hard drugs like crack and methamphetamine did to people—the innocent and the not-so-innocent.

Hazel Mosley was among the most innocent.

Detective Sgt. Horace Womack, who was a member of the Drug Task Force, was the DeSoto Parish Sheriff's Department investigator on duty that weekend. Womack got the call from Logansport P.D. at ten o'clock Sunday morning.

"After being advised by Chief Clark that he had a homicide, he stated that the scene was secure," Sgt. Womack wrote in his report. "I contacted my office and advised Captain Mike Lee of the situation. It appeared to be a homicide and robbery. Logansport P.D. would be handling the case since it was in the city limits but had requested our assistance."

Arriving at Hazel Mosley's house, Womack checked the exterior of the property, looking for evidence of forced entry. There was none.

"The window to the bedroom of the victim was open but the screen was intact and there was no indication of any forced entry," the investigator reported. "Officers stated that both doors were locked when they entered the residence. A dead bolt on the kitchen door was locked from the inside. The front door was found to be locked but was not completely pushed shut. No indication at this time that the house was broken into. No signs of forced entry."

Sgt. Womack noted the kitchen light as well as the lights in Hazel's bedroom and an adjacent bedroom were on. Both bedrooms had been ransacked: dresser drawers pulled out, the contents dumped on the floors and beds. Everything had been rifled through. Paperwork, envelopes, clothing, jewelry, purses—everything in both bedrooms had been turned topsy-turvy.

Who besides Hazel could possibly know what was missing?

The condition of the room made it clear someone was looking for something. But what?

The ransacking and robbery was the least of it. Hazel's body lay face down in a pool of blood in the doorway between her bedroom and kitchen. It appeared she had been either stabbed in the head or beaten with a blunt object.

Metal was embedded in her head, as if a knife had been thrust with so much force that it pierced the skull then broke off, the tip stuck inside her skull. Other than that piece of blade protruding from Hazel's skull, there was no trace of a murder weapon and a search of the residence and yard did not produce one.

Hazel had fought back. There were defensive wounds on her arms and hands. A blood-soaked pillow was at the foot of the bed.

"One pillow was completely soaked in blood," the deputy noted. "The blood was soaked through the pillow, through the bedding, and into the mattress. Also laying on the bed were two small metal pieces that appear to be broken from a knife. These two pieces do match together."

If Hazel had been stabbed in her sleep, how was it that she was on the floor?

Her nightgown was pulled up around her chest. Womack suspected this seventy-nine-year-old woman had been sexually assaulted.

Investigators began seizing evidence, finger-printing the table, the telephone, the pie safe, and kitchen cabinets. The problem would be that so many people were invited into Hazel's house, unless the prints were in blood, they would be of little investigative value.

Sgt. Womack walked outside, needing the cold air. He rubbed his eyes and face, looking up at the sullen sky with a silent prayer for answers. Bad things happened to good people the investigator knew too well. But what happened to Hazel Mosley made even the veteran lawman shake his head in disbelief. Who did this and why?

"We worked murders," Womack recalled. "But most of the victims and suspects we handled were directly involved with drugs. We just didn't see murders like this. This lady was someone's mother. Someone's grandmother. She was someone who liked people and someone the people of Logansport liked. Hazel Mosley's murder was a tough one."

Based on the degree of violence, Sgt. Womack believed this evil was probably the work of an addict. Unfortunately, in Japan Quarters of Logansport, Louisiana—that left plenty of suspects.

Time was of the essence. That time of year, it was dark at five-thirty and the sun didn't rise until almost seven in the morning, leaving more than twelve hours of darkness during which this evil could have taken place. Sharletta Duncan spoke to Hazel between five-thirty and six o'clock, she was certain. Hazel had not answered the telephone for Lula Barnes at ten-thirty.

We theorized Hazel Mosley's murder occurred in that window. Any number of people had been seen outside in the neighborhood during that time. Most of them were known to smoke crack. Back then three drugs plagued DeSoto Parish: crack was primarily a black man's drug. Methamphetamine, speed, was the preferred high among backwoods whites manufactured in isolated shacks and trailer houses. Marijuana was passed around between all of them.

The first potential suspect Sgt. Womack and Logansport Police Chief Gary Clark called on Sunday afternoon was Tal Gray, a small, wiry black man who bought and sold small quantities of crack, who had been seen by several people walking in the Quarters Saturday night. Gray would sell just enough dope to keep himself supplied. He had been picked up for one petty crime or another many times.

"Myself and Chief Clark went to the residence of Tal Gray's mother," Womack wrote in his report. "Tal Gray answered the door. He was sleeping on the couch. He stated that he had just arrived home that morning and went to sleep. No one else was present at the time. Tal Gray is known to myself and Chief Clark as being involved in illegal drug activities, admitted cocaine addict, and also a suspect in numerous burglaries and thefts recently."

The investigator went on to note Gray "acted extremely nervous."

On the chair beside the couch, Womack spotted an Army jacket.

"Is that yours?" Womack nodded at the khaki-green jacket.

"Yessir," Gray responded.

"Would you mind if I look inside it? In the pockets?" Womack asked.

Gray's eyes now wide open, nodded. "Go ahead," he

said. This was a familiar dance for Tal Gray. Had he said no the investigator would just get a search warrant.

Shoving his hand into the left jacket pocket, Horace pulled out a crack pipe.

Gray shrugged. "It's mine. I's got a problem with that."

The deputy reached into the right front pocket, pulling out a knife. They took Tal Gray into Logansport PD for questioning in Hazel's murder.

"Gray gave us a statement that he had been at a Jimmy Garrett's residence along with another female and several brothers from approximately eight-thirty Saturday night until nine o'clock the next morning, at which time he stated he was told of the death by a neighbor. He couldn't remember her name," Sgt. Womack wrote, adding, "note for report purposes: Mr. Gray seemed extremely nervous, made numerous comments about the knife and/or blood. At this point no information has been released as to the means of the death of the victim."

Gray's alibi partially held up—some people placed him at Garrett's residence that evening—but some of the times and statements were inconsistent, the detective noted. They also found a second knife with a broken blade inside Gray's residence, which Sgt. Womack noted, was little more than a shack behind his mother's house.

"It [the knife] had blood close to the broken-off portion of the handle," Womack noted.

Tal Gray's crack pipe and two knives were bagged and tagged and turned into the crime lab for forensic testing. Tal Gray was let go after questioning.

Gray was an addict who had committed a plethora of petty crimes. He was seen out and about in Hazel's neighborhood the night of her death and was in possession of a knife with a broken blade and bloodied handle. It was very early in the investigation and not enough evidence existed to hold him, but in Sgt. Horace Womack's mind, Tal Gray was a likely suspect.

But other known druggies were running in the

neighborhood that night. One of them had a personal beef with Hazel Mosley.

In November before her death, Hazel Mosley evicted a couple from one of her rental properties. Womack found the eviction notice and Hazel's proof of ownership of the property among the many papers in her house. Even though the pair, Terry Wise and Ruby McKeever, had basically squatted on Hazel's property, refusing to pay rent after moving in, they had not taken being evicted well. Terry Wise was another person who had been seen in the neighborhood the night of the murder. He was with Darren McKeever, Ruby's son. Now, McKeever drew Sgt. Womack's suspicion more than Wise because McKeever was known around town as a pervert, having exposed himself to more than one person on the street.

The first time Sgt. Womack spoke with Terry Wise and Darren McKeever about Hazel Mosley's murder, he noted McKeever was defensive and denied even knowing Hazel. When confronted with the eviction notice, McKeever crawfished saying well, maybe he knew Hazel, okay, but he had never been inside her house.

The second time Sgt. Womack questioned McKeever the story had changed. Womack asked if he would be willing to be fingerprinted.

"Okay, okay," McKeever volunteered, "I was in the house."

"When?"

"Monday, before the murder," he said.

"Why was that?"

He said he helped Miss Hazel carry four bags of groceries home from the Big Star Grocery and that she paid him fifteen dollars for his help.

The information was not right. Sgt. Womack confirmed Hazel bought groceries the Monday before her death, all right—but it had been in Center, Texas. She had ridden there and back with a friend.

"Mrs. Hazel never purchased more than two bags of groceries when walking," Sgt. Womack noted in his well-kept daily case diary. "She regularly paid Charlie Abraham two dollars to help carry her groceries. Why would she pay McKeever fifteen dollars?"

McKeever's story did not add up.

The cruelty of Jeff Rodgers' murder four months earlier rattled the community. Details of that crime had been trickling out week by week through news media coverage of pre-trial hearings. The attack on Hazel Mosley so soon after the Rodger's murder sparked outrage across the parish, particularly from the people of Logansport who demanded justice. The sheriff promised Sgt. Horace Womack all the help he needed. Me.

We re-examined the crime scene and items seized from the Mosley house, which included an empty bank bag. Hazel was the treasurer of St. Luke's Baptist Church. Was she killed for money in the church bag? Reverend James Jones said deposits were always made the afternoon after the church gathering when a collection was made—on Sunday or Wednesday. Hazel deposited the Sunday collection no later than Monday afternoon and she had the Wednesday night collection in the bank Thursday afternoon, the Reverend said. The bag would have been empty on Saturday, waiting for Hazel to bring it with her to church on Sunday.

Sgt. Womack and Chief Clark had learned from two of Hazel's girlfriends that she liked to collect old money. They said she had many old silver dollars and half-dollars. She also collected two-dollar bills and silver certificates. She was known to give her Sunday School students silver coins on special occasions. That information helped explain the many empty envelopes that were found torn open and strewn across Hazel's bedroom.

The federal government started making silver certificates in 1878. They could be used to redeem silver coins. Once the federal government stopped production of certificates in 1964, they became collector's items, normally bringing little more than face value. But some, just like any currency, could fetch a surprising price, depending on their rarity. A $1,000 silver certificate from 1891 sold at auction in 2018 for slightly less than two million dollars, simply because there are only two of them known to be left in the world.

One friend told us Hazel kept her antique money underneath her mattress, a secret she did not think Hazel shared with others. Since we had not heard that from anyone else, we asked the woman to guard that secret. Perhaps whoever had stolen Hazel's coins and rare money was the only other person to know where it had been hidden.

Who knew the dates and value of Hazel Mosley's silver certificates? How many were there? How many silver dollars and half dollars had been taken? Chief Clark got word out to the local businesses: let him know if anyone came in spending old money. To a person, everyone agreed they would do whatever they could to help find Hazel Mosley's murderer.

On the Tuesday after Hazel's murder, Logansport Police Chief Gary Clark took a telephone call from the manager of Bill's Dollar Store in town. A woman, Sylvia Coleman, paid for some household items with some old two-dollar bills. Even more unusual, the manager noted, Sylvia Coleman had a silver certificate.

If the silver certificate Sylvia Coleman used at the dollar store was, indeed, stolen from Hazel Mosley, it was almost certainly taken by someone who mistook it for a dollar bill. Sylvia Coleman tried to spend it just like a dollar. She had no idea it might be more valuable.

Time to talk to Sylvia Coleman.

Sylvia Coleman lived in Joaquin, Texas, just across the Sabine River from Logansport, but she spent the night of Hazel's murder with friends, Josie Singleton and M.C. Chancellor in apartment number thirty-eight of The Seasons, a government housing project within walking distance of Hazel's house. The Seasons more resembled a single-story red-brick motel than an apartment complex, nothing more than a row of apartments facing a sidewalk and parking lot. In each apartment you walked into a living room with the kitchen-breakfast room behind, two bedrooms and a bath off to one side or the other. Tile floors, a double window in front with tattered plastic window blinds. There was a kitchen backdoor. You had to have two exits.

Sylvia said she was given the money Saturday night while she was at Josie's apartment by a man named Darrell Ballard, another well-known druggie.

"Why would Ballard give you that money?" Sgt. Womack asked.

"He didn't *give* it to me," Sylvia said. "He gave me four two-dollar bills and he asked me to exchange them for two fives."

"Was it old money?"

"You know, two of them were faded and it was, uh, I think the other two were real crispy," she said. "But the first money, you know, when he was counting it, he put the crispy money, you know, on top, 'cause it looked like kind of new. But, when I got to looking through it to count it—you know the dollars was, you know, faded and stuff."

"Did Darrell say where he got the money?"

"He wanted me to hold it. Well, I was thinking when he asked me to hold it that he probably stole it from his mamma. But it was too late 'cause he already got my money. But I was just gonna tell her, if she said something about it later, that he had brought me the money and wanted some change for it—which, I didn't understand 'cause, you know, two

two-dollar bills and a dollar is five dollars."

"Yes," Sgt. Womack said. "What time was this?"

"Late," she said. "Maybe one-thirty or two o'clock in the morning. We was playing dominoes."

"Did Darrell act strange or anything to you? Anything out of the ordinary?"

"Darrell's just a strange man," Sylvia said. "I've seen him. I've spoken to him. I gathered— I mean— I don't think he, you know, they just put his bread in the oven. They didn't let it bake long enough."

"Okay, but he said he was going to come back and get that money? He didn't want you to spend it?"

She nodded. "He said, 'I don't want you to spend it. Hold it for me. In the morning, I'll come back and get it. He asked, 'What time are you leaving?' And I said, 'I'm going to leave as soon as M.C. gets ready to take me home.' I said, 'If you don't get here by then, I'm not coming back over here. You just going to have to miss me.'"

"He never came back that night?"

"No, sir. He never came back."

"And it's my understanding you used this money to buy some stuff at the dollar store in Logansport?"

"Yes, some things for my house and everything."

"Mr. Chancellor gave us an old one-dollar bill that he said Darrell dropped or he believed Darrell dropped outside his door. Did you ever see that?"

The silver certificate M.C. Chancellor turned over to Chief Clark was a 1935F series. He turned it in voluntarily when he learned what it was and that it might be connected to Hazel's murder.

Sylvia shook her head. "No, I never looked outside."

"So, you don't know how Darrell got there?"

"No. He said he had to give a white boy five dollars out there," she said. "I didn't know if they came together or not."

It was time to talk to Darrell Ballard, but before we got a chance, another disturbing clue came to our attention. It was spray-painted on the rusted, corrugated tin covering of a bus shelter in the Quarters. Alarmed townspeople called Police Chief Gary Clark, who called Sgt. Womack to come look.

"It was bizarre," the sergeant admitted, and disturbing.

Scrawled in black spray paint on the back of the bus stop, where children waited for the school bus, was a rambling, mostly incoherent message, much of which was covered up with big, fat, black "B.P." spray-painted on top. Still, many of the words were clearly legible: "Fuck everybody. Every bitch. That's how I feel." The message rambled on, until it concluded, "I think I've been dreaming of fucking an eighty-year-old woman. It's sick, but it's in my dreams."

Womack's suspicion that Hazel Mosley might have been sexually assaulted had been a very well-guarded secret. The list of suspects was growing.

The known pervert popped into our minds. We questioned Darren McKeever again. Pressed, McKeever broke down and confessed to scribbling the obscene message on the bus stop. "It was just a fantasy," he insisted.

"His alibi is extremely weak," Womack noted. "It has been changed by times and locations twice by him and by his witness Terry Wise."

The next time Womack ran into McKeever, he noted, "He was extremely nervous and defensive, but he agreed to a polygraph. Note: McKeever was wearing a gold necklace similar to the jewelry at Mrs. Hazel's house. When asked about it, he said he found it."

Tal Gray had the knife with a broken blade and bloodied handle.

Terry Wise carried a grudge against Hazel.

Darren McKeever had a gold necklace and a twisted sexual fantasy.

They were all under suspicion but until forensics came back there was not enough evidence to detain any of them on suspicion of murder.

But Darrell Ballard had been in possession of Hazel's hidden money. That was enough to bring him in for questioning.

Ballard was an odd fellow, but then again, no more so than Darren McKeever. At the age of thirty, Ballard had been in and out of jail for a decade in DeSoto and Caddo parishes on charges like burglary, simple battery, unauthorized use of a motor vehicle, illegal possession of stolen items. In 1990 he was convicted and sentenced to two years in the Department of Corrections for possession of stolen items. That sentence was suspended. He served two years on probation.

He stood five-foot eight and he weighed 130 pounds soaking wet. He spoke with a stutter. Ballard went through school in special education, worked a short time killing chickens at a poultry plant, then lived with his mother drawing Social Security Disability, much of which went to buy alcohol or drugs.

He was wanted by Caddo Parish on an outstanding warrant for unauthorized use of a moving vehicle and failure to appear, so Horace and I picked up Ballard at his mother's house on the Caddo Parish warrant. That was Friday, February 3. We questioned him about the murder of Hazel Mosley, specifically asking about the old money he gave Sylvia Coleman.

Ballard was a person who jerked—his head, his shoulders, his legs were always twitching, jerking unexpectedly. We brought him into my office, with the video camera setup to begin our questioning about Hazel Moseley's robbery and murder.

His twitching and stuttering became uncontrollable when we started asking about Hazel's money.

"I's, I's got it from a white dude," he picked at his fingernails, which were chewed to the quick. When he stopped picking at his nails, he clicked his fingertips together frantically.

"When was that?" I asked.

"Uh, uh, about two-thirty."

"In the morning?" I asked. He nodded.

"Why would some 'white dude' give you old money?"

"I didn't know it was old," Ballard said, "He wanted me to buy him some crack."

"Why did you want Sylvia Coleman to exchange the two-dollar bills for two fives?"

The more we talked with Ballard the more obvious it became he was flying by the seat of his pants, making it up as he went until finally, he made no sense at all. He was just rambling incoherently.

Bottom line, Darrell Ballard did not deny having the antique money but insisted he got it from a white man, and he used it to buy crack from Sylvia Coleman.

Because that money had been inside Hazel's house before her death and Ballard had been in possession of it, Womack got a warrant to take him to the Northwest Crime Lab in Shreveport to obtain physical evidence— fingerprints, samples of blood and hair.

When Ballard learned that, he lost it.

"He asked me numerous questions about the tests and what the tests would reveal," Womack wrote.

I had a voodoo doll that came from Marie Laveau's House of Voodoo in New Orleans that had been given to me years before by an informant. It was nothing more than a cloth rag doll maybe four or five inches long sewn from fabric of a feed sack, stuffed with 'magic herbs.' The eyes, nose, and mouth were stitched on. I always thought it looked like a stuffed gingerbread man and I'd kept it for years as a souvenir. I never noticed it bothering anyone like it did Darrell Ballard. Several times during the interview Ballard would sneak a look at it, his darting eyes wide, unable to look at the menacing doll for any length of time.

On impulse, as Womack continued questioning Ballard, I pulled a strip of Scotch tape from a dispenser on the desk, walked over to Ballard, and touched the Scotch tape to his hair. I then wrapped the tape that had touched Ballard's hair around the head of the voodoo doll and stuck a straight pin through it.

"Darrell," I said, "If you don't tell us the truth, you'll be dead in twenty-four hours."

That was late Friday afternoon.

A certain amount of trickery is acceptable when you are trying to get a confession. I picked up a suspect in Franklinton, near the coast, who was wanted for killing a DeSoto Parish woman and stealing her car. We had issued a statewide BOLO for the car and when Franklinton PD spotted it at a nightclub, they notified us, asking what we wanted them to do.

"Nothing," I said. "Just sit on it. When someone gets in, pick them up on a warrant for the stolen car."

The victim in that case was a retired teacher who had been on the telephone with a friend when she said, "Hold on. There's a black man walking up the driveway in white tennis shoes. Let me see what he wants."

The man asked for a glass of water, so the woman told her friend she would call her back. The friend became worried when she never did. When she was found murdered all we had to go on was a black man with white tennis shoes and the stolen car.

It turned out the thirsty man was a gangbanger hitchhiking from Oklahoma to his home in Franklinton about an hour from New Orleans. When the woman brought the man a glass of water, he hit her in the head with a fence post he'd picked up while she was inside. Then he stole her car. He was tired of hitchhiking. Her last deed on this earth was to bring a thirsty man a drink of cold water. I get mad all over again just remembering it.

I worked that case with Capt. Marvin Melton. On the drive to Franklinton, we discussed how we wanted to handle things and decided we would play it this way: The suspect was picked up for motor vehicle theft. On the drive back we all got to talking. I mentioned, "You put a pretty good knot on that woman's head."

"Yeah," he volunteered. "I hit her with that stick and took her car."

When we got to the jail, I said, "I failed to mention that she died. You are under arrest for first degree murder." That man is still in Angola. If I had told that man from the start that the woman was dead and he was under arrest for murder and car theft, he would never have told us a thing. We could have gotten him for car theft but without his admission, probably not for the woman's murder. Ask me if I regret tricking him.

In another case, a Mansfield man confessed to killing a mobster found naked on the interstate in DeSoto Parish. The victim had been shot six times with a nine-millimeter—three bullets to the head and three to the heart. This wanna-be bad guy in jail on some petty crime told the jailers he wanted to confess to the killing, so they brought him to me to take his statement.

"Who shot him with the .45?" I asked.

"Oh, that was the guy with me," he said. "I met him in a bar. I don't know his name."

That busted the false confession.

So, it is legally acceptable to use trickery in order to get to the truth. I could not be sure how the district attorney or judge would look upon me using the voodoo doll, and I was pretty sure a defense attorney might throw a fit—but we needed the truth and Horace and I both believed Darrell Ballard had it.

People in Logansport were calling the sheriff's department, the district attorney, and or the judge every day, demanding we find Hazel Mosley's killer.

The fact that Darrell was the man with the money put him inside her house sometime after she got off the telephone with Sharletta Duncan. Until forensics came back on Tal Gray's knife to see if the blood on it matched Hazel Mosley's blood type, until we found out if she had been sexually assaulted, and if so, if her assailant's blood type matched any other suspect, Darrell Ballard's possession of Hazel's antique money made him our number-one suspect.

When I did it—when I put the tape to his hair then taped it to the voodoo doll— I could not be certain if Ballard believed in voodoo, but based on his reaction to the doll, I figured he did. Voodoo. Hoodoo. They used them interchangeably. Whatever they called it, black magic was as much a part of the poor black culture of the Big Woods as poke sallet and collard greens.

We routinely arrested people who were carrying what they called mojo bags or gris-gris bags, good luck charms, in their pockets. Some carried the flattened, dried, skeletal remains of a small little bird or frog in their billfolds as a talisman to ward off evil, not unlike those who carry a rabbit's foot or hang an upside-down horseshoe over the door. The question is, how deeply do they believe in it?

We busted a marijuana plantation with 7,000 plants. When we arrested some of the workers, Hondurans and Mexicans, we discovered they had a duffle bag hanging from the ceiling of their bunkhouse. Each man slapped that bag on the way out each morning and uttered a chant for good luck. It didn't work. They all got busted and one worker was shot by a DPS trooper after he pulled a gun during the raid.

A certain drug dealer in the DeSoto Parish jail once received an envelope with the head of a little mojo doll inside. It had been pinched off the body. The next day the jailers had to take that man to the hospital. He said he had a headache that was "killing him."

Another drug dealer was in jail awaiting trial. When we ran a search warrant on his house, inside the freezer, we found a cow heart wrapped in white freezer paper with the name of the judge who was hearing his case written on it— District Judge Charles Adams (who retired from the bench in 2020 and was subsequently elected District Attorney.) The wrapped cow heart had a tag attached stating, "Bury this heart the day before the trial and chant 'I'll be set free' nine times and you will be set free." During that same trial someone spread ashes on the judge's bench and desks of the attorneys during a break one day.

So, given past experience and the way Ballard eyed the voodoo doll, I knew there was a good chance he believed me when I said he'd be dead in twenty-four hours if he didn't tell the truth.

Noon the next day, Womack got a call at home from Deputy Doris Youngblood at the jail. Ballard wanted to talk. "He said he wants to tell you the truth," she said.

Horace and I interviewed Darrell Ballard together, again, on videotape. We got the Miranda warnings and legalities out of the way first.

"You want to talk to me, Darrell?" Womack said.

"Yessir."

"What do you want to talk about?"

"I did that, sir," Ballard said.

"Did what?"

"Uh, I did that. I was drunk. I was drunk."

"*What* did you do?" Sgt. Womack repeated.

"Uh, I went in there at Miss Hazel's. I did that, drunk. I don't supposed to be drinking."

"And you think because you were drunk, that's what happened? I mean, you just lost control?"

"Yessir."

"Well, start it again," Womack said. "And tell me what happened that day."

"Uh, I been, uh, my mama been on me about that drinking, you hear about that."

"I know that. I know you have a problem with your drinking."

"Uh-huh," Ballard grunted.

Poor guy. He trembled. He stuttered. His body jerked. Some of it was just withdrawal and if I didn't know what a horrible thing he'd done, I'd have felt sorry for him. Hell, I did feel sorry for him. He was such a pathetic creature. What was it that Sylvia Coleman had said? "They put his bread in the oven, but they didn't bake it long enough."

"It affects your mind when you're drinking?" Womack went on.

"Then she went there. She tried to put me away one time."

"I know that."

"Man, man, I went down that road. I passed up through there and got to drinking heavy and heavy, you know, like I had a problem. I got to crying. The next thing I know I was across the tracks to the woman's house over there. I was at the door. I said, 'It's Darrell.' She let me in. Sat down. Talked to her. Then I just cracked up."

"What happened? Did she make you mad?" I asked.

"No."

"You just snapped?"

"Just snapped. I don't know. I don't even know how I snapped. I just snapped."

"Well, tell me what you remember happening," Womack said.

"I remember I sat down and talked to her. Then the next thing I know I had got a knife and hit her, and I was going to tell my mama about it and…"

"Do you remember how many times you hit her with the knife, Darrell?" I asked.

"No, sir."

"Do you remember what you did with the knife?"

"No, sir, I sure don't. Then I got back on my bike and went and got me another drink."

Womack asked, "Well, did you take any money from her house?"

"No, sir, I ain't take no money now. That been somebody had to come behind me do that. Now, I ain't take no money. I'm telling you the truth. I'm the one did it, but I ain't take no money."

Womack and I looked at each other. He said he didn't take the money, but he had the money. Why would you admit to killing her but not admit to taking the money?

"Nobody was with you? You sure?"

"Somebody had to be watching me, somebody had to. I didn't take no money."

"You don't reckon you could have taken it and just don't remember?" Womack asked.

Ballard tapped his fingers together, his feet tap, tap, tapping on the floor as he stared at the desk. "Probably did," he said. "I don't know."

"Well, you know, Darrell, the house was pretty torn up. It was ransacked. Somebody was looking for money and stuff," Womack said.

"Yes, it probably been me. I don't know, sir. It probably was me. See, Mama tried to get some help you know, tried to get…"

"I understand that."

"You know, I'm trying to get some."

"Well, I'm going to try to get you some help, you know? What time was it when you went to that house? Was it dark yet?" Womack just wanted to keep him talking. The more Ballard talked, the more the truth came out, in bits and pieces.

"Yessir, it was dark."

"How did you know Hazel? You just knew her from seeing her around Logansport?"

"No. By my mama."

Darrell and Sgt. Horace Womack continued to talk for thirty minutes. "Did Darren McKeever have anything to do with this," Womack asked.

"No." Darrell said he was alone.

"You knocked on the door and she let you in? What did y'all talk about?"

"We were talking about my problem that I have."

"Okay."

"I've got a problem."

"Were you upset when you went to her house? You said you were crying."

"I was just, I got— I do that. I think about my daddy I crack up sometimes."

"Yeah?" The deputy needed to keep Ballard talking.

"I cracks up."

"Where did you get the knife from, Darrell?"

"It was laying, it was laying right there."

"On the table? On the counter?"

"On the table and I done dropped it."

"What kind of knife was it?"

"It was, uh, a butcher knife."

"Well, describe it for me." The videotape was recording, and Womack and I were both taking notes. "How long was the knife," Womack asked.

"About that long." Ballard held out his hands indicating four or five inches.

"Was it like the knives you used at the chicken place?"

"Uh-huh. Then I dropped it. I mean, someone had to come."

"You dropped it in the house, you think?"

"Uh-huh."

"You don't remember taking it with you? Where did you go when you left Mrs. Hazel's house?"

"I went home."

"Back to your mama's house?"

"Yeah. Went outside. I stood around. I was going to tell, I was going to come on down there and tell you, but something kept on telling me, 'Naw. Naw.'"

"You were scared. Okay. I understand. Did you have sex with Mrs. Hazel?"

"No. Didn't have no sex with her, sir."

"Are you sure?"

"Uh-huh. That mean somebody had to come behind me."

"You reckon you just don't remember, Darrell?"

"I just don't remember."

"Maybe you just snapped and don't remember what you did because somebody had sex with her."

"Yeah. I may have did it, sir."

Womack tried to assure Ballard. Like me, Womack just wanted the truth. The whole truth. "Well, that's what I'm saying. I understand that. I don't want you to sit here and not tell me stuff because you're afraid to tell me that I may think badly of you or something like that. I don't, okay?"

"All right."

"Well, we're here to get to the truth, okay? And find out what happened and try to help you," Womack said.

They kept talking. Darrell said he didn't take the money, then he did take the money, then he didn't remember. He did not have sex with her, he did have sex with her, he did not remember.

After that initial statement in the DeSoto Parish jail on February fourth, Darrell Ballard called either Womack or me on several different occasions, wanting to talk. Each time, he said he remembered more about the night and gave more details. He said he remembered putting Hazel on the pillow. Perhaps she had tried to get from her bed to the telephone and collapsed on the floor. He said he went to the house two times that night and it was on the second trip that he had sex with her on the floor.

Several times we asked Ballard about McKeever— could he have been involved?

Each time, Ballard said, "No."

The autopsy showed that Hazel Mosley was stabbed in the front part of her skull. "This subject's death was the result of severe cranio-facial injuries," according to forensic pathologist Dr. George McCormick. "She had sustained multiple lacerations of her forehead, with underlying fractures of the skull and lacerations of the brain."

Ribs one through four on her left side were fractured and ribs one through five on her right side were fractured. Hazel had tried to defend herself.

Hazel was blood type B. The pillow and the bedding, down through the mattress were soaked in her blood, and it was pooled on the floor beneath her head.

Her nightgown was on wrong side out and backward. She had been raped by someone who was blood type O. Darrell Ballard was blood type O. Darren McKeever was not.

The blood on Tal Gray's knife was not Type B.

Ballard was indicted by the DeSoto Parish grand jury on a charge of capital murder. Steve Thomas was appointed to defend him. Thomas was a graduate of LSU Law School who began his career as a public defender in Shreveport. He worked a few years for the DeSoto Parish District Attorney's Office then went back to public defense. He now manages a team of public defenders who represent the indigent.

"I remember being surprised when Darrell was arrested on this kind of charge. It just seemed out of character," Thomas said. Before the Mosley murder, he had defended Ballard on several lesser charges.

In 1995, Thomas was handling several other cases, two of which were capital cases, so he filed a motion to withdraw. Herman Lawson and Richard Goorley were then appointed to defend Darrell Ballard against the capital offense.

The first thing they did was file a motion for a sanity commission hearing, which was granted by 11th Judicial District Court Judge Robert Burgess. Then they filed a motion for a hearing to suppress the voodoo confession.

Judge Burgess, a third-generation Louisiana District Judge, granted both defense motions. The sanity hearing would be first. If Ballard was found mentally fit for trial, there would be a hearing to suppress the evidence.

Ballard was analyzed by three clinical psychologists: Dr. Jack Grindle, Dr. Joe Ben Hayes, and Dr. George Seiden.

Dr. Seiden evaluated him first, on August 3, 1995: "Prior to conducting the interview, I reviewed the transcript of a statement given by Mr. Ballard to Sgt. Horace Womack of the DeSoto Parish Sheriff's Office on February 4, 1995 and an offense report prepared by Womack dated February 7, 1995," Dr. Seiden wrote in his report to the court.

"Mr. Ballard stated, 'They accuse me of killing somebody. A woman named Ms. Hazel.' He stated that he did not know Ms. Hazel and that he had never met her. Later in the interview, however, he indicated that Ms. Hazel was a woman who lived in a house down the road from his home and that he passed by her house every day and various people had told him that was the home of Ms. Hazel. He insisted, however, that he had never met her."

Dr. Seiden reported that Ballard said he did not know what he did or what they said he did; that he believed the event took place on a Saturday, but he did not know what month.

However, Dr. Seiden reported Ballard said, "Somebody in the Mansfield Police Station pulled out a voodoo doll and told him that something bad would happen to him if he didn't tell them what happened. He also stated that he remembered someone threatening to blow his head off."

Dr. Seiden wrote a lengthy report detailing Ballard's account of the day of Hazel Mosley's murder. He said he started drinking that morning, first beer then bootleg gin. He stated, "I don't remember all I did." He then added, "I remember going where they play dominoes," and "where the winos hang out."

"He then added 'one of my friends gave me something and made me start doing weird stuff.' When Mr. Ballard was confronted with the transcript of the statement he had given as well and the report of Sgt. Womack, he stated that he now remembered making the statement but that he only made it because of the voodoo doll. He said that he remembered the things at the time of the statement but that they then gave him some strong pills which wiped out his memory."

According to Dr. Seiden's report, Ballard said he had been sexually abused by a stepbrother and had been picked on because of his intellectual limitations. He reported he began hurting himself when he was nineteen, that he did it 'for something to do,' that he ran into a truck, cutting his head, jumped off the roof of his house, and had, in November 1994, cut off his left big toe with a chainsaw because he got mad at himself.

Most notably Dr. Seiden wrote, "Mr. Ballard then stated that he had never been a violent person and so he could not understand why he did what he did on the day of the murder. He stated that he felt bad about doing it."

The bottom line, Dr. Seiden wrote, "I have also concluded that at the time of the alleged offense, Darrell Ballard, despite his report of intoxication, knew the nature and quality of his acts and knew whether they were wrong." He concluded Ballard did, indeed, have the ability to assist his attorney in his own defense.

Dr. Hayes reached a different conclusion when he met with Ballard on Oct. 30, 1995.

"I spent approximately an hour with him [Ballard] alone and attempted to take a history and discuss his charges and ability to proceed to trial. You also asked me to address his mental state at the time of the alleged crime and I must admit that I could not do much with this as he alleges a complete blackout of what happened at the time that the event was to have occurred. He states he woke up that morning and began drinking and using cocaine that a friend gave him and continued to drink all day. He does not remember events of that afternoon or that night and states that he was arrested the next day and told that he murdered and raped a woman in 'the quarters' in Logansport where he lived. He states that he was told that he was going around 'knocking on everybody's door' but he does not remember any of this."

Dr. Hayes noted Ballard "related to me somewhat like a child and rocked back and forth in his chair somewhat like a retardate does during the interview," concluding the man could not assist his defense attorneys and was not capable of taking the stand in his own defense.

Dr. Jack Grindle agreed with Dr. Hayes that Ballard's IQ was very low and that he was mentally retarded due to some form of organic brain syndrome. "I suspect this person was delivered at home and probably suffered cerebral oxygen lack at birth.

"It took him three minutes counting on his fingers to answer my question as to how many brothers and sisters he had (five sisters and one brother). He went to special education school only and he does not know for how long. He does not know how to read or write—he can sign his name.

"He never had a regular job; he stutters often when he talks; hesitates that he does not know why he is in jail and does not ever remember having robbed or killed anyone. He states that he used alcohol and drugs from an early age. He states that when he tries real hard to remember something that he gets a severe headache; he can't sleep well, and he is very nervous. It is observed that he bites his fingernails to the quick. He also alleges both visual and auditory hallucinations. He also has told his friends and they told him he is crazy.

"It is my opinion that this person was mentally incompetent at the time of the alleged crime and that he is mentally incompetent to assist his lawyer in his defense," Dr. Grindle concluded.

On February 8, 1996, Judge Burgess declared Darrell Ballard to be mentally incompetent to assist his defense counsel and was incapable of understanding the proceedings against him. He was sentenced to confinement at Feliciana Forensic Facility, to be held without bond for treatment and observation until such time as he could regain mental capacity.

As I had suspected, both defense attorneys considered my voodoo doll as 'over the line.'

"I couldn't believe they tricked a mentally challenged man into confessing with that kind of subterfuge," Thomas said.

I did not consider it subterfuge. Darrell Ballard had Hazel Mosley's money and he knew it came from underneath the mattress of her bed. The woman had been savagely attacked. She was raped by someone with Ballard's blood type. His inability to remember what happened that night was a convenience, an act, a ruse. His way of saying, 'It's not my fault.'

"It was a coerced confession," said Richard Goorley, who handled Ballard's case all the way through. It was Goorley who filed the motion to suppress the voodoo confession.

In March 1997, the 11th Judicial District Court was notified by the Superintendent of the Feliciana Forensics Facility that Ballard was now mentally competent to stand trial.

"That's what they do there," Goorley said. "They don't treat the people sent there. They school them on how to work with the lawyer and answer questions so they can get them out of there and on to trial."

"We were shocked when we got notice that Ballard was ready to stand trial," Judge Burgess said. "I don't believe any of us—not the D.A. or the defense attorney or sheriff's office—none of us thought he would ever be competent for trial."

A second sanity commission hearing was ordered. On September 4, 1997, Darrell Ballard was examined by psychiatrists Dr. Mark Vigen and Dr. Michael Johnson, who reported, "According to Mr. Ballard, after he was arrested, the police put a gun to his head and threatened to shoot him if he did not confess. He also reported that they pulled hair from his head and threatened to harm him by making a voodoo doll if he did not confess. He confessed, believing that the police would put a curse on him if he did not."

The two psychiatrists tested Ballard via three standardized tests. Dr. Vigen and Dr. Johnson concluded, "We have two measures showing Mr. Ballard as competent and one showing him as not competent. By the State's standards we are of the opinion that Mr. Ballard is minimally competent to stand trial. However, careful pre-trial education with and for him will most likely be needed."

Dr. Hayes and Dr. Grindle also performed evaluations. This time Dr. Hayes concluded Ballard was 'well-schooled' at Feliciana and was able to assist his counsel. However, "Because he cannot report any recollection or memory of any of the alleged events, it is impossible for me to render a definitive opinion on his mental state and/or sanity or not at the time of the alleged event."

Dr. Grindle essentially agreed. "It is my opinion that the defendant has the capacity to proceed with his trial. Since he has been off alcohol and drugs, Mr. Ballard is obviously more alert and able to speak and be understood. I doubt that he would be effective, since all he would say would be I had a black-out the entire episode."

Based on the recommendation of the three psychiatrists, Judge Burgess ordered the criminal prosecution of Darrell Ballard would proceed to trial.

The hearing on the motion to suppress the voodoo confession was held April 9, 1998.

Both sides presented testimony. Judge Burgess heard the arguments but did not issue a ruling.

"I had concerns," the judge said later. "I never made up my mind. I was going to send them back to brief the issue to allow both sides to bring in the psychiatrist to understand his ability."

But it never came to that. The two sides reached a plea agreement.

"When you are dealing with a capital case, if you can get a plea to life it is considered a victory," Goorley explained. He should know. Goorley is the former executive director of the Capital Assistance Project of Louisiana, a non-profit that provided legal defense for indigent capital suspects across the state.

"If you can get a plea to a determinate sentence, that is a real victory," he added—which he did in the Darrell Ballard case. Ballard agreed to plead guilty to manslaughter and forcible rape.

"When push came to shove, they had some compelling evidence, not the least of which came from his (Ballard's) own mouth," Goorley said. "The damning evidence wasn't what Robbo had from the voodoo confession, but what Darrell Ballard kept giving them in those follow-up interviews when he called Robbo. It's called the fruit of the poisonous tree. If Robbo had used the voodoo doll over and over again, nothing Ballard said would have been admissible. But he didn't. Once Ballard reached out to Robbo wanting to talk, all of that was an admissible, free, willing statement. And he did that more than once."

September 1, 1998, Judge Burgess sentenced Darrell Ballard to forty years in prison on the guilty plea to manslaughter and thirty years in prison for the guilty plea to forcible rape. The two sentences were to run consecutively. Darrell Ballard died in prison in 2002.

Trusting, kind-hearted Hazel Mosley opened her door one dark winter night to a neighborhood kid she had known since birth. Evil walked in with him. Hazel was buried beside her husband outside Logansport. Her home has since been razed, nothing left but the giant oak that provided her shade.

Reginald Jones said he always believed a second person was involved in his mother's death. He said he did not learn his mother had been so brutally murdered until he arrived in Logansport from Houston for the funeral.

If there was a second killer, as Reggie Jones said he believes, I wish someone in the community would have come forward and told us who they suspected. If anyone had given us any suspect to proceed with, we would have worked as hard as possible to bring that person to justice. We did everything we legally could to get Ballard to tell us if someone was with him. He always said no.

As for the controversy of the voodoo doll confession, I still argue if I had not done that, Darrell Ballard would have continued to say he had no memory of the night and no one might ever have been brought to justice for the murder of a woman who was beloved by so many people.

Steve Thomas called it unconscionable and Judge Burgess admitted having serious misgivings about the voodoo confession, but I stand by it. In 1930 the US Supreme Court ruled "criminal activity is such that stealth and strategy are necessary weapons in the arsenal of the police officer" and in 1973, in a case involving an undercover narcotics agent who actually helped make speed that the suspect was arrested for selling, the justices agreed the mere fact of deceit will not defeat a prosecution "for there are circumstances when the use of deceit is the only practicable law enforcement technique available."

The rule of thumb in law enforcement is, unless the trick is calculated to produce a false confession, it is admissible. Darrell Ballard's confession was not false. Remember what Dr. George Seiden wrote in his psychiatric examination of Ballard? "Mr. Ballard then stated that he had never been a violent person and so he could not understand why he did what he did on the day of the murder. He stated that he felt bad about doing it."

Ever since Adam got caught in the garden people have lived with regret. My experience has been their regret was more about getting caught than remorse for a bad deed done. In all my years, I never found a Lady Macbeth running around trying to wash out the damned spot. It was my job to catch them red-handed. If that called for a trick, so be it.

Home of Hazel Moseley - January 1995
    —Courtesy DeSoto Parish Sheriff's Office

Former DeSoto Parish
Sheriff Frenchie Lambert

Former Louisiana
District Judge
Robert Burgess

Voodoo Doll Used

Night Hunt

Guided by a distant porchlight, four officers felt their way through the blackness of midnight in the Big Woods toward Faye Simpson's house, careful to make no sound that might be heard above winter wind stirring the trees. No lights shone from inside the old house that sat high above the forest floor in one of the most remote regions of Louisiana.

Near the clearing, with weapons drawn, one man circled to the back as others moved to the porch, each familiar with the layout. We'd all been there before.

Years earlier, I'd been dispatched to Faye's house to find a bleeding man who was missing the tip of his pecker. I can't recall if it was her husband or boyfriend, and I'm not certain exactly what he did but—whatever it was— Faye put an end to it with a .22 caliber rifle.

Myrtle Faye Simpson was a woman to remember.

The case opened four days earlier: Monday, December 29,

1997. My phone rang about 9:30 p.m. A man and woman were at the DeSoto Parish Sheriff's Department to report a missing person.

I went in to meet a couple who had driven about an hour from Doyline to Mansfield searching for their friend, David Levi Solomon.

Bobby Crawford and April White were in their late twenties or early thirties. It can be difficult to judge age. Some people wear better than others. The girl was a boney blonde with hair halfway down her back, almost as tall as the man. He, too, was angular, average height, dark shaggy hair.

They said it was their second trip to DeSoto Parish since Friday when they drove down for David Solomon's birthday party.

"But when we got there, David wasn't there," April said. "Connie—his girlfriend—said David had just gone to the liquor store—"

"So, we waited," Crawford talked over her. "We waited more than an hour, and finally said, 'We're going home, tell David we were here.'"

"The party was at the girlfriend's house?"

They both nodded.

"And you say your friend, David, left and never came back?" I asked.

"She said he went to the liquor store with some other guys who were at the party," April said.

"In his own car?"

"No. She said they all went in another guy's car."

"Did *they* come back? The others?"

"No. None of them ever came back to the party," Crawford answered. "So, finally we said hell with it. We drove back to Doyline. It was odd, but we didn't think that much about it. They could've gotten into a pool game or something. But here's the thing: David's mother called me yesterday. He was supposed to be at work Sunday, and he wasn't. *Nobody* has seen him."

It was my habit to make notes when taking any kind of statement. I looked up from my scribbling to study their faces. I got paid to read faces. Each looked at me directly when speaking, offered up information eagerly, consistently, their faces open, anxious for answers. They were telling the truth.

"Any chance you got the names of the people David left with?"

April said, "Debo and Danny—"

"Wilkins?" I interrupted her.

"Yes!" April answered. "That's it. After we talked to Connie earlier today, we found Danny and asked him about David, and he said they got into an argument after they left the liquor store, and David got out of their car near some battlefield."

"Mansfield Battlefield Park?" I was still scribbling, trying to get everything down legibly. Sometimes I struggled the next day to read my own hen-scratching.

"I think so," April said.

"And where did the girlfriend live?"

"Pelican," Crawford said.

That would be one hell of a walk on a winter night.

"What's the girlfriend's name? Full name?"

"Young," April said. "Connie Young."

"Did she say why *she* hasn't reported him missing?"

April shook her head. "She said she didn't know where he was. Said she thought maybe he went off somewhere."

Odd. But you never know when you're dealing with a missing person. Sometimes people do just walk away. Still, this didn't meet the smell test. It sleeted Friday. Nobody was walking from Mansfield Battlefield Park to Pelican Friday night.

"If no one has heard from David Solomon since Friday, he's been missing long enough for an official report. I'll put out a BOLO tonight and get to work on this first thing in the morning," I said.

David Solomon was a white male, blonde hair, blue

eyes, five-nine, about 170 pounds, they said. He turned thirty on Friday, December 26.

Son of a gun. He disappeared on his birthday.

"This ain't like David," Crawford said.

"I know you're worried about your friend," I tried to reassure them, "I'll get to the bottom of it."

I was barely in the office Tuesday morning when David Solomon's mother called the sheriff's department. There was fear in her voice.

"Something bad has happened," Rebecca Solomon said. "David would never do this. He's never done anything like this."

David Solomon worked as a floor hand on an offshore oil rig in the Gulf of Mexico. Seven days on, seven days off. He travelled to and from work in New Iberia with his brother-in-law. They all lived in Gibsland, in Bienville Parish—the parish made famous by the capture of Bonnie and Clyde. The Bonnie and Clyde Ambush Museum is about all there is in Gibsland, which sits just south of Interstate 20 about halfway between Shreveport and Ruston. Gibsland never had a thousand citizens but the Solomons were some of them.

Rebecca said her family celebrated Christmas early in Gibsland, then David left with Connie to spend Christmas Day and his birthday in Pelican.

"She had a party planned for him," Mrs. Solomon explained. "He was excited about having a birthday party."

"Mrs. Solomon, is there any reason someone would want to hurt your son? Any enemies?" I asked.

She paused, I assumed giving honest thought to the question. Then she replied, "Not that I know of. But I don't like that girlfriend. You know she's a widow. I understand she had a husband who got killed in a car wreck not too long ago, under suspicious circumstances."

It was understandable that his mother was frantic and would try to put blame anywhere she could. I had three daughters. Your child is your child whether age five or fifty.

She rattled on, "You know, David had money on him. He got paid. He gave me some money, but he still had close to $500 on him when he left with her last week."

"Finding your son is my top priority" I said. "You'll be the first to know whatever I find out."

Later that morning we huddled in C.I.D. —me, Pat Cobbs, Horace Womack, Judson Rives, James Clements, Toni Morris, and Donnie Barber.

We all knew the Wilkins brothers.

They had a hard-scrabble upbringing. Never really knew their biological dad. Raised by a heavy-handed stepfather with little patience. Debo dropped out of school and went out on his own in the ninth grade. Danny quit school in the tenth.

Both were brawlers, in their early twenties, who worked construction and outages. Danny, the younger, stood just under six feet tall and weighed well over 200 pounds. His litany of petty arrests included burglary and possession of drug paraphernalia.

Debo was the more imposing personality. His countenance implied Native American heritage: long, coal-black hair pulled into a ponytail tied at the nap of his neck. Smooth brown skin, broad shoulders, black eyes. Debo carried himself with a self-assurance that drew his peers to follow him—often into trouble. He'd been arrested repeatedly for battery, assault, criminal damage to property, disturbing the peace.

Detective Donnie Barber knew the Wilkins boys better than the rest of us.

Before joining the department, Donnie and his wife owned a little grocery store in Catuna, a community between Mansfield and Many where the Wilkins were raised.

Catuna disappeared when the state widened Highway 171 to four lanes, gobbling up the old grocery store in highway right-of-way. But for decades before, it was the hub of the community, where old men gathered daily around a wood burning stove (whether it was fired or not), chewing tobacco, smoking cigarettes, drinking coffee, pontificating about the problems of DeSoto Parish and the outside world.

The shotgun wooden building was built in an earlier era and never modernized. Stepping through the doors was a walk back in time—on wide plank floors beneath a creaky slow-moving ceiling fan. Double screen doors stayed propped open, weather permitting. The walls were lined with wooden shelves filled with sacks and cans of cooking basics: flour, cornmeal, sugar, beans, and lard. They cut and sold meat on a big round butcherblock table. Lots of bologna, salami, and ham. Customers could buy fresh eggs and milk. Plenty of penny and dime candy for the kids. Frosty, ice cold sodas in thick blue-green bottles were sold from a chest-type drink machine—the slider bottle kind.

From a back room, Catuna Grocery sold feed, fertilizer, and dog food. They also had small living quarters in the back where their kids could nap, and one or the other of them could take an occasional break.

Under the front portico were two gasoline pumps, the kind with a crank handle you had to turn to roll each sale back to zero. By the time the Barbers bought the store, most people pumped their own gas, but Donnie would still do it for the older women. They even sold kerosene from a pump under the portico. It may be hard to believe but some families in rural DeSoto Parish still used kerosene lamps in the 1970s and early '80s.

Air for tires and water for radiators were free.

The Wilkins kids grew up within walking distance of Catuna Grocery. There was a passel of siblings—five boys and two girls. Debo got his moniker as an infant when the oldest brother, Charlie, struggled to pronounce his given name, Dennis Barry. Somehow, it had come out as Debo, and stayed that way.

After a discussion in C.I.D., we agreed to talk to Danny first without Debo's knowledge. Danny was the more approachable.

"Before we talk to Danny, I want to talk to the girlfriend," I said. "Let's get Connie Young in here. I'd like to know why she didn't report her boyfriend missing when he disappeared from his own birthday party."

Connie Marie Young was an attractive woman in her mid-to-late twenties. Small. Five-foot three or four. Thick caramel-colored hair fell to her shoulders. Big blue-gray eyes searched my face as she entered the office, looking for answers of her own.

Donnie Barber was with me. There were always two detectives present when we questioned anyone. We thanked her for coming in and I offered her a chair.

"We just need to ask you some questions about David Solomon. When was the last time you saw him?"

"Friday night," she said.

"What were the circumstances?"

"Well, it was David's birthday party and he left with some guys and went to a liquor store and none of them ever came back."

"Where was this party?" I asked.

"My house."

"And where is that? Where is your house?"

"I live on Highway 177 in Pelican."

I caught her watching us taking notes but each time I asked a direct question, she glanced away, looking at her hands or out the window, picking at her purse. Why wouldn't she look me in the eye?

"Who lives with you?" I asked.

"I live with my father and my children and David stays with me when he's not working. When he's not offshore."

"Okay. So, David Solomon lives with you: It didn't worry you that he left his own birthday party and just didn't come back? This is Tuesday. You haven't seen him since last Friday. Other people reported him missing, not the person he lived with."

She struggled to reply. It was more of an accusation than question so I re-phrased, "Why have you not reported him missing?"

"I mean—yes—it worries me. But I don't know. I guess I thought—maybe he just went off."

I couldn't fathom that mindset. Someone you live with disappears and you do nothing. I wasn't seeing any tears. She didn't show near the concern for David Solomon that Bobby Crawford or April White had shown and there was not the anxiety in her voice I'd heard in Mrs. Solomon's.

"Where would he 'go off' to? And why?" I asked.

Connie Young finally looked me squarely in the face, squinting, fed up with the questioning. "Maybe we'd fussed a little. Maybe he just decided he didn't want to come back to me."

"Were you having trouble?"

"You know. Everybody has their ups and downs."

"Who all was at this birthday party?"

"Me and David and my son and Debo and Danny Wilkins and Scotty Wisely. April White and Bobby Crawford, but they didn't get there till late. They weren't there when David left—and they went back to Gibsland without seeing him. My sister was supposed to come."

Donnie asked, "Is David a friend of the Wilkins?"

"Oh, no. We'd just met them."

"When?" I asked. "When did you 'just meet them'?"

"Christmas Eve. At the car wash. The carwash on Highway 509. April is a friend of mine and she introduced us to Debo and Danny. And then, we saw them again at the video store later that day and David invited them to his party."

"Why would he do that? Why would David invite people he just met to his birthday party?" I asked.

"Because David is very outgoing. Very friendly. That's very like David, to meet someone and invite them to his party."

It just didn't feel right.

"Miss Young—what is it you're not telling me?" I asked.

Her eyes flashed. "Why? Do you think? Are you accusing me—"

"I don't think anything, except that David Solomon is missing. He hasn't been seen since last Friday. He didn't show up for work Sunday or Monday. He lived with you. And you never reported him missing."

"I called Debo and asked about him—about David," she said.

"When was that?"

"Sunday. He said David got mad after they left the liquor store and told them to let him out of the car near battlefield park."

"And you believed that?"

"Why wouldn't I?"

I leaned in, holding her gaze. "Because it was cold and raining and battlefield park is ten to fifteen miles from where you live. Why would he get out of the car at battlefield park and not where he could call you?"

She shrugged. "I don't know."

"Don't go anywhere, Miss Young. I may need to ask you more questions."

Donnie and I drove to Southside Video in South Mansfield.

The temperatures had been unusually cold. Sure, it was late December, but Louisiana winters don't normally stay below freezing very long. For the past week it had been bitter cold, gray, damp.

"What do you think about the girl?" Donnie asked.

"I don't know. Seems odd she didn't report him missing."

"You say Solomon's mother said he had $500 on him?"

I nodded.

"I was just thinking, that's a lot of money to people like

200

Debo and Danny. I hope those boys didn't do something stupid."

I was thinking the same. Working offshore paid good money compared to wages in western Louisiana. A big chunk of DeSoto Parish lived in poverty and most of the rest weren't far above it.

Southside Video was a white frame building on Highway 171 with an apartment attached in the back for sleeping quarters. That's where we found Danny Wilkins.

He was built like a lumberjack with tousled brown hair. I never saw Danny that he didn't look like he'd slept in his clothes, just woke up without washing his face or brushing his hair. I think disheveled would be the word.

"How are you doing, Danny?" Donnie smiled. I think he had a genuine fondness for the kid, knowing him so long. "It's been a while."

"I'm good," Danny replied. "You?"

"Good, good," Donnie answered. "How are your folks? Your mom? Grandmother?"

"They're all good."

"Danny, I need for you to come down to the office and talk to us," Donnie said.

"Okay."

He didn't hesitate or ask why. I couldn't help but think Debo would've told us to come back with a warrant then high-tailed it out of town while we were gone.

Because he had a relationship with Danny, I was happy to sit back and let Donnie do the talking on the drive to the sheriff's office, and it was Donnie who led the questioning in my office. He read Danny the Miranda Warning.

"Danny, we're just trying to find out about this David Solomon. We understand you and Debo went off with him from a birthday party Friday night and no one has seen him since. Can you tell me anything about it?"

"I don't know what happened to him. He got mad because we wanted to ride around before we went back to the party."

"Who was driving?" Donnie asked.

"Scotty. Scotty Wisely. It was Scotty's car."

Scotty Wisely was another troublemaker. At twenty-five, his arrest sheet was as long as the dining room table: criminal damage to property, possession of stolen property, fighting, domestic violence, resisting arrest.

Wisely and the Wilkins brothers—what a dangerous mix.

"So, what happened to Solomon?" Donnie asked.

"He was hollering and everything. Then he said, 'Just stop the car and let me get out!' So, we did. We stopped and let him out."

"Where was that?" Donnie asked.

"By battlefield park."

"Mansfield Battlefield Park?"

"Yeah."

"Danny—that's *bullshit!*" Donnie said. "You know it's bullshit. That park is halfway across the parish from Pelican! Where is David Solomon?"

To our dismay, Danny Wilkins burst opened like a floodgate. "I didn't kill him! But I watched them do it!"

He dropped his shaggy head into his big, grease-stained hands, his elbows on the desk, shoulders shaking.

Donnie and I were dumbfounded—not to learn that David Solomon was dead or even that Debo and Scotty killed him—they were outlaws—but Danny Wilkins' spontaneous emotional breakdown was disarming. We hadn't pushed him at all. He appeared deeply disturbed by whatever happened and he'd been dragging the guilt around like an anvil. He drew in a deep breath, as if relieved having unloaded it.

"Where is David Solomon?" I asked.

"At an old gravel pit. Near Pelican."

"Can you tell me how to get there?"

He drew a map on the yellow paper of my legal notebook then agreed to take us to the murder weapon.

Donnie and I walked out of the office, beyond Danny's

earshot.

"That's the easiest confession we'll ever get," Donnie said.

"One for the records. I'm going to the gravel pit. Will you get Pat and y'all take Danny to find the murder weapon?"

"Yeah," Donnie replied. "See you later."

I radioed directions to Captain Andy Anderson, telling him I was on my way.

Hiring Andy Anderson was the best thing Sheriff Hugh Bennett ever did.

Bennett defeated Frenchie Lambert in 1992 in a grudge match to be remembered. For whatever reason, Lambert and Bennett were two dogs scrapping for the same ham hock. Two big egos wanting to be king of one hill.

In 1988, Frenchie had coaxed a man into running against Bennett for tax assessor. Frenchie's candidate gave Bennett a good run for his money but lost the election. Four years later, when Frenchie came up for re-election, Bennett decided he'd teach the coonass sheriff a thing or two about revenge. Bennett announced *he* was running for sheriff of DeSoto Parish.

Frenchie had been sheriff so long—three terms—he had become arrogant. I think he thought he was unbeatable. He didn't consider the tax assessor a serious opponent. After all, other than working as a patrol deputy several years under Sheriff Roy Webb, what the hell did Hugh Bennett know about being a sheriff, Frenchie scoffed.

Frenchie wouldn't go to candidate forums. He'd send someone else to represent him. There was a men's group that met every Monday morning in Pelican, my father-in-law was one of them, so I encouraged Frenchie, "Go drink coffee and talk to them."

"Who the hell's running this department?" Frenchie growled. "You or me?"

"You are," I answered.

"All right then. You go talk to 'em for me."

And that's how it was until Hugh Bennett beat Frenchie Lambert with fifty-four percent of the vote in November 1992. He took office in '93 and turned everything upside down.

Frenchie was dead right about one thing: Hugh Bennett didn't know much about sheriffing, but he proved himself to be a popular politician.

In Louisiana, the sheriff is king of the parish. He answers to no one but the people who elect him every four years. He can fire anyone and everyone in the department for any reason or no reason. He can fire you if he doesn't like the color of your wife's lipstick and you have no recourse. A deputy serves at the sheriff's pleasure.

When he was running for office, Bennett told the TV stations and newspapers that the DeSoto Parish Drug Task Force was a black eye on the department, and he was serious about disbanding it. Frenchie hired me in 1980 to create it. We had taken down thousands of pounds of illegal drugs through the years, but in doing so, we chaffed some of Bennett's supporters, whose kids had been ensnared along the way.

After Bennett won the election, word got back to me that when he took his oath of office, I'd be out of a job.

I'd worked part time for the Louisiana Sheriff's Association for five years. Frenchie assigned me that duty at the request of Bucky Rives, the executive director of the sheriff's association. Bucky and I worked undercover together back in '73 and '74.

There was no extra pay, but they furnished an apartment in Baton Rouge. During each legislative session, I worked in Baton Rouge Monday through Wednesday or Thursday, assisting the sheriff's association on proposed bills that might affect law enforcement by talking to lawmakers, sometimes testifying before committees. I'd drive home and work at the sheriff's department Friday and

Saturday.

I mentioned to Bucky what I'd heard. Maybe he'd be on the lookout if I needed a job in a few months?

Bucky told me later that after our conversation, he called a well-connected oil and gas man who needed Bucky's help getting a bill passed through the legislature.

"I can pass it, or I can kill it deader than a hammer," Bucky told the man. "If Robbo doesn't have a job—your bill is dead."

I held onto my job long after Hugh Bennett retired and the DeSoto Parish Drug Task Force kept trucking along, to Bennett's chagrin. For whatever reason, Bennett disliked us so much, he sent word down through the ranks that the task force should leave the Logansport bus station alone. His reasoning? The drugs we were seizing there were headed for the East Coast and we were clogging up the DeSoto Parish Jail with unwanted prisoners he had to feed.

Sheriff Bennett never once asked me about a case I was working. He let other people take care of law enforcement while he focused on politicking, budgets, and administration. But he did hire Andy Anderson as his chief deputy.

Andy was a retired Army sergeant major—served thirteen years as U.S. Army special forces, starting in Viet Nam in 1963. When Andy retired from the military he was serving as the Senior Enlisted Advisor for the Louisiana National Guard. He personified military discipline: flattop haircut, six feet tall, solid 200 pounds. He brought a lot of professionalism to the department. But two years after being named chief deputy, Andy grew tired of politics. He resigned as chief deputy and took over command of the patrol division. Andy knew the turns and curves of most every DeSoto Parish road.

When I radioed Andy the directions Danny Wilkins scrawled on my notepad, he knew exactly where to go. Before I could get to the abandoned gravel pit, Andy found David Solomon's body face down in a stand of scrawny pines. He radioed all units to park on the asphalt road a quarter mile away and walk into the area, as he had. Preserving evidence was now top priority.

Using his radio, Andy guided me to the body.

"I followed the tire tracks, saw the pool of blood, followed the drag marks, and saw him." Andy pointed. "As soon as I did, I backed up. Nothing's been touched."

He didn't have to tell me that. I trusted Andy.

I moved in to look more closely.

Solomon's left knee was pulled up under his stomach, his right cheek rested on pine straw, elbows at his shoulders. Had he died while trying to crawl?

Donning latex gloves, I squatted down to examine his wounds: A hole the size of my thumb at the base of his left jaw. A wound that size was fired from very close range. There was a second hole in his skull just behind his left ear and several scattered smaller open wounds to the side and the back of his head, all typical of a shotgun blast at close range.

Shotgun pellets separate with distance. The farther apart the pellets, the greater the distance from the target at the time of firing. Solomon's wounds were in a tight circle.

I turned over his body.

Glazed, pale blue eyes were partially open, the eyelids fringed with pale lashes that matched the color of his hair. Strawberry blonde, they call it. He wore a trimmed mustache. Freckled porcelain skin. David Solomon was medium height and weight but stout. Thick-chested. Muscular. That man could lift a lot of weight.

Solomon was dressed in brand new blue denim overalls with straps at the shoulder, the kind with metal buckles in front. He had on a sweatshirt underneath. A close-range blast hit the right buckle of his overalls, embedding it in his chest.

A new gold watch glistened on his left wrist.

The blast to his chest came first. It would have been debilitating but not necessarily lethal. He most likely could have survived that shot. But the shot that made that hole in his neck—that killed him— I'd say instantly. Probably severed the jugular vein and carotid artery, then travelled on into the brain.

It had been so cold since Friday that Solomon's body was well-preserved, no obvious signs of decomposition.

After my examination, Judson Rives took over handling the body and transferring its custody to the coroner while I walked off through the scrubby pines and broom sage, searching for evidence if anyone asked.

Looking into David Solomon's frozen eyes, I heard his mother's voice.

"Something bad has happened," she'd said.

Mothers seem to know things like that. I'd seen it before.

She'd mentioned how excited her son was about his birthday party. I drew in the chill December air. Hell of a birthday party.

Then I remembered, I promised Rebecca Solomon I'd tell her what I found.

That never got any easier.

I'd been wrong in my initial thought that David Solomon died trying to crawl—not with that wound under his jaw. Besides, it was obvious his body was dragged to where it was found.

Half a dozen of us processed the crime scene from the asphalt road, mapping, measuring, photographing everything. Several others stood guard along the road to keep the curious at bay.

Tire tracks led into and out of the gravel pit. We took plaster of paris molds of the tracks and molds of several different shoe prints.

It was clear where the car had backed up and turned around in the damp earth. Why?

I picked up, bagged, and tagged all the evidence: I took samples of blood where it stained the earth. I believed it to be Solomon's blood, but tests would make the determination.

An empty, red 12-guage shotgun casing lay on the ground three feet away from where the blood pooled—the spot where we believed he had been mortally wounded.

One dollar and eighty-five cents in change was scattered in the grass, sixteen feet away in the direction of the drag marks.

Solomon's body had been dragged a hundred-some-odd feet, with several stops and jogs along the way. It appeared two people dragged awhile, rested, dragged some more. I took samples of the bloody pine straw beneath his head and I bagged a blood-soaked pinecone beneath his chest.

I picked three cigarette butts off the ground near where Solomon had been shot, something I considered a lucky find. We were using DNA evidence then, so I'd be able to determine who left the cigarette butts behind. Then a young deputy pointed my attention to Chief Deputy Mike Lee, standing near where Solomon had been shot, smoking a cigarette. We watched Lee flick his butt on the ground. I went over and picked it up. *Son of a bitch.* Same brand as the ones I'd picked up a few minutes earlier. Were the ones I picked up Lee's or had they been left by the killers? I'd have to get a sample of Lee's DNA to find out. That would not sit well.

While I and other deputies worked the crime scene, Danny Wilkins guided Donnie Barber and Pat Cobbs to a mobile home near Grand Cane where he and Scotty Wisely hid the murder weapon. They recovered the Stevens shotgun on the ground, tucked under the back side of a fallen tree. It was photographed, bagged, and tagged.

Then they brought Danny Wilkins down to the gravel pit to meet me. I wanted him to show me exactly what happened that night. Reconstruct it. Show me, who stood where? Who did what?

"Gives me the creeps to be here," Danny said, looking

around. "I can still hear him trying to breathe. It made a whistle—him breathing—there at the end."

I knew that sound. I heard it when I was a medic in the military. It is not a sound you forget.

"I still hear it," Danny said, his eyes haunted, "I can't get it out of my head."

We probably spent an hour there, reconstructing the events of the night David Solomon was murdered. Then, scuffing the ground with his new Nike tennis shoes, Danny said, "You know, you won't take Debo alive."

"What do you mean?" I asked.

"I mean, Debo said he won't be taken alive," Danny replied. "I know my brother."

Donnie and Pat drove Danny Wilkins back to DPSO where Donnie and Detective Toni Morris did the questioning. We all had our areas of expertise—mine was narcotics. Donnie and Toni were the department's best interrogators.

Donnie read the Miranda Warning to Danny a second time. They both signed and dated the document that detailed the suspect's legal rights, then Toni led the questioning standing beside the video camera mounted on Donnie's desk, forcing Danny to answer each question looking into the camera lens. Donnie sat in his desk chair with Danny directly across from him.

"This is Deputy Toni Morris. Today's date is December 30, 1997. The time is now 2:26 p.m. Also present during the taping is Lt. Donnie Barber with the DeSoto Parish Sheriff's Office. State your name please."

"Danny Carroll Wilkins."

"Danny, how old are you?"

"Twenty-one."

"How far in school did you go?" Toni asked.

"Tenth grade."

"Where did you go to school?"

"Mansfield High."

"Are you under the influence of any drugs or alcohol right now?"

"No, sir."

"A few days ago, did you meet an individual by the name of David Solomon?"

"Yes, sir."

"Where did you meet him?" Toni asked.

"At the car wash on 509."

"How did you meet him?"

"They pulled up and asked us if we wanted to go to a party Friday night."

"Who is 'they'?"

"Uh, David, Connie, and some girl named April."

"April White?" Donnie asked.

"Yeah."

"Where did you know her from?"

"Met her in a bar in Keithville one night."

"Does she live down here somewhere?" Donnie had taken over asking questions.

"She, uh, lives with Chris Wilkerson in Carmel," Danny replied.

That surprised Donnie. I had been under the impression April White lived in Doyline with Bobby Crawford and had told Donnie the same. It wasn't as I had surmised. She'd acted like she didn't know the Wilkins brothers.

"Uh-huh. And this girl you knew, April, was with two other people you didn't know?"

"I didn't know Connie or David," Danny said.

Donnie looked at Toni. "Go ahead, I just wanted to ask about April White."

Toni steered the questioning back to the carwash. "Did they just drive up and start washing their car or something and y'all got into a conversation?" he asked.

"They seen we had Debo there, I guess, and they pulled up."

"Who is Debo?"

"Debo is my brother— Dennis Wilkins."

"Right," Toni said.

"And they just asked y'all to a party? Where?"

"Out at their house on 177."

"Who is 'their' house?" Toni asked.

"Well, David was living with Connie out there."

"Connie who?"

Donnie spoke up again. "I believe it is Connie Young. We took a statement from her this morning."

They went back and forth pulling brief answers from Danny about the initial meeting Christmas Eve: Connie, David and April were in Connie's father's truck.

"So, tell us about the party Friday—who was there?" Toni asked.

"Well," Danny began, "the party was cancelled. They were supposed to have a keg party, but it was cancelled because it was raining earlier that day."

"Pretty lousy weather on Friday, wasn't it?" Toni said.

"Pretty much. And, uh, we sat out there. We had a fifth of Jägermeister, and we went to drinking on it."

"Who? Who had that?"

"David. And we went to drinking that and we had a couple of beers and then they smoked some pot."

Connie's son, about seven, was there. Apparently, as Danny told it, the party wasn't exciting enough for the likes of Debo and Scotty and they were running low on alcohol.

David offered to buy more, but he didn't have a car.

Scotty offered to drive. The men piled in— Debo riding shotgun, Danny and David in the back seat. They headed to a liquor store about three miles from Connie's house.

"Debo and David got out and went inside the store," Danny narrated. "Debo went to use the bathroom and David was buying the beer. Come back out and got in the car and left and we told him we were going night hunting."

"Night hunting? You've got to explain that to me," Toni said.

"Me, Scotty, Debo. Well, Scotty and Debo said they wanted to go night hunting and I said okay so we was all going night hunting."

"Everybody agreed to that?"

"Everybody except David. David didn't want to go. He wanted to go back to his house. And they said— Debo and Scotty said— 'No, we're going on down here and do this and then we're going to come back to the party.'"

Toni commanded the questioning. "What kind of night hunting did y'all want to do?"

"Looking for deer."

"Did you have guns in the car?"

"Yes, sir."

"What kind of guns?"

"I had a .308 rifle, a 12-gauge and ah, another 12-gauge."

The two officers exchanged looks. They knew where this was going.

"Pumps? Automatics?" Toni asked.

"Two pumps."

"Who did the .308 belong to?"

"Scotty Wisely."

"Who did the shotguns belong to?"

"One belonged to Scotty and one to, uh, me. I mean, I had it."

"Okay, go ahead," Donnie prompted. He was ready to get to the meat of the story. "What happened after you told David you were going night hunting?"

"Well, he didn't want to go. And he got kind of belligerent. Debo said he didn't want to take him back home, they wanted to go on and hunt then they'd take him home."

As Scotty drove deeper and deeper into the thicket, Danny said, away from Connie's house, David grew increasingly angry, demanding, "Turn this car around and take me home!"

"Did David try to get out of the car?" Toni asked.

Danny let out a snort. "No, man—he didn't try to get out of the backseat of a moving car. Besides, there was only the two doors. He couldn't get out."

They continued to drive, Danny said, with David protesting the whole time until Scotty finally pulled off the paved roadway into an abandoned gravel pit used for mudding—off-road racing through mud.

As soon as Scotty stopped the Mustang, he and Debo got out.

"And this is where they wanted to go night hunting?" Donnie asked.

"We wasn't going hunting," Danny said. "They were going down there to do exactly what they done."

"I'm not sure I understand what you are telling me," Toni said.

Donnie understood. He told Toni about taking Danny to the gravel pit earlier that afternoon.

"What happened after the car stopped?" Donnie prompted.

Danny said he and David followed the other two and walked to the rear of the vehicle. Scotty popped the trunk, Debo grabbed a shotgun and walked off into the woods, Scotty following him.

David and Danny remained at the trunk, David continuing to shout that he wanted to go back to Connie's house.

"At that point, I thought they was going hunting," Danny said. "But then I heard them whispering and I got the feeling something else was happening. Then I seen Debo cut around behind a tree and that's when I knew, you know, he wasn't playing around. I moved out of the way and that guy jumped in the car. He wouldn't get out of the car till Debo made him."

"How did Debo make him get out?" Toni asked.

"Just telling him he didn't want to mess up the car and to get out. Just kept hollering at him."

Finally, David Solomon got out of the car and Debo ordered him to kneel on the ground.

Solomon got down on his knees, hands in the air, the shotgun aimed as his face—then he stood up.

He turned, started to run— Debo yelling at him.

Solomon stopped, turned around and faced Debo.

"You son of a bitch!" he yelled at the man holding the shotgun. "If you're gonna shoot me, you're going to have to do it looking at me!"

Blam!

The shotgun blast hit David Solomon in the chest, knocking him off his feet. He landed on the ground on his back. The air knocked out of him, momentarily stunned.

"Did he say anything?" Toni asked.

"Never heard him say nothing."

"What did you do?"

"I just stood there looking. I couldn't believe it happened."

Toni asked, "How far away was your brother when he—"

"About ten feet."

"About the length of this room?"

"Yeah."

"What did you see?" Donnie asked.

"I seen him lying on the ground. I seen blood."

"What did you hear?"

"I didn't hear nothing. Nobody said anything till Scotty run around the car. Scotty didn't know what to do. I think it shocked him as much as it did me."

Danny said Scotty got in the car, got back out, and Debo yelled, "Don't start trippin' on me! Come here! Come here!"

"Start what?" Toni asked.

"Trippin'. He didn't want either of us to blank out on him. Well, Scotty went over there, and I got in the back seat of the car. I was sitting in the car and they were standing over this guy's body and I seen the guy's hand throw money. That's all I seen. They were standing over the body and the guy's hand threw money."

"The guy's hand threw money?" It was Toni asking.

"Yeah. He threw money at 'em. It just fell in a pile. And they got it and counted it."

"Counted it? How could they see to count it, in the dark?" Donnie asked.

"Scotty had turned the car around to shine the headlights on him, on the ground."

"Whoa! Wait," Toni said. "Hold up! When did the car get turned around? Who moved the car?"

"Scotty."

Toni repeated, slowly, to get it straight in his mind, "Scotty moved the car so that the lights would shine onto where this guy— David—was laying on the ground. Then you saw the money come out of his hand and you saw them count it?"

"Right."

"So, David was still alive."

It was a statement, not a question, from Donnie.

Both Toni and Donnie struggled to reconstruct the sequence of events, which wasn't unusual. Witnesses often left out important details in retelling an occurrence.

"Yeah," Danny replied. "He was alive on the ground. On his back, on the ground. The shotgun was back in the front seat of the car. Debo put it there. And then— I can't tell you which one said it—but I heard one of 'em say, "Do you want to do it or do you want me to do it?' and I guess it was Debo 'cause Scotty said, 'I'll do it'—and he got the gun out of the car."

"What gun?" Toni asked.

"*The 12 gauge in the front seat*," Danny said. "He put a shell into it and went over there and shot him in the head."

"He had to actually put a shell into it?" Donnie asked.

"Yeah, it's a pump shotgun. We didn't have all three shells in there. We just had one shell in it."

The two officers exchanged looks, absorbing the brutality of the scenario Danny Wilkins just described: Debo shoots David Solomon in cold blood, leaves him wounded on the frozen ground, walks to the car, and sets the shotgun inside. Scotty Wisely gets in the car, turns it around to shine headlights on David. Wisely gets out, he and Debo stand over Solomon—who is still alive at that point—and they count his money in front of him. Wisely walks to the car, loads the shotgun, walks back, stands over David Solomon, and shoots him in the head at point- blank range.

The spine-chilling sound Danny Wilkins mentioned earlier at the gravel pit, the sound he said he couldn't get out of his head, was the piercing whistle of air being sucked in and forced out of a punctured windpipe until the victim finally drowns in his own blood. That sound came after the second shot.

"Then what did they do?" Donnie asked.

"Scotty put the gun back in the car, in the floorboard of the front seat. Then they grabbed his arms and pulled him off into the woods."

Awhile later, Danny said, Debo and Scotty returned. Using the glow of the headlights, they picked up beer cans and cigarette butts.

"I told 'em—you're gonna get caught 'cause you left that shotgun shell out there, but nobody wanted to go back to the scene of the crime, so forget it. I knew it was gonna happen," Danny said.

Toni asked, "Do you know how much money they ended up with?"

"Four hundred some odd dollars. I can't tell you exactly."

"How do you come up with that figure?"

Danny said, while Scotty drove to the truck stop on Interstate 49 at Carmel, Debo used the interior lights in the Mustang to count the money—three one-hundred-dollar bills, five twenty-dollar bills, and assorted smaller bills.

He said they filled up the Mustang with gasoline at the truck stop. Debo went inside and asked for a girl who worked there.

"They said she didn't come on till midnight," Danny said. "So Debo left fifteen dollars in an envelope for her."

From there, the three rode around several hours, Danny recalled, riding to Keithville and back. Then to Coushatta, where Danny threw his tennis shoes over the bridge railing into the Red River.

"We knew there were shoe prints out there and we didn't want them traced back to us."

Scotty dropped off Debo at a house on Shell Street in Mansfield sometime before dawn. At that time, Debo gave Scotty and Danny each a one-hundred-dollar bill. Scotty and Danny went to get something to eat then drove to Southside Video where they slept in the rear living quarters.

"What did you do with your money?" Donnie asked.

"Bought me some new shoes."

We issued an all-points bulletin for Dennis (Debo)Wilkins and Timothy (Scotty) Wisely. Wilkins, five-foot eleven, long black hair, dark brown eyes, 170 pounds. Wisely six feet tall, 185 pounds, brown hair, blue eyes. The bulletin warned all law enforcement agencies that Dennis Barry Wilkins said he wouldn't be taken alive. Both men were considered heavily armed.

They were not.

Word got to Debo that we picked up Danny from Southside Video, probably before we got him to the station. Debo and Scotty stashed the Mustang near Grand Cane, drove to Shreveport where Scotty pawned his rifle and shotgun to his stepbrother for fifty dollars. Then the pair headed east in Debo's Chevrolet.

While our deputies and Mansfield police officers crisscrossed DeSoto Parish looking for the murder suspects, they were driving farther and farther east.

The next day was New Year's Eve. The Mansfield and Shreveport newspapers carried the story of David Solomon's murder, the arrest of Danny Wilkins, and the search for Debo Wilkins and Scotty Wisely.

A man named Paul Conley telephoned the sheriff's office, telling me that if the shotgun used to kill Solomon was a Stevens 12 gauge, it was his. He said Danny Wilkins borrowed the shotgun about two weeks earlier.

That same day, J.C. Wise, Scotty Wisely's stepfather, called to tell me he had two weapons Scotty left in Shreveport—the .308 Infield with a scope and a Springfield 12-gauge pump shotgun. Wise said he knew where Scotty's 1988 Mustang was hidden and agreed to take me there.

We met in Grand Cane. Wise handed over the two weapons as evidence, then led me to the Mustang, which was parked beside an abandoned house a few miles east of Grand Cane. It was locked. Wise had to get his own key, which he gave to me. We had the vehicle towed to DPSO.

Chapter Two

Midnight January 2, 1998, my phone rang.

Scotty Wisely was at the DeSoto Parish Sheriff's Office. He'd come in voluntarily to surrender.

Scotty told Donnie and me that he and Debo drove to Florida to meet a friend of Debo's in Tampa. Scotty called his mother from a pay phone there, and she persuaded him to come home. He and Debo drove back to Louisiana, left Debo's car at a roadside park on Interstate 10 in Slidell where one of Scotty's friends picked them up to bring Scotty back to his parents' house.

Debo rode along.

"I'm willing to give a statement," Scotty said. "But I want my lawyer present when I do."

That was that. We had to wait for Scotty to get a lawyer to ask him any questions.

"Where is Debo?" I asked.

"At Faye Simpson's house," Scotty replied.

On the return drive to Desoto Parish with Scotty and his friend, Debo asked to be let out on Interstate 49 west of Pelican. Not realizing Scotty was going home to surrender, thinking they would meet the next day and head to Texas, Debo told him, "I'll meet you at the railroad tracks. If I'm not there, you know where I'll be."

There was something Debo needed to do before he left town for good.

He walked all New Year's Day to reach Faye Simpson's house in Benson, arriving after dark. She was a second mother to him, but Faye wasn't the reason he walked so far. It was her daughter Raven he came to see one last time.

The yard was full of cars. There was a birthday party for one of Faye's grandchildren so Debo hid in the woods until the cars were finally gone and the last light was turned out.

Then he walked to the porch.

"Momma had a front door with four glass panes that were covered by a curtain," Raven Waters remembered. "I had just laid down for the night when there was a knock on the door. I thought who in the world can that be? I pulled back the curtain to peak out—and there was Debo. I froze. I knew he was on the run. They were hunting for him and he shows up here."

Raven opened the door.

"He came inside, and we hugged," she recalled.

There had always been something soulful between them. Sweethearts when they were younger—the only thing that kept them apart was Debo's lifestyle. His parties and drugs, Raven would not abide. She loved the man but not his ways.

"We just held onto each other," she said.

The petite nineteen-year-old with long, ebony hair looked up at this man she loved.

"Why, Debo, why?" she asked. "Why did you do this?"

She waited for an answer that was slow to come, looking up into his eyes. He would not meet her gaze, she recalled. He lowered his head, looking away, answering at last, "I don't know."

Debo shook his head slowly, took the door handle to leave, saying again, "I don't know."

"Debo, wait," Raven held onto him. "Don't leave. Stay. Please. I want you to stay."

Raven woke her mother.

Faye got out of bed, put on her house robe, came into the living room, assessing Debo. She'd seen the news. She knew what he had done. But Faye Simpson had known the boy his entire life. She wasn't afraid of him.

"Are you hungry, son?" she asked.

He nodded.

Leading him into the kitchen, pulling food from the refrigerator, Faye asked, "Son, what in the hell have you done?"

"I don't know, Aunt Faye," he replied. "I don't know."

They sat at the table, the three of them, in silence.

Neither woman peppered him with questions or blame. They just let him eat, feeling the warmth and security of their home. Faye struggled to understand the anger that must live inside him, for him to have done such a thing. She had never seen Debo that way—to have killed a man the way they said he did.

After a while, Faye leaned in, forcing Debo to look into her eyes.

"Son," she said, "you know you've got to turn yourself in. You can't run forever. You've got to face what you did."

Sitting at Faye's familiar kitchen table, a half-empty plate of food before him, Debo Wilkins gazed wide-eyed straight ahead, through Faye, as if she weren't there. He stared into whatever visions were inside his head—shooting David Solomon? The prospect of what kind of life now lay ahead of him? No matter how fast or far he ran, he could never outrun what he had done.

It felt forever, Raven said, until Debo answered her mother.

"Yes ma'am," he said. "I know. I will."

"We didn't have a telephone," Raven said, "so, Momma walked down the road to my uncle's house and called the police. While she was gone, we just held each other. He told me he had to come see me before he left for good or turned himself in, as it happened. I told him I'd always be here for him. I hugged him and we just held each other for a long time. I remember I told him I loved him, and we kissed goodbye."

At 2 a.m. on January 2, 1998, DPSO officers James Clements, Horace Womack, Pat Cobbs and Mansfield Police Sgt. Gary Hobbs converged on Faye Simpson's house. Although she called police saying Debo was ready to surrender, that word had not gotten to our officers already in Benson. The last they were told, Debo Wilkins said he wouldn't be taken alive—and he'd already killed one man.

The house was dark except for the front porch, illuminated by the yellow light. With eyes adjusted to the darkness, the men advanced on the house, weapons drawn, careful to make no noise that might alert those inside.

Pat Cobbs moved to the back while the others moved onto the porch. James Clements tried the front doorknob. It didn't move. Locked.

Then the knob was pulled from Clements' hand.

Faye stood in the doorway, between the officers and Debo.

"He's here," she said. "He's ready to give himself up."

Then she stepped aside.

Clements looked past the woman into the dark room where Debo was smoking a cigarette, looking squarely back at the detective, his face eerily illuminated by the orange glow of the burning cigarette.

It was too dark for Clements to see if Debo had a weapon. No matter: Debo Wilkins was staring into the barrel of Clements' .357 magnum revolver and he knew James Clements was willing to use it.

"Debo! Show me your hands!" Clements yelled. "Walk to the porch!"

Only a man with a death wish would do otherwise.

He hesitated, staring at the gun. He did not move.

Did Debo want to die?

"Show me your hands!" Clements ordered again. "Walk to the porch!"

"You're under arrest," Horace Womack said as Debo reached the light of the porch, his open hands in the air, his face devoid of emotion.

He had said goodbye to Raven.

It was done.

"You have the right to remain silent," Horace Womack recited the Miranda Warning as Clements cuffed Debo. "Anything you say can and will be used against you in a court of law."

With the snap of the cuffs, Clements asked, "Do you understand your rights?"

Debo nodded.

"You have to say it," Clements said. "Do you understand your rights? You have the right to have an attorney present. Anything you say can—"

"Yes," Debo interrupted the officer. "I understand my rights."

Under the porch light, Clements patted him down: one large black-handled knife in the right back pocket, a brown knife in his left back pocket, a small knife in his right front pocket. They were bagged into evidence, then James Clements transported Debo Wilkins to the DeSoto Parish Detention Center, where Donnie, Toni, and I waited—where he refused to give a statement.

Faye never saw Debo again. She died in 2006. She probably saved lives that night. Her calm command, "You can't run forever. You have to face what you've done," got through to Debo when nothing else had.

So many years later, Raven Sepulvado Waters remembers her mother's calm strength and she still struggles to accept what the man she so adored did to another.

"Debo and I were so close," she said, "but I knew Scotty and Danny, too. We all grew up together. Did they fight? Yeah, if you grew up in Pelican, you fought. You had to take care of yourself. But Debo would give anybody the shirt off his back. He was funny. He was kind. I just never could understand why he did what he did. It just wasn't the Debo I knew."

Since neither Debo nor Scotty would talk, all we had to go on was what Danny Wilkins told us the first day. We went to work corroborating the evidence.

Chapter Three

January 15, 1998 the DeSoto Parish Grand Jury indicted all three men— Danny Carroll Wilkins, Dennis Barry Wilkins, and Timothy Scott Wisely for capital murder and armed robbery.

They would be tried in the Louisiana 11th Judicial District before District Judge Stephen Beasley. A trial date was set for October 26, 1998.

Soon thereafter, District Attorney Don Burkett announced he would seek the death penalty against all three men. He would try Danny Wilkins first. Debo and Scotty would be tried together.

Facing the death penalty, none of them cooperated with the prosecutors. Debo and Scotty never had. Once Danny was given a public defender, he went mum as well.

Alan Harris was appointed to represent Danny and Stephen Glassell, another public defender, represented Debo.

Scotty's family hired Daryl Gold.

The first thing any good defense attorney does is try to have the confession and any statements thrown out. Alan Harris was a good attorney. He argued that Danny's confession was illegally obtained because we promised leniency if he would confess and cooperate.

Everything had been recorded, proving otherwise. People can complain about video cameras and I can't image wearing one all day—but a video camera protects innocent cops. If you do it right, the video camera is your friend.

Legal maneuverings went on throughout 1998 and 1999 while all three men were held in the DeSoto Parish Jail and the Solomon family waited for justice.

September 8, 1999, Debo Wilkins agreed to plead guilty to the lesser charge of manslaughter and armed robbery. He was sentenced to forty years at hard labor for manslaughter and fifty years for armed robbery. Judge Beasley allowed the sentences to run concurrently.

Danny Wilkins pleaded guilty to the reduced charges of accessory after the fact second degree murder on September 27, 1999, for which he was sentenced to five years in prison. He also pleaded guilty to the charge of conspiracy to commit armed robbery, for which he was sentenced to seven years in prison. The sentences ran concurrently. He was given credit for time served and has been released from prison.

Scotty Wisely did not agree to any plea offer. He opted for a bench trial before Judge Beasley, which was held May 22, 2000. It was not until then that the whole truth came out.

All was not as initially told.

Under oath, Danny Wilkins testified during the December 24 meeting at the car wash Connie asked Debo to buy her some pot. The two had met before and knew each other well enough for her to feel comfortable asking him to score her some marijuana.

Prosecutor Clifford Strider quizzed Danny about the meeting on the witness stand.

"Mr. Wilkins, you saw them (Connie, April, and David) at the carwash on December 24, 1997, did you see them later that day at any place?"

"Yes, sir, they met us over at Southside Video. They came over there to talk to us."

"Do you know what the purpose of that was?" Strider asked.

"They was looking for drugs."

Debo couldn't find his supplier, so he returned the money he'd been given to buy marijuana, Danny testified.

"While you were at the carwash or while you were at the video store, did they invite you any place?"

"They asked us if we wanted to come to a party."

"Who invited you?" Strider asked.

"Connie Young invited us out to David Solomon's birthday party out there at her house," Danny said.

"When was the birthday party going to be?"

"December twenty-sixth."

Danny testified he, Debo, and Scotty were at Connie's house about two hours before heading to the liquor store. During that time, he said, Connie made Colorado Bulldogs, a mixed drink with Vodka and Kahlua, David had a fifth of Jägermeister, a syrupy German liqueur with licorice and ginseng. The guests brought Budweiser.

They all drank, popped fireworks, and smoked weed, Danny testified.

"Who smoked weed?" Strider asked.

"Scotty, David, Debo, and Connie."

"Did you smoke the weed?" the prosecutor asked.

"I had to go back— I was supposed to be scheduled to go back to work in Oklahoma so I couldn't smoke," Danny replied. Earlier, Danny testified he worked a construction job in Oklahoma for H.Z. Zachary.

"Do they do drug tests at your work?" Strider asked.

"They do drug tests, yes, sir."

When the booze ran out, Danny said, David offered to buy more. By then it was around 10 p.m. The men drove to

Grandma's Old Towne Store to buy more. While Debo and David went inside, Danny said, Scotty asked him, "Do you think Debo is serious?"

Danny said he asked, "Serious about what?"

Scotty answered, "Debo said he's going to take this guy out."

Danny told the judge he interpreted 'taking him out' to mean beating him (David) up.

"Debo said that plenty of times and we ended up fighting a bunch of people," Danny testified. "You know, I didn't know what he meant by taking him out."

They drove around, as Danny had told Donnie and Toni December 30, 1997, all the while David protesting that he didn't want to go night hunting, he wanted to go back to Connie's house. When they finally pulled into the gravel pit, Danny testified, Debo and Scotty hopped out of the vehicle, went to the rear, and opened the trunk.

David followed, slamming the trunk closed. Scotty re-opened it. Debo grabbed a shotgun and walked into the woods, Scotty trailing behind.

David and Danny remained at the back of the car, David demanding to be taken home.

"He was getting hostile with me about going home. I couldn't carry him home. It wasn't my car," Danny said. "Scotty asked me for a cigarette, and he walked up, and we met halfway between where they were standing and where I was standing and that's when I see Debo come out from behind the tree. He had run around, made a circle, and come out and pointed that gun at David."

"Where was David while you were taking a cigarette out?" Strider asked.

"Still standing behind the car."

"So, he didn't move?"

"No, sir," Danny replied.

"What happened next?"

"He come and pointed the gun at David. Then David jumped inside the car and Debo made it around the car and pointed the gun on that side of the car and kept saying 'don't make me mess up the car, get out of the car.' David finally— he finally talked David out of the car and told him to get down on his knees."

For what felt like thirty minutes, he said, Debo and David argued before Debo shot the unarmed man, blowing Solomon off his feet onto the cold ground on his back.

Other than the Christmas Eve meeting being about buying dope, Danny Wilkins' testimony was true to the statement he made on the day of his arrest.

Connie Young was a different matter.

I'd had a sense she was hiding something, leaving something out of her story when she came to my office that day. I'd even asked her, "What is it you're not telling me?"

The part about sending Debo to buy her dope—that had been omitted.

The fact that she'd met Debo and Danny at some mutual friend's shop in Mansfield earlier had been omitted from her statement to me as well as the fact that she'd run into Debo at bars before their Christmas Eve meeting. She had not been forthcoming about any of that in my office.

She brushed it aside as having seen them before but not having been formally introduced but Cliff Strider pried it out of her on the witness stand.

"Did you and Debo have any kind of conversation at the carwash?" Strider asked her.

"A small amount," she said. "I was just introduced to him by a friend and then we sat there, and we were talking about—he was—we were talking about he could go get a bag of marijuana."

"Who introduced you?"

"April White."

April White had not been forthcoming with me, either. She gave me the impression she met Debo and Danny at David's birthday party, yet she was the person who introduced Connie to them. April White fooled me.

There were conflicting versions of who invited whom

to the birthday party. Danny said it was Connie and April who invited them, not David.

On the witness stand, Connie said it was David. She also testified Debo asked her out during David's birthday party. That was another thing she left out in my office.

When Debo testified, Cliff Strider asked about meeting David Solomon Christmas Eve.

"When he came to the video store was he with someone?" Strider asked.

"He was with Connie and a girl named April," Debo replied.

"Connie and April. When they came to the—while they were at the video store, did they invite you any place? Did Mr. Solomon invite you any place?"

"I don't think it was David that done that. It was April and Connie that had invited us to the party at the carwash," Debo answered.

Under cross-examination, Daryl Gold repeatedly questioned Debo about David Solomon's girlfriend, implying his desire for the woman was the motive for the murder.

"When did you first meet Connie Young?" Gold asked.

"I've seen her a couple of times at a bar and spoke to her," Debo answered.

"What bar?"

"It's a bar in Carmel. I don't know the name of it."

"You ever talk to her?" Gold asked.

"I've spoke to her, you know."

"Did you ever—when did you learn that she either lived with or had a relationship with David Solomon?" Gold went on.

"The day I met David Solomon at the carwash."

"So, you didn't know before that time?"

"No, sir," Debo replied.

"Did you want to go out with Connie?" Gold asked.

"I thought she looked nice."

"Did you want to go out with her?" the defense attorney

repeated.

"Not really. I had a girlfriend at home."

"Did you ever ask her to go out?"

"Not that I recall," Debo answered.

"On the day you shot David Solomon, did you ask her to go out?" Gold asked.

"Not that I can recall."

The defense attorney wasn't giving up, asking again, "Did you tell her that sometimes when David wasn't around that you'd like to go out with her?"

"I might have," Debo said. "I was drunk."

"Pardon me?"

"I said I might have. I was drunk."

The crux of Scotty Wisely's defense was that Debo— not Scotty—fired the fatal shot. Both of Solomon's wounds were inflicted by Debo Wilkins, Gold said.

When Scotty Wisely took the witness stand, he insisted he warned Solomon to run for his life before the first shot.

"You told him that?" Gold asked. "To run?"

"Yes."

"Did he ever run?"

"No," Wisely answered.

Scotty Wisely testified that after the initial shot, Danny misheard or misunderstood what was said between he and Debo.

"He asked me if I was going to do it or was he going to do it. I told him 'I'm *not* doing it.'"

In closing, Daryl Gold argued the Wilkins brothers conspired on a story to lay ultimate blame on his client: that Danny's initial statement shielded Debo from total responsibility for David Solomon's death, that Debo's attorney allowed him to see Danny's statement, thus Debo parroted what his brother had told.

Gold also maintained robbery was never a motive in the murder. It was never discussed before Debo shot David Solomon, and they left the gold watch. Taking the money was an after-thought, he said, an unexpected plus, when the money flew out of David Solomon's hands.

Cliff Strider argued Danny Wilkins wasn't that bright.

Strider told the judge, Danny told the truth to me and Donnie Barber initially, cooperated by telling us where to find the body and the murder weapon, and that he followed up truthfully in his recorded statement to Donnie and Toni Morris.

Strider also emphasized the point that the Wilkins brothers accepted responsibility for their actions while Scotty Wisely never had. His argument to the judge was compelling.

"The state will acknowledge there were plea negotiations in this matter, and I will state for the record that those plea negotiations took place with the approval and the knowledge of the victim's family in this matter. And I will also state the discussions with the victim's family were predicated—the plea offers were predicated on two things: The first is acceptance of responsibility. The family was hoping there would be an acceptance of responsibility from this defendant as it were from the other two defendants. That has not happened. The other reason, Your Honor, was a matter of closure. This family did not want to sit through a trial where they had an explanation of how their son or brother died—the extent of the injuries, the circumstances surrounding it. They wanted to resolve the matter if possible with an acceptance of responsibility and closure without sitting through a trial. Neither one of those things happened."

The next day, May 23, 2000, Judge Stephen Beasley found Timothy Scott Wisely guilty of manslaughter.

July 11, 2000, Judge Beasley pronounced sentence: forty years hard labor in the Louisiana Department of Corrections. Scotty Wisely remains in prison.

Chapter Four

David Solomon was two years in his grave in Gibsland Memorial Cemetery before his family got the closure Cliff Strider referred to—if closure is even possible for people grieving the loss of loved ones.

"It's been more than twenty years," Rebecca Solomon told me, "and I still think about my son every day. He was the only one I had. I could depend on David."

Now elderly and frail, Rebecca remembered the last time she saw her son.

"David loved my hot rolls and homemade macaroni and cheese," she said. "Every time he came home, he'd throw me over his shoulder and say 'Momma, you better have my homemade hot rolls and homemade macaroni and cheese.' It took me five years to make them again after he died. I loved my son. He was there for me."

He wasn't a perfect man, she said. Like his assailants, David Solomon had seen the inside of a jail cell himself. He'd been arrested for drinking and driving, battery, even burglary.

"My son had got out in August (1997) for DWI, from a penal farm in Bossier Parish," Rebecca said. "He went to work with my son-in-law on the oil rig. He was turning his life around till he met that girl."

David Solomon's supervisors on the oil rig spoke highly of his ability and work ethic. In just a few months of working there, David had already been promoted.

Rebecca Solomon told about a conversation she had with Debo in 1999. She travelled to DeSoto Parish to ask him to testify against Scotty. She said Debo apologized at that time for his actions.

"I told him, you know, you not only ruined my family's lives, but your life. You destroyed too many lives. It was senseless, for $480 and a girl. That girl wasn't worth it."

David's sister, Lori Hay, dismissed Rebecca's bitterness toward Connie Young.

"Momma didn't like anyone who liked David," she said. "He was her baby. He was my brother. I miss him every day. Every single day."

Debo still insists the murder had nothing to do with Connie Young.

Speaking from Wade Correctional Center in Homer, Debo was emphatic. "That had *nothing* to do with it."

The killing stemmed strictly from the argument between the two men, he said.

"I don't really remember much of anything about that night," he said. "It's painful. I don't want to think about it. The person I was twenty-two years ago is not the person I am today. I was messed up drinking and drugging—marijuana, methamphetamine, LSD—drugs were a daily thing. If I knew then what I know now, I wouldn't be here today."

Debo was a bitter young man when he was sentenced to Angola Prison in 1999 at the age of twenty-six. He stayed that way until 2004.

"After so many years, I put everything in the good

Lord's hands and turned it over to him. And I've been growing ever since. I pray for him (David Solomon) every day."

He completed his GED in prison.

"My momma was very happy about that," he said.

He serves on the steering committee of the prison's Alcoholics Anonymous Narcotics Anonymous groups and even teaches Celebrate Recovery.

He talks to young people coming into prison who walked paths similar to his.

"I tell them, think about your family first. Put Christ in your life."

It's worked for Debo.

Scotty Wisely said basically the same thing, minus the religion.

"It's a bad memory I'm trying to forget," he said. "I'm sorry it happened. I wish it never did. I think if I weren't so drunk that night, I wouldn't have done it. I'll take blame for it—but I do believe, if I weren't so drunk, I wouldn't have done it."

"Do you think of David Solomon?" I asked.

"Pretty much every day," he said.

Danny Wilkins was released from prison but that doesn't mean he's free. He lives with an inescapable torment: the chilling sound of David Solomon's dying breath.

"I still hear it when I'm driving down the road," Danny said. "Sometimes I hear it in the middle of the night—that piercing whistle. It wakes me up. It is a sound that will never leave me."

Investigators remove body of David Solomon from crime scene near Pelican December 1997
    —All photos courtesy Mansfield Enterprise

Danny Wilkins

Dennis Wilkins

Scotty Wisely enters courthouse for trial.

Scott Wisely

Bloody Rivers

We could hear the hounds coming way before we saw the trucks.

Smart enough to know, once loaded up they would soon have a hunt, the dogs were chafing to be set free, telling us all about it with earsplitting, high-pitched howls, yowls, and bays that clashed off-key with guttural barks of snarling curs locked among them.

Their deafening discordance was actually a welcome sound.

We'd waited what felt like hours for the man-tracking team to arrive. A glance at my watch gave me a reality check: it was actually less than two hours since the sheriff sent for them. Minutes can feel like hours when you're broiling beneath a white-hot sun that bleaches even a cloudless sky. It distorts your perception of time.

That was beside the point now. The waiting was over. The howling hounds were finally here.

Some people, like DeSoto Parish Sheriff Rodney Arbuckle, cherished that sound. Flashing his boyish grin, the sheriff slapped me on the back with his enormous paw.

"That's music to my ears!" he said.

Arbuckle, a big man in size and stature, beamed as the caravan pulled into a wellsite that doubled as a staging area for the manhunt. The trucks, pulling gooseneck trailers with horses and dogs, could go no farther down the parish road. It was lined with law enforcement vehicles from DeSoto and Caddo parishes, Louisiana State Police, Texas Department of Public Safety—even deputies from Panola County Sheriff's Department had come to help us keep our fugitive cornered.

Arbuckle called for the Winn dogs when our department's K-9 Belgian Malinois gave out. Kira, they called her, had a hell of a nose but she was used for quick sprints and take downs, a bite dog never intended to be used in such an extensive hunt as this turned out to be. Dew was on the grass when Kira started tracking but as the sun rose, so had the heat and humidity. There was not a dry shirt to be seen—a credit to the thick-coated Malinois that she worked as long as she had in those conditions.

Winn Correctional Center, a privately run prison located south of Winnfield in the Kisatchie National Forest, used tracking dogs in the same way as the Texas Department of Corrections. Arbuckle—a pro with hunting dogs—had been impressed years before watching TDC tracking dogs work and was similarly impressed seeing a demonstration of the Winn tracking team. It turned out the Winn dog handler had come out of TDC.

"They turn 'em loose and let 'em hunt," Arbuckle said.

In contrast, Angola Prison hunts their bloodhounds on leash and our Malinois worked on leash as well.

"They had better results in Texas," the sheriff said. "They use a pack of eight to ten dogs, different breeds, blue ticks, redbones, Catahoula curs—they let 'em run down a man just like a hog or deer. And those dogs will bite."

Had we been looking for a missing child, Arbuckle said, he would not want the Winn dogs. He would want the bloodhounds on a leash. But we were not looking for a missing child or even a wandering senior citizen.

We were on the trail of a killer and the longtime sheriff was not worried in the least about what the pack might do to Stephen Rivers when they found him.

Before sunrise, Rivers had killed two women—sisters—gutting them like fish.

Every available law enforcement officer in the parish was called to help find him.

Rivers was sighted near Keatchi about 7:30 a.m. Under fire, he had skirted away, hiding somewhere in a dark forest on the back side of a cow pasture of calf-high Bermuda grass.

Should Rivers continue making his way deeper and deeper into those woods, we would be here awhile, dogs or no dogs. The woods of western Louisiana just do not end in that direction— South.

But woods like these are particularly difficult to navigate, so dense that sunshine never reaches the ever-damp floor. It is sewn together with saw briars, blackberry vines, poison ivy, poison oak, grapevines, Virginia creeper, honeysuckle, trumpet vines, even wild roses that twirl up and around most every tree then intertwine with vines from the adjoining tree. This vegetation fabric creates a mat that requires a machete to get through.

Saw briars and wild roses cut like barbed wire.

Equally threatening—low-lying woods like those are snaky, teaming with cottonmouth water moccasins that nest in shallow streams meandering throughout. There would be plenty of rattlesnakes, copperheads, and coral snakes in there, too.

It is a fact that outlaws will take the path of least resistance.

Chances were, Stephen Rivers would keep to where the going was easiest, moving along the periphery, making for a house or barn, a culvert or cave or road. Deputies checked all area residences to see if there was anyone around who might offer him shelter.

Arbuckle briefed the Winn dog handler, who took two dogs to the approximate place Rivers was last seen. Silently, the hounds ran in circles, noses to the ground, lifting their heads to sniff the air, searching for the scent until—at once—both dogs opened up—jumping, baying, howling, signaling to their handlers and the rest of their pack— they had *the* scent and *the* direction of travel. The remainder of the pack was set loose to join them, and they all ran, noses to the ground, at break-neck speed.

Horse-mounted, rifle-toting K-9 officers trotted behind with heavily armed members of the SWAT Team on foot, bringing up the rear.

Arbuckle gave a thumbs up as we exchanged looks.

"They'll get him now!" He grinned. "Listen and wait."

He had no doubts. There would be no stopping until the dogs cornered Rivers. That pack would not give out. They could hunt for hours if need be. We just had to continue holding the perimeter. The Winn guards would fire a shot to let us know when and where the chase ended.

If Rivers stayed in the woods, sooner or later, the dogs would get him.

If he came out, we would get him.

A man cannot do what Stephen Rivers did and not pay a price.

Detective Corporal Dusty Herring was the DeSoto Parish Sheriff's Office investigator on duty that morning, called out about 2 a.m. on the burglary of a liquor store in Mansfield.

Wrapping up the burglary scene, Dusty heard DeSoto Emergency 911 Dispatch, "DeSoto Parish all units. Two females stabbed. 1001 Speights Road. Life air en route."

Calling 'all units' was unusual. So was the Life Air helicopter out of Shreveport.

"DeSoto 312, did you catch that traffic?"

It was the Sheriff's department dispatcher.

"I did," Dusty answered. "I'm headed that way."

It was 5:07 a.m. on Sunday August 8, 2010.

The next thing the dispatcher did was call me. I was Chief of Criminal Investigations at that time. It was just a courtesy call to keep me in the loop.

From where Dusty was in Mansfield, driving full speed with lights flashing, Speights Road was a good twenty minutes away.

Arriving at a manufactured home sitting deep in the woods away from the parish road, Dusty was relieved to see several units from Logansport Fire Department already there along with DeSoto Emergency Medical Service paramedics and two DPSO patrol units.

He assessed the scene: An unusually large, manufactured home, gray with white trim and forest green shutters. An above-ground swimming pool in the front yard. No front porch, just steps leading into the front door.

Every light in the house appeared to be on.

Center stage, paramedics were rushing in and out of the open front door. They appeared not to notice a toddler crawling over the motionless body of a woman sprawled on her back just inside the front door.

The child was crying, "Mamma, Mamma, wake up!"

Doing his best to shake his mother awake, the boy sobbed, "Stop playing, Mamma! Wake up!"

Medics dared not take time to stop and console him.

Recounting that morning ten years ago, Dusty—now Captain of DeSoto Parish Emergency Operations—admitted, "It still gives me chill bumps to see that baby crawling on his mother crying, trying to wake her up and her covered in blood. I knew, had she been alive, EMS would be working on her. They were not."

Knowing he could not permit those raw emotions to

take over, Dusty grabbed his camera and started taking photographs.

"There were so many people already there, I needed to preserve as much of the crime scene as I possibly could," he recalled.

Inside, he stepped around the victim in the doorway to see firemen and paramedics working on a second blood-covered woman in an adjoining room. They were doing chest compressions, he recalled, anything and everything they could to keep her alive until the Life Air helicopter arrived from LSU Hospital.

"I observed blood all over the house including the walls, ceiling, carpet, and furniture," Dusty wrote in his official case report. "Due to the expansive crime scene and possibility of multiple victims I advised dispatch to call out the entire Criminal Investigations Division. Then I had the victims' mother, Virginia Anne Knight, identify everyone in the house."

The daughter dead in the doorway was Diane Knight Rivers. She was twenty-five. A tall woman, about five-foot ten. Thick, long blonde hair was pulled into a ponytail.

The daughter on the couch—the one who might survive—was Virginia Lee Knight, twenty-three. They called her Jenny. Not as tall as her mother and sister, Jenny had dark brown hair. She, too, was soaked in her own blood, flowing from puncture wounds across her chest and abdomen. Her blood soaked the couch and carpet.

Mrs. Knight told Dusty that Stephen Rivers and Diana had a child together. Diana had filed for divorce on July 29. The district court issued a restraining order against her estranged husband after he (Rivers) attacked her (the mother) and there was to be a custody hearing later that month.

Apparently, she believed, Jenny had been awakened during her sister's struggle with Rivers and was stabbed herself.

Virginia, who slept in the far back of the house, was not

sure what woke her up—the scuffle? Screams? A door slamming? Her car driving off? Whatever it was she had rushed down the hallway to the living room to find her daughters in their condition at the same time as their children did.

Stephen Rivers and her car were gone.

The Logansport Elementary School teacher called 911.

The first responders to arrive, paramedics from Logansport, found Virginia Knight on the living room floor, cradling Diana in her arms.

"She's gone," Mrs. Knight wept, "she's gone."

Her arms wrapped around one daughter, she pleaded for the other.

"Please, help Jenny," she cried. "Please save Jenny."

When Patrol Deputy Ken McCoy got there, Mrs. Knight told him, "It had to be Stephen Rivers who did this."

"She (Mrs. Knight) was in shock, I'd say," Dusty recalled. "She wasn't screaming or carrying on. She was terribly upset about the children. She would go back and forth from the children to the table to her daughters. She would cry then compose herself then give us more information then cry again. It was just a terrible, heartbreaking scene."

All the while there was a withered old man sitting at a table in the dining room shaking his head, bewildered, bumfuzzled, getting up and down, bumbling around. That was John Colley, Mrs. Knight explained, her father-in-law, whom she helped care for.

And then there were children everywhere—five children under the age of seven in the home. One of the older boys told Deputy Casey Hicks he saw "Uncle Stephen running through the house with blood all over him."

"There was a bedroom off the living room that was full of toys," Dusty recalled. "It didn't have blood all over it. I put all the kids in that one room and said, 'I need for you to stay in this room.' I couldn't stand the thought of those kids seeing anything more."

At the time, Dusty's children were three and one. He was cut to the quick by the children's situation. "They were going to be scarred enough emotionally by what happened. They did not need to see any more."

A few moments later, Dusty went into the room with the children, opened a window, and passed each to a patrol deputy waiting just outside to care for them until family members arrived to take them.

"It was surreal," he recalled.

From across the parish road, Bill Speights watched the frantic goings on after the roar of the helicopter awakened him and his wife, Kay. It was still dark. Maybe a dozen emergency units, lights flashing, crowded the Knight's front yard—a broad area left open as a landing pad for the chopper.

"When we saw them passing kids through a window, I became really concerned," the retired dairy farmer said. "Whatever it was, it had to be bad."

Bill Speights had no way of knowing just how bad it was.

Each woman had been slashed and stabbed—face, neck, chest, abdomen—again and again and again.

The assault began in the bedroom where Diana slept, moved into the living room where her body was found, and continued into an adjoining den with a fireplace where Jenny was found. The bed covers and mattress in Diana's room were soaked in blood. Bloody handprints, smears and splatters across the walls and doorway, into the living room. On the couch, carpet, ceiling, and walls—as if Diana fought, slinging her arms the entire time she was being assailed.

Deep slices across the palms of her hands showed, at one point, she actually grabbed the knife blade.

"I did not realize there was that much blood in the human body," Dusty said. "There was blood everywhere. I guess with me, at that point, it was strictly 'I've got a job to do. I've got these two—one dead and one dying—we've got to find this guy.' I had to make sure my ducks were in a row.

I never worked a double homicide before. There were lots of moving pieces. The main thing is, we've got to catch him."

Dispatch called me a second time at 5:30 a.m., telling me Dusty said call out everyone in C.I.D. —something that had never been done before. They weren't asking permission, just giving me the heads up.

"Do it," I said, "I'm headed that way."

Dusty Herring joined us five years earlier, after working almost ten years with Shreveport PD. Fifteen years in law enforcement, but he still had a boyish look of innocence about him. Tall, slender, square shoulders, sandy hair. He was as sharp as they come, raised in law enforcement. His father was a retired Shreveport Assistant Police Chief, and his uncle a Caddo Parish Sheriff's Deputy.

If Dusty Herring said, "Call out the calvary," he had good reason.

My faith in his common sense and know-how was reinforced when I arrived.

Dusty started, "I just felt like I needed—"

"You did the right thing," I said.

An abundance of people were coming and going, others had already come and gone: the fire department personnel, paramedics, air flight attendants, the first four patrol deputies, all had been in and out of the front door.

Nine people from four generations were inside the Knight house at the time of the crimes.

Now every member of DeSoto Parish C.I.D. was arriving, along with other members of the victims' family. Even neighbors were beginning to show up.

The crime scene had to be protected and preserved for processing.

An extensive crime scene like that one, involving multiple people, covering multiple rooms, yard, cars— would take hours to process. The more people to work it, the faster it could be completed.

Everybody else had to get out.

At that point we could not worry about footprints in and

out of the front of the house, but we had to keep people away from the back yard where the car had been parked and stolen. There would be footprints, handprints, and other usable evidence back there.

We had to photograph then measure and record each blood splatter, handprint, footprint, each pool of blood, then measure and document size and distance between each.

We have to take a sample of each splatter and smear for blood typing: whose blood was it? Diana's? Jenny's? Rivers'?

There is a process called stringing. Each blood droplet has a tail and each tail is at its own unique angle. Using an algorithm, you triangulate where the victim was when each splatter occurred and at what angle the blow was struck. You can reconstruct a crime scene, but it is painstakingly tedious, and it takes a lot of personnel.

Before the body of a deceased victim can be removed from the crime scene, you must photograph every wound, measure each for width and length, measure the distance between each wound, record the angles of each wound.

The exact processing of a crime scene is crucial to a successful prosecution. You cannot rush or take short cuts. The more detail, the better for the prosecution.

A little after 6 a.m. an oilfield tanker truck stopped in front of the Knight home, telling Deputy McCoy there was a vehicle parked in the middle of a nearby lease road that was not there earlier that morning and he could not get by it. Ken McCoy went to check it out.

"I approached the vehicle with my duty weapon drawn and noticed blood on the door and shined my flashlight inside and noticed blood on the inside of the vehicle," McCoy wrote in his case report.

The car, a tan Buick sedan, was registered to Virginia Knight. Like the house, it was covered in blood: It looked like the steering wheel had been painted red. Blood had pooled on the floormat. Bloody handprints on the driver's door. Streams of blood dried after running down the driver's door.

Drenched in blood, Rivers drove his mother-in-law's car from her house to the wellsite, abandoned it, and got into another vehicle to escape. The patrol deputy radioed for an investigator to meet him. This had been planned.

This was a pre-meditated attack.

What Rivers had not planned on was the adrenaline dump.

During a crime spree like he went through—fighting and fatally stabbing his wife and sister-in-law, stealing his mother-in-law's car, racing to the wellsite, getting into his own pickup truck, racing off to Texas— Rivers was operating on sheer adrenaline.

The human body cannot function at that harried pace long. When the body runs out of adrenaline, it crashes. People can black out. At the very least, they suddenly become weak and disoriented.

"There is just a hell of an adrenaline dump when you go like that," Dusty said. "Your body cannot sustain that level of arousal."

During a post-adrenaline dump, a person gets cotton mouth, becomes sweaty, feels lightheaded.

Just after he crossed the Texas line, Rivers lost control of his pickup truck, crashing head-on into a tree. The airbag deployed. Disoriented, he started walking back into Louisiana. Had Rivers continued traveling west—who knows, he might not have been caught. But his mind was muddled by whatever he had been on before the murderous attack and then by the adrenaline dump.

He walked right back into the area he had just fled.

DPSO Detective Corporal Adam Ewing, on his way from the crime scene to LSU Hospital in Shreveport to check on the condition of Jenny Knight, came upon Rivers walking on Stateline Road.

Although Ewing did not have a photograph of the suspect, he had a description: white male, mid-thirties, black hair, wearing a black T-Shirt, blue jeans, and boots. It had to be him. He slowed and pulled alongside Rivers.

"Who are you?" Ewing called out his window.

"Stephen."

Rivers continued walking.

"Stephen *Rivers*?"

"Yes."

"Get on the ground!" Ewing ordered as he stopped his vehicle and jumped out.

Rivers had already scrambled across the ditch and was through the barbed-wire fence. The deputy opened fire, but Rivers was running on adrenaline again, bent low, weaving, bobbing, dodging as he got farther and farther away.

Fight or flight. Rivers was making his way to the forest.

Ewing called for backup. It was 7:34 a.m.

Dusty and several others left to join Ewing while I and a few other investigators remained at the Knight home, continuing to process evidence. When that was complete, I would move to the manhunt on Stateline Road.

This was Dusty's case. I would support him.

When I took over as Chief of C.I.D., Sheriff Arbuckle let me pick my own team of investigators. I had everybody there I wanted, and I'd told them, "I know you all have experience. You've all been to school. I'll send you to more schools. I am going to let you handle your own cases. I'm not going to rag you, come in behind you asking, 'What did you do today?'"

If they asked for advice, I'd give it. If I felt they were taking a wrong turn, I was prepared to tell them—but I never had to. I had a good, solid C.I.D. team. This was Dusty Herring's case.

On the way to meet Ewing, he called SWAT and our K-9 Unit to Stateline Road.

It was a sure bet Stephen Rivers was exhausted, hiding in the thick undergrowth of the forest where air does not reach. It was stifling. He had not had time to recoup from the adrenaline dump that led to losing control of the truck and crashing into the tree. Now he was running again, on foot with a deputy firing at him.

From the time Ewing opened fire on Rivers about 7:30 a.m. until the Winn dogs arrived, about three hours elapsed.

I had time to go to the site where Rivers crashed his truck into a tree just inside Texas. He plowed through several small trees before smashing into one big enough to stop the Ford crew cab truck. He had been driving fast enough that, when he lost control on a curve, careening into the woods, he hit something—a hole or a tree—hard enough to rip the front passenger side wheel off the truck. Not the tire, the whole wheel. Both doors on the driver's side were crushed as if he'd been T-boned. With the airbag deployed, Rivers was fortunate to get out and walk away.

Ordering a rollback to take Rivers' truck to the sheriff's department garage, I joined Arbuckle and Dusty on Stateline Road where they were waiting for the Winn tracking team.

During the wait, a Louisiana state trooper noticed a man with a dog walking along a pipeline right of way on property leased by a hunting club. Suspecting it might be Stephen Rivers, the trooper approached but saw quickly, it was not Rivers.

The man was a member of the hunting club who had come before daylight to scout the property. The trooper warned the hunter to be careful, briefing him on the situation with Rivers. The hunter decided to take his dog and go home. Driving out of the hunting club, he saw a man wearing a black T-shirt and jeans walking along a deer trail. As the hunter neared, the man darted back into the woods, but as the hunter drove by—as Rivers realized this was not law enforcement—he emerged from the woods and ran after the hunter, waving his arms, calling for him to "Stop!" He needed a ride out.

Having been forewarned, the hunter sped off to find the nearest law enforcement officer. When the news got to

Dusty, he widened our perimeter. Disoriented in the woods, Rivers had come full circle. He was almost back to the Knight house.

It was the hunter who guided the Winn handlers to the approximate place where Rivers tried to flag him down. Once they caught his scent, their sound must have been numbing to the man they were after.

The rest of us held the perimeter—the sounds of the dogs growing more and more distant—until one of the guards radioed, "We've got him!"

Arbuckle let out a hoot. Just under an hour had passed.

As he knew they would, the Winn dogs pursued Stephen Rivers until he collapsed and lay down at the base of a big pine tree. Sprawled on his back on the forest floor, surrounded by the dogs, seeing armed officers approaching, Stephen Rivers pulled a knife from his pants pocket and plunged it into his abdomen.

Then he slashed both wrists.

SWAT officers radioed Dusty they needed an ambulance.

That was impossible. There was no way an ambulance could get anywhere near Rivers and the guards. Fortunately, DPSO Deputy Tommy Williamson was there in his own four-wheel drive Jeep. He and Sgt. Pat Jones jumped in, navigating their way in from the back side.

Sgt. Jones read Rivers his Miranda Rights, confiscated the pocketknife and a Samsung cellphone, which, it turned out, belonged to Diana. They put Rivers in the Jeep and brought him back to the wellsite where an EMS unit was waiting to take him to the hospital in Shreveport.

Sheriff Arbuckle read the Miranda Rights to Rivers again, with plenty of witnesses.

"Do you understand these rights as I have read them to you?"

Rivers nodded.

"I need for you to acknowledge verbally," Arbuckle ordered. "Do you understand your rights?"

"Yes," Rivers said.

Arbuckle nodded, signaling for the ambulance attendants to take off.

That was a little after noon.

Jenny Knight was pronounced dead at LSU Hospital in Shreveport not long after her arrival. Like her sister Diana, Jenny Knight bled to death. If a person is bleeding from an arm or leg, you can slow the blood flow with a tourniquet but when she is stabbed across her chest, abdomen, and in the back deeply enough to pierce internal organs and arteries, it is impossible to stem the blood flow.

Rivers underwent surgery at the same hospital for self-inflicted stab wounds to his abdomen and the slashes to his wrists. None of his injuries were serious. He didn't cut himself badly enough to bleed to death. His wrists were slashed horizontally. A person who really wants to die cuts their veins lengthwise. None of us believed Stephen Rivers really tried to kill himself.

That night, Dusty Herring went to the hospital to get a statement from him.

Like I've said before, when you work a homicide investigation, nobody looks at the clock. Dusty was twenty hours on duty.

Recovering from his surgery, Rivers was held in a semi-private room with another male prisoner from a different jurisdiction and a private guard with him. He was handcuffed to his bed. His feet were shackled.

It was 8 p.m. This was Dusty's first really good look at his suspect.

Physically, Stephen Rivers was not as tall as his wife. He was thirty-six years old, five-foot six inches tall. Thick.

"He was built like a body builder who put on a few too many pounds around the paunch," Dusty recalled. "Maybe a beer gut. But he was muscular."

Rivers had that south Louisiana black hair, black eyes,

olive skin.

Introducing himself as the deputy in charge of the investigation, Dusty asked Rivers if he wanted to make a statement.

"Off the record," Rivers said.

"I don't need a statement off the record," Dusty replied. "Whatever you tell me is for the record. Before you say anything, let me tell you what I know."

Then Dusty laid out what he had put together from the statements he got from Virginia Knight, John Colley, the children, and from our crime-scene analysis.

Stephen Rivers appeared to listen intently.

"I know you came in the back door. You knew it would be unlocked," Dusty began. Diana and Jenny would go outside on the back porch to smoke, so the back door was usually unlocked, Dusty had learned from Mrs. Knight.

"You walked past Jenny—she was asleep on the couch. You went into Diana's bedroom and began stabbing her. As she was screaming, you decided to leave. On your way out you ran into Jenny as she was headed to her sister's bedroom to see why she was screaming. And you then stabbed her— because she could identify you.

"You grabbed Mrs. Knight's car keys, stole her car, drove it to the wellsite about one-third mile down the road, where your truck was parked. Then you got into your truck and headed west on Speights and Stateline roads. I know where you crashed your truck. You started walking north on Stateline Road. You stopped at a house to ask for water. A short time later you were approached by a deputy and took off running."

Rivers nodded.

"When you crashed your truck were you trying to kill yourself or did you just lose control.

"I was trying to kill myself."

"Did you stab yourself in the woods or earlier?"

"Before I crashed the truck," Rivers replied.

Idiot, Dusty thought. Do you know how many people

watched you stab yourself when the dogs cornered you?

Then Rivers began giving his version of what happened inside the Knight house.

"What you said was true," he said.

Earlier that morning, Rivers said he had been with another man, drinking alcohol, smoking crack cocaine. He said he took a pill the man gave him that was supposed to be stronger than methadone.

"I want a drug test," Rivers said.

"I'll get a court order for the blood they've drawn," Dusty said.

Rivers said Diana texted him from a phone number he did not recognize, asking him to come over.

"Rivers stated that he knew there was a restraining order against him, that he was not to be around Diana. So, he parked at the well location and walked down to the house. He said Diana told him the back door would be left unlocked and for him to just come in," Dusty wrote in his case report, summarizing River's details of the early morning.

Once inside, Rivers said, he saw Diana asleep in bed, her cellphone charging on a bedside table. Rivers said he scrolled through the text messages, saw a texted photo of a penis that was not his.

"This added to his anger," Dusty paraphrased Rivers' statement. "Rivers then stated he got in bed with Diana. She woke up and they began to talk. He confronted her about the messages and the picture, and she got mad at him for going through her phone.

"Rivers said Diana slapped him in the face and told him to get out. This enraged Rivers and he began stabbing her. Rivers stated he did remember running into Jenny but did not remember actively stabbing her.

"Rivers stated that he appreciated me being 'cool' about the whole thing and then he asked me 'How are they?'

"How are *who*?" Dusty asked.

"Diana and Jenny," Rivers replied.

"How are they? They're dead!"

Rivers hung his head, a tear running down his face.

"I didn't mean for that to happen," he said.

"I'll be back tomorrow," Dusty said as he walked out the door. "You need some rest."

And so did he.

I went home that evening to a house full of kids.

My daughters and their families had come to Mansfield from Shreveport and Tyler for the weekend. They were all in the pool when I got home, not a care in the world.

We had five grandchildren at that time— Reece, Bryce, Sadie Belle, Aaron, and Juliana, all under the age of eight —about the ages of Virginia Knight's grandchildren.

They were red as lobsters, happy as little clams, glad to see me.

"Papa! Papa! Come get in the water!"

"In a few minutes," I called back. "I've got to go inside a minute."

Linda understood. I needed a few minutes.

I'd heard all kinds of excuses for domestic violence— 'I love her so much I just couldn't lose her,' 'If I can't have her nobody can,' 'She can't get away with that,' 'No one's gonna take my kid away from me'—none of those excuses ever explained the real why for me.

What had happened inside the Knight house was just plain old evil. My mind wandered to a sermon we'd heard not long before—that our struggle isn't against flesh and blood but against the spiritual forces of evil.

Diana and Jenny had damned sure struggled against flesh and blood.

They lost the fight.

But it was true, I believed: spiritual forces of evil exist and some people, for whatever reasons, listen to them, give into them, as Stephen Rivers had.

It took a dark soul to do what he had done.

I went to our bathroom, locked the door, splashed water on my face, then got on my knees to thank the Lord for all I had—my wife, our family, health, work, and well-being.

I prayed for Virginia Knight. I had that image of her sitting on the floor, crying, cradling her dying, bloodied daughter in her arms, begging deputies to save Jenny. I thought of my own daughters—what would Linda or I have done had it been our daughters?

I shuddered at the thought.

Most of all, I think, I prayed for the children who had been in the house.

What Dusty and I and the others had seen—it was bad enough for adults—but children had been there. They had seen it all. The toddler crawling on his mother, crying for her to wake her up—shaking her to wake up—could he ever overcome that?

Looking back, I think that was my moment of realization—you cannot unsee what you have seen.

The next morning Dusty was back in Stephen Rivers' hospital room.

The suspect's demeanor had changed. There was no trace of those tears from the night before.

"After he knew they were both dead, there was a soulless look in his eyes," Dusty remembered.

He handed Rivers a Miranda Rights waiver to sign, which he did, adding, "I want to speak to my father."

"When I'd try to talk to him, he would smirk, with a half-cocked grin—eyes that look through you. There was nothing behind them, like a great white shark—there was nothing there."

Dusty called Stephen Rivers' father using his own cellphone, explained who he was, why he was calling. Then he handed his cellphone to Rivers. When the conversation ended, Rivers looked at Dusty saying, "I want to talk to a lawyer before I say any more."

Then he smiled.

That was the end of Stephen Rivers' cooperation with law enforcement.

"I just wanted to punch him in the mouth," Dusty recalled. "But I knew, if you do that, all this is out the window."

Rivers had already admitted what he did.

He was identified by one of the boys in the house and we learned from the first emergency responders at the Knight's residence that Jenny Knight whispered, "Stephen did this," before she lost consciousness.

The clothing taken from him at the hospital was sent to the crime lab for analysis. Whose blood was on his clothing, in addition to his own?

Dusty got a search warrant for Diana Knight's cellphone, which, as it turned out, was registered to Stephen's mother, Sharon Rivers.

"I also contacted the suspect's mother, Sharon Rivers, and asked her about the cell phone account and she gave me verbal permission to seek out any and all information I needed from the victim's cellphone."

The phone was taken to the Bossier City Marshal's Office, Internet Crimes Against Children's Office for help retrieving information from it. Since it was locked with a password, only SIMS card information could be pulled. That data was placed on a CD and logged into evidence.

Later, Dusty spoke at length with Rivers' parents.

"They indicated to me that they were truly sorry for what their son had done, and they would assist in the investigation any way they could. However, they could not tell Stephen to say anything that could later cause him to get the death penalty," Dusty wrote.

Friday, August 12 Dusty collected blood-stain cards from both victims as a control sample against Rivers' blood. With a court order in hand, he collected Stephen Rivers'

DNA and delivered all evidence he and the C.I.D. team had collected from the crime scenes, the victims, and suspect to the crime lab for analysis.

That same day, mourners filled Logansport High School gymnasium to attend funeral services for Diana Knight Rivers and Virginia Leigh (Jenny) Knight. It was the largest facility in their hometown.

Both girls went through school at Logansport, they each graduated from high school in Kilgore, Texas after their parents moved there. When Virginia returned to Logansport, the girls' father remained in Kilgore. Virginia was still teaching at Logansport Elementary School in 2010. She has since retired.

Jenny was living and working in Kilgore. Her decision to visit her mom that weekend proved fatal. Had she remained in Kilgore—she might be alive today. With every case there is that one decision someone makes that changes their fate.

Television news stations from Shreveport and Tyler covered the case, with one television news reporter speaking to Jenny's friends and co-workers at the Kilgore restaurant where she had worked seven years.

This was posted on the station KLTV-TV website August 13, 2010:

"Thursday, a picture of Jenny and her sister Diana was displayed on the cash register at the restaurant, next to a jar, asking people to help the family with the enormous cost of two funerals. Jenny's boss says it's the least they can do.

"That's a good family. That's a good family," said Juan Prado. "Especially her momma, she's been really good. But you know, there's nothing you can do when those things happen."

Diana and Jenny were two of six sisters. Their tight-knit family raised the children who were left without their mothers.

Stephen and Diana Rivers had a tumultuous relationship, a textbook case of codependency.

Stephen had become addicted to drugs—he was high on crack cocaine the morning of the murders. His toxicology screen showed only cocaine in his system—whatever pill he said he took that was supposed to be stronger than methadone was not in his system when his blood was drawn in the hospital.

They both had accused the other of physical abuse.

After Stephen attacked Mrs. Knight in July, Diana filed for divorce and got a restraining order. Still—be it because of the children or their own chemistry, the two remained in contact until her murder.

Stephen Rivers was indicted by the DeSoto Parish grand jury on two counts of capital murder. He was looking at the death sentence.

Blood tests showed he was high on crack cocaine at the time of the murders while neither of his victims, asleep in their mothers' house, showed any trace of alcohol or drugs in their systems.

Diana suffered ten stab wounds—any one of several, inflicted alone, could have killed her: one four-inch wound to the right upper chest pierced her heart. Another cut into a lung, a third ripped open her abdominal wall. Her spleen was pierced by a four-inch-deep stab wound in her lower back and a wicked slash to her right flank cut six inches deep.

She was slashed across her face, stabbed in the neck, cutting into her thyroid.

The coroner noted Diana had ten other defensive wounds—those deep slices—across both hands and arms.

Jenny was cut across her scalp, the knife was plunged four inches deep into her chest in two different places, piercing the right atrium of her heart and interventricular septum of the heart. In other words— Stephen Rivers literally sliced Jenny Knight's heart apart. Another wound sliced through her liver.

The photo Rivers said he saw on Diana's cellphone was never found. Forensics retrieved text messages between the two right up to a few hours before Diana's death and having obtained the password, they got photos off the cellphone, but the photo Rivers said he saw, the one he used as an excuse for his deadly rage, was never found. There is no evidence it ever existed.

Rivers was defended by lawyers of the Capital Assistance Project of Louisiana (CAPOLA), who filed motions for us to produce that photograph, but you can't deliver what you don't have.

"When I'm working a homicide, it's like putting together the pieces of a puzzle," Dusty said. "I have to use the pieces I have. I can't make them up. If I'd had that photograph, I would have used it. It would have gone to motive. It also could have been used as evidence that he acted in rage, not aforethought. Either way—had the forensics lab found it, I would have used it. It was not there. Either it never existed, or he (Rivers) erased it in his rage."

The case never came to trial.

CAPOLA lawyers and the 42nd District Attorney's Office reached a plea agreement: the prosecution would take the death sentence off the table in exchange for a guilty plea to two counts of capital murder. The sentences were to run concurrently.

That plea was entered on December 12, 2011 before District Judge Robert Burgess.

Rivers later filed to have the sentence reduced, a motion which was denied.

Stephen Rivers—who killed his wife and her sister out of a possessive rage to keep her and to keep her from taking his son in a custody battle—would spend the rest of his life without either.

He remains in Angola Prison as of this writing, sentenced to hard labor for the remainder of his life.

A man cannot do what Stephen Rivers did and not pay the price.

Stephen Rivers

Former DeSoto Parish
Sheriff Rodney Arbuckle

DPSO Criminal Investigations Division 2009—from left: Cpl. Dusty Herring, Sgt. John Cobb, Lt. Horace Womack, Judy Freeman, Sgt. Brett Cooper, Det. Garland Heansley, Cpl. Ray Sharrow, Lt. Robert Davidson, Cpl. Adam Ewing, Sgt. Keith Banta

You Just Never Know

An old friend of mine— I'll call him Joe—came into my office early one morning in the summer of 1991. He was in a froth, his ebony skin paled, eyes wide, and jaw gaped open. He made me think of a largemouth bass.

"I was fishing on Grand Bayou last night," Joe said, "and you won't believe what happened."

He didn't give me a chance to guess.

"I was way up in the bayou—back where most folks don't go—fishing off the bank—when I came around a bend and ran smack-dab into a bunch of marijuana plants. I heard some noises, so I crouched down and looked around. On up, there was a big tent, and two or three men on horseback— and they was all toting rifles. So, I backed out real easy."

"No doubt in your mind it was marijuana?"

"No, sir! It was that crazy weed, sure enough."

"And you say three men on horseback with guns?"

Joe nodded.

"Could you draw me a map of how to get there?" I

asked.

"You bet. I'm telling you, Mr. Robbo—there was a lot of them plants and the men had guns and I was scared. Hell, I dropped my pole! Get it for me if you go back out there, would you?"

Grand Bayou is a marshy wilderness on the eastern edge of DeSoto Parish, north of Coushatta, which flows into and is fed by the Red River. It's a resort area now but back then it was just a sportsman's paradise year-round. Fishing, duck hunting, deer hunting. You name it.

I followed the map Joe scrawled for me.

The land where he spotted the marijuana was on the backside of an antebellum plantation. Two thousand acres that once grew cotton had been turned into a different kind of cash crop.

I learned four men had leased the land: a former police chief from a small town in Northeast Texas, a south Louisiana man, one man from Guatemala, and the fourth from Mexico. I don't recall now exactly how they got together but the four built a partnership working remote, fertile farmland that had laid fallow for years. They'd propagated acres and acres of marijuana grown shoulder high. A man could get rich on that crop. Four men were counting on it.

I called in the Drug Enforcement Agency, Louisiana State Police, and Red River Parish Sheriff's Department to help us watch the operation around the clock. We laid low for weeks, studying their movements, learning their routine.

With the sun rising over the cypress bayou one steamy July morning, we converged on the old sharecropper's house where the men slept. About twenty of us fanned out around the clapboard shack.

Knowing the men were heavily armed, we'd secured a no-knock warrant.

A state trooper and I kicked in the door, both yelling, "Police!"

As the door fell open, we were face to face with a big,

blonde, bare-chested man pulling a gun from his shoulder holster, his eyes wide with fright as the trooper fired, hitting his shoulder, spinning him around.

The room reeked of gunpowder.

My heart pounded in my throat as I eased off the trigger of my nine-millimeter Glock. The man was down. No need for me to fire my weapon.

Apparently, he'd slept with his gun in the holster. We woke him from a deep sleep, yelling and kicking in the door. The trooper and I both rushed to pick him up off the floor, sitting him in a chair, working to slow his bleeding.

How many times, through the years, I've laid in bed at night going over the events of days like that. What went right? What went wrong? What could I have done better?

When I was young and first got into law enforcement, I thought I was bulletproof. It wouldn't happen to me. *Not me.*

The older I got, the more times I dealt with guns drawn, the more clearly I saw—you just never know. Is this the day I will save a life? Or take a life? Or lose my own?

Back in the 1980s, we executed a search warrant on a drug dealer in Longstreet in the wee hours of the morning. Longstreet is another isolated crossroads community in rural DeSoto Parish, north of Logansport.

I banged on the door yelling, "Police! I have a search warrant!"

As the door cracked opened, I shouldered my way through, grabbing the man, forcing him to sit on the couch.

Charlie Frazier was beside me. Charlie reached down and took a .38 caliber handgun out of the man's hand. *I never saw that gun in the dark.*

I didn't break a sweat until I tried to go to sleep that evening. My God! How easily that man could have killed me.

There was another time the Louisiana State Police called Sheriff Frenchie Lambert, telling him they had a tip that a contract had been put out on my life. A man arrested in Beaumont told investigators a mobster known as 'Heavy' from Bayou Blue paid him to kill me.

I had no idea why.

Frenchie insisted I get my wife and kids out of town while they investigated, so we went to Oklahoma to stay with a distant relative of Linda's.

In the meantime, state police started watching this man in Bayou Blue, who owned several strip joints and bars between Zwolle and the Gulf Coast. I'm not sure if he was called Heavy because of his big gut or his deep mob connections but either way, the name was appropriate.

With me in Oklahoma, Frenchie sent a deputy to Bayou Blue.

"We know about the contract on Robbo," the deputy told Heavy. "If anything happens to Robbo or his family— it's *you* we're coming for."

As it turned out, one of Heavy's connections in Zwolle—a town infamous for its lawlessness—was the sister of someone I had arrested for selling drugs. She had pleaded with me to drop the charges. I'd told her, "No way."

Then she called the prosecutor at his home, asking the same thing.

When Herman Lawson told her, "It's not happening," the woman threatened to tell his wife they were having an affair.

Herman said, "Go ahead. She's right here. Honey, someone wants to talk to you."

That next week that woman borrowed $3,500 from the local bank to remodel her bathroom. It never got remodeled.

Frenchie and the state police theorized she paid Heavy, who hired the guy who was nabbed in Texas. No one was ever prosecuted. I didn't get shot. Frenchie couldn't prove the connection and not long afterward, Heavy was found murdered, two of his strip joints torched.

His line of work was more dangerous than mine. Or he just wasn't as lucky.

Once, when my oldest daughter answered the telephone

on a Friday night, a man on the other end said, "You tell your f-'ing daddy I'm gonna kill him if it's the last thing I do."

Allison was a teenager.

"You wish!" she said, slamming down the phone. Then she burst into tears. It's not always easy being the child of a cop.

When Allison was just a toddler, I had to work in New Orleans for about a week one time. When I got back to town, an informant came to my office, telling me he'd overheard two men talking about hiding in the woods behind my house while I was gone. They were waiting there to kill me when I came home from work. The informant said he heard them saying my wife was pregnant and they watched her carrying a little girl on her hip. Have you ever felt your scalp tingle?

Weary of the waiting, one of the men said he'd just kill Linda and be done with it, but the other man stopped him.

"No, you won't," he said. "She's got nothing to do with this."

They were members of the Bandidos biker gang. Four months earlier, a hunter found a body buried in a shallow grave near Pelican. He literally tripped over a hand sticking out of the earth. We were able to identify the murder victim by fingerprints. He was a Bandido from Houston.

A couple of us went to talk to some members of the Houston Bandidos. They were glad to hear the guy was dead, said he'd stolen heroin from them, and they told us who did the killing. They named five people, one from Coushatta, another from Mansfield.

It was the guy from Coushatta who said he'd off Linda instead of me. We had been watching him after we came back from Houston and he was tired of it. He'd killed his biker friend. What was a cop to him? Or a cop's wife?

He was a meth head who ended up being shot in the head by his own wife. She was afraid of him.

That second biker who staked out my house, the man from Mansfield, told me all about it a few months before he died of cancer. He was the one who kept Coushatta from killing Linda. It was his deathbed confession to me. That man served two tours in Special Forces in Viet Nam, got messed up on speed when he got back. He was a good guy when he was clean but dangerous as hell when he wasn't.

There was another drug dealer I chased for years. They called him Sugar Boo. Big brickhouse of a man. Rodney Hamilton—he was notorious. The number-one drug dealer in this part of the state. I arrested Sugar Boo four or five times on drug charges.

Word got out that Sugar Boo was carrying in his car, so we pulled him over at a gas station parking lot. My weapon drawn, I ran up to his car, yanked opened the door and there sat Sugar Boo with a pistol between his legs and a Tech Nine thirty-round Uzi at his side.

A few months ago, I ran into Sugar. He's done his time. Lives in Houston now, but he still has family over here and comes to visit from time to time.

Sugar came up to me and said, "Man, I just want to thank you!"

"Thank me? Thank me for what?" I asked.

"Do you remember back when you pulled me over with all those guns?"

"I sure do."

"Man, I was thinking the other day. You could've killed me with all those guns I had, and nobody would've ever said a word. Nobody would've known if you'd just shot me dead, all those guns I had. But you didn't. I appreciate that."

I never thought about shooting Sugar Boo. It didn't make any difference how many guns he had. He didn't draw on me. The truth is, so many of the people I dealt with like Sugar Boo, I liked. They were likable people. The problem was, they were breaking the law and it was my job to stop them.

The only time I was ever injured on the job was my own mistake. I was questioning a man who was strung out on crack. He started getting rambunctious, resisting, wrestling, so I grabbed him around his neck, tucking his head against my shoulder, trying to restrain him to walk with me.

That guy— Daniel Chamberlain was his name—was maybe eighteen or nineteen at the time and I was much older. He was shorter than me but stout. When I wrapped my arm around his neck, Chamberlain bent down, picked me up over his head, and body-slammed me onto the concrete. Fractured my hip. That's how quickly and unexpectedly it can happen. I thank God Horace Womack and Donnie Barber were there.

I cannot count the nights I've stared into the blackness over my bed, going over my own mistakes. I think about today's law-enforcement officers. They make mistakes, just like I did. If we are lucky, we live to learn from our missteps. If we are not, we die. Or are permanently disabled. Or someone else dies or is permanently disabled.

We went through a lot of active shooter/assault training over the years. They used to tell us, even if you have a loaded gun, a man with a knife standing twenty feet away can kill you before you fire your weapon.

I never believed it.

Then they put me in a simulation with my weapon (loaded with blanks) against a knife-wielding assailant across the room. One, two, three—go. I fired a shot, but he was on top me with a knife in seconds. In real life, he would have been wounded but just as likely, I'd be dead.

Being forced into instant life-and-death decisions is the stuff of nightmares.

People have recurring dreams—about flying or falling, taking a test they're not prepared for, being naked and no one notices. For years, my recurring dream has been about an active shooter call. I rush to North DeSoto Elementary School where Linda taught third grade for almost twenty years, pulling up to chaos in the school yard.

I run through the entry, down a corridor, following screams and gunfire, past one bloodied body after another, the sounds of chaos deafening—moans, screams, cries, gunfire.

Reaching a classroom door, I see a gunman holding a

child against him as a body shield—his left hand over her mouth, firing an automatic weapon with his right, executing one child after another.

In my nightmare, the only shot I have is through that little girl. Kill one child or let a madman keep killing other children.

I awake with a jolt, every time.

It's not something we talk about—people in law enforcement—our nightmares, our anxieties, our fears of making a wrong decision in a split second. I thank the Lord I'm retired. I never worked in a pressure cooker like what exists today: Every move law-enforcement officers make is recorded on a body camera or by some civilian on a cell phone. Video doesn't lie but video taken at one random angle cannot necessarily tell the complete story and it can be downright misleading.

When we first got video cameras in our patrol units, we didn't like it. But we quickly learned, video is a good cop's best friend. I can't tell you how many times video protected me when defense attorneys argued a confession was coerced. Honest cops should not fear video, be it from a dash camera, body camera, or cellphone.

On the other hand, the public should not judge a cop by twenty seconds of video recorded from an arbitrary angle, taken out of context of what happened earlier.

My time in law enforcement has come and gone. Our children are our future. They will rise to meet the demands of their times as has every generation before them. They will evolve new techniques and practices to make sure the law is enforced without bias or malice.

But people will still make mistakes.

And people will still die.

Conclusion

On rare occasions when I want to retreat from the world, I seek the solace of a magnificent bald cypress that rises a hundred feet above our hunting camp outside Grand Cane.

Its trunk is twenty-one-feet in circumference.

They tell me this tree is almost 300 years old, a seedling shortly after the French came ashore along the Gulf Coast, claiming this land in the name of King Louis XIV. I like knowing this tree was here then, when Natchitoches Caddo ruled the land.

I like knowing the cypress was here before the United States bought Louisiana.

It would have been a sprawling shade tree by the time my mother's ancestors settled here in the 1830s, when DeSoto Parish was just an ecclesiastical division of the Roman Catholic Church.

In 1843, the Louisiana State Legislature began a tradition of taking the route of least resistance, which they uphold today, by simply proclaiming Catholic Church parishes to double as governmental jurisdictions. By that time, my mother's grandfather was farming about 600 acres of this land.

We were here before, during, and after the Civil War. My mother's people listened to the gunfire and roar of the cannons of the Battle of Mansfield in early 1864 from their home, which is a quarter mile from the one I live in now.

The Battle of Mansfield was the last victory for the Confederacy west of the Mississippi River. For a hundred years, people around here bragged that it was their ancestors who soundly whipped the Union forces in their march from Baton Rouge to take Shreveport— Port Shreve on the Red River—which, Union generals planned, would be their launching spot for an invasion of Texas.

Twenty-one-thousand men shot at each other for two days, less than a mile from my home. When the fighting was done 3,117 men lay dead—twice as many Yankees as Rebels. I found a cannon ball in a creek on my property a few years back. We were that close. I can't imagine how my great-great-grandmother felt as she listened to the roar of that battle, her father, and her husband off fighting in Tennessee.

My ancestors— Davidsons and Joneses—clung to this red dirt through the Great Depression and weathered every crisis that has faced this nation for almost 200 years. Yes, I am content knowing my roots run almost as deep in the rich red dirt of DeSoto Parish as do the roots of this ancient tree. The parish cemeteries are filled with my family members and I am destined to join them some day.

I had triple bypass heart surgery a few years back.

There is nothing like facing your own mortality to make a man take an unvarnished inventory of his life and beliefs. Under orders to relax and take it easy for a while, I've spent a lot of time sitting in the shade of this cypress, often in deep contemplation.

I can't say I sorted out all the whys of the world but a few things I've concluded:

Everything changes around us—except us.

We have not changed since Adam and Eve got caught

in the garden with fig leaves on, since Cain killed his brother in a jealous rage, Noah got drunk when he finally got off the Ark, David lusted after Bathsheba, having her husband killed, and the Jews killed the one man who came to save them.

Evil has always existed, as has good. It is the eternal struggle faced by every generation.

That will never change.

What has been done cannot be undone.

A word, once uttered, cannot be taken back any more than a bullet, once fired, can be put back into its chamber. Both lay waste to the human heart.

Carnage seen is not forgotten and a life lost is gone forever.

Healing from heart surgery, enjoying the quiet of the hunting cabin, I indulged in time for such thoughts. For so many years, being in my business, I couldn't afford the luxury of philosophizing about the frailty of the human condition. Guys who did that ended up drinking themselves out of a job and family—or worse.

You deal with it. You don't dwell on it.

It's just what people who stay in law enforcement do.

In the process, most of us grow a mighty hard bark—like the cypress.

I feel a kinship to this tree. Its tough bark has enabled it to endure what others around it could not.

Its bark is gray and furrowed, as is mine.

Its branches offer shelter to those who draw near it, as I long to do for my family.

The bald cypress has outlived all my ancestors and it will surely outlive me. Hopefully, it will be around to shade my grandchildren as I rest not far away beneath this lush Louisiana earth.

Having sat here long enough to face my ghosts, telling their stories, I have found a peace recognizing I did my best to bring each of them justice.

Now, I'm looking forward to a good night's sleep.

Bald cypress at hunting camp near Grand Cane—trunk is twenty-one-feet in circumference—estimated to be almost 300 years old.

9 781633 635104